The philosophy of
F. P. Ramsey

The philosophy of
F. P. Ramsey

NILS-ERIC SAHLIN

DEPARTMENT OF PHILOSOPHY, LUND UNIVERSITY

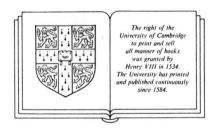

The right of the
University of Cambridge
to print and sell
all manner of books
was granted by
Henry VIII in 1534.
The University has printed
and published continuously
since 1584.

CAMBRIDGE UNIVERSITY PRESS

CAMBRIDGE

NEW YORK   PORT CHESTER   MELBOURNE   SYDNEY

Published by the Press Syndicate of the University of Cambridge
The Pitt Building, Trumpington Street, Cambridge CB2 1RP
40 West 20th Street, New York, NY 10011, USA
10 Stamford Road, Oakleigh, Melbourne 3166, Australia

© Cambridge University Press 1990

First published 1990

Printed in the United States of America

Library of Congress Cataloging-in-Publication Data

Sahlin, Nils-Eric.
The philosophy of F.P. Ramsey / Nils-Eric Sahlin.
p.   cm.
Includes bibliographical references.
ISBN 0-521-38543-1
1. Ramsey, Frank Plumpton, 1903–1930.   I. Title.
B1649.R254S24   1990
192–dc20   90-31042
                              CIP

British Library Cataloguing in Publication Data

Sahlin, Nils-Eric 1954–
The philosophy of F. P. Ramsey.
1. Mathematical logic. Ramsey, F. P. (Frank Plumpton), 1903–1930
I. Title
511.3092

ISBN 0–521–38543–1 hardback

To Vivianne, Hampus and Linnea

Contents

Preface

During the first decades of this century the intellectual atmosphere at Cambridge was exceptionally lively and creative. Thinkers such as the philosophers C. D. Broad, W. E. Johnson, G. E. Moore, Bertrand Russell, Ludwig Wittgenstein and the economist J. M. Keynes have had a decisive impact on modern research and social debate. Their ideas have become generally known from numbers of scholarly essays, books and biographies. But the greatest of them all is scarcely known outside a small circle of specialists. Frank Plumpton Ramsey, who died in 1930 at the age of only 26, in a series of brilliant essays laid the foundations of several new and flourishing theories in philosophy, mathematics and economics. However, not until recently, decades after Ramsey's death, have we gradually realized what unprecedented originality his work contains. When intellectual vigour began to ebb away from Cambridge in the years following his death, his genius did not show to full advantage.

My aim in this book is to give a comprehensive picture of Frank Ramsey's philosophical and scientific research. I have tried to present and discuss as straightforwardly as possible his often difficult ideas and theories, put them into a historical context and demonstrate their importance for modern research. My hope is that the reader who does not have any previous knowledge of the subjects discussed will be able to profit from the book, and that the specialist will also enjoy it. For those who feel they want to know a little about Frank Ramsey as a person, I have added a short biography, in Chapter 10.

Acknowledgements

I still vividly remember how, almost 15 years ago, I went as a new graduate student to one of my first meetings with my supervisor Professor Sören Halldén. Having discussed my interests we concluded that I should do some work on probability and decision theory. Professor Halldén then went to the library and returned after a few minutes with a not too thick book with black covers – *The Foundations of Mathematics*. That episode was the very beginning of the present book. But it took me many years to realize what an outstanding philosopher Frank Ramsey was, and what a great book *The Foundations of Mathematics* is. Since then Sören Halldén has supported this project in innumerable ways, and his encouragement and constructive suggestions have been invaluable to me.

Professors Peter Gärdenfors and Bengt Hansson have also discussed this book in detail at a number of informal seminars. They have also patiently listened to me whenever I reached a deadlock (though I am sure they sometimes hoped I would soon find a new passion).

Professor Hugh Mellor has read every chapter of my manuscript and made many constructive suggestions. He has a very clear view of Ramsey's philosophy and without his comments this book would probably have contained several misinterpretations and mistakes.

Mrs Jane Burch, Frank Ramsey's daughter, was kind enough to let me see some of Ramsey's unpublished manuscripts and letters, and kindly allowed me to use the photograph on the cover. She and Mrs Margaret Paul, Ramsey's sister, also helped me with the details of the biographical chapter.

In 1987 I briefly visited the Archives of Scientific Philosophy in the Twentieth Century, University of Pittsburgh, where Frank Ramsey's manuscripts are collected. Professor Nicholas Rescher assisted me in every way during this visit. He has also given me valuable comments on parts of this book.

Acknowledgements

Professor Isaac Levi's detailed and valuable comments and his constructive suggestions have helped me to revise and to avoid mistakes in the final version of my manuscript.

This book has existed for some time in manuscript. It was first written in Swedish and later translated into English. Mrs Muriel Larsson translated most of the chapters, and I have translated the rest. In the course of translation, I have considerably expanded and rewritten the original text.

Professors Ingemar Hansson, Risto Hilpinen, Sten Lindström, Ulrich Majer, Björn Thalberg, Anders Tengstrand and Mr Paul Hemeren have read various parts of this book at some stage in its composition and have given me their critical comments.

I wish to thank all of these people most sincerely.

This project has been supported by grants from the Erik and Gurli Hultengren Foundation, Anders Karitz Foundation, New Society of Letters at Lund, and Knut and Alice Wallenberg Foundation, all of which I gratefully acknowledge.

I conclude this preface by letting Ramsey himself state his version of the Paradox of the Preface:

> [We] cannot without self-contradiction say p and q and r and . . . and one of p, q, r . . . is false. (N.B. – We know what we know, otherwise there would not be a contradiction.) But we can be nearly certain that one is false and yet nearly certain of each; but p, q, r are then infected with doubt. But Moore is right in saying that not necessarily all are so infected; but if we exempt some, we shall probably become fairly clear that one of the exempted is probably wrong, and so on.[1]

Introduction

Frank Ramsey's bibliography contains 18 published works. Eight of these are fairly extensive philosophical and scientific essays; the rest are reviews, short notes and articles for the *Encyclopædia Britannica*. The bibliography would, however, be incomplete if one did not add the articles published posthumously in 1931 and 1978 in *The Foundations of Mathematics and Other Logical Essays* (edited by R. B. Braithwaite) and *Foundations: Essays in Philosophy, Logic, Mathematics and Economics* (edited by D. H. Mellor). Thus the core of Ramsey's philosophical and scientific work consists of no more than, say, 15 papers. But they are 15 remarkable papers, profound and full of originality. Today most of them are recognized as the foundation of flourishing theories in logic, mathematics, philosophy of mathematics, statistics, probability theory, decision theory, semantics, scientific method, cognitive science, metaphysics and economics. But they are more than 15 brilliant essays on 15 disparate subjects. They all contain the same view of philosophy – a method of analysis – merging a sound portion of realism (or, as Moore preferred to put it, 'the soundest common sense') with Ramsey's kind of pragmatist philosophy.

In 1922, when he was only 19 years old, Ramsey published three short articles, two of them in the *Cambridge Magazine*. One of these, 'Mr Keynes on Probability', is a review of Keynes's *A Treatise on Probability*. Ramsey's criticism of Keynes's theory that a probability says something about the strength of an (inconclusive) inference from one proposition

1

to another was so forceful that Keynes himself abandoned the project.[1] Ramsey's dissatisfaction with this type of probability theory later led him to develop his own theory, published in 'Truth and Probability'. The other *Cambridge Magazine* article, 'The Douglas Proposal', is a brilliant discussion of the so-called social credit proposal of Major Douglas, which was hotly debated at that time. There is no doubt that this short essay must have impressed the economists at Cambridge, including Keynes. The third of Ramsey's 1922 articles was a review in the *New Statesman* of W. E. Johnson's *Logic Part II*.

In 1923, Ramsey reviewed Ludwig Wittgenstein's *Tractatus Logico-Philosophicus*, a book which Ramsey himself had to a great extent translated into English (see Chapter 10). This review, which has attracted much attention ever since, contains some of the criticism that eventually led Wittgenstein to abandon his *Tractatus* philosophy. In the introduction to *Philosophical Investigations* Wittgenstein mentions the significance which Ramsey's 'certain and forcible' criticism had for his philosophical reorientation:

> For since beginning to occupy myself with philosophy again, sixteen years ago, I have been forced to recognize the grave mistakes in what I wrote in that first book. I was helped to realize these mistakes – to a degree which I myself am hardly able to estimate – by the criticism which my ideas encountered from Frank Ramsey, with whom I discussed them in innumerable conversations during the last two years of his life.[2]

In spite of Ramsey's criticism of the *Tractatus*, it was undoubtedly the book which, together with *Principia Mathematica*, had the greatest impact on Ramsey's philosophy. It took up most of his time; and in the following year, 1924, Ramsey published only a review of C. K. Ogden's and I. A. Richards's *The Meaning of Meaning*.

Ramsey's longer essays fall into three categories: philosophy, economics, logic and mathematics – which I discuss in that order.

Philosophy. Dissatisfied with Keynes's theory of probability, Ramsey in 1926 developed his own theory in 'Truth and Probability'. In this paper he shows how people's beliefs and desires can be measured by the use of a betting method. He shows that if we accept a number of intuitive principles of rational behaviour, a measure used to represent our 'degrees of belief' will satisfy the laws of probability. Ramsey thus laid the foundations of the modern theory of subjective probability, and also those of modern utility theory and decision theory. 'Truth and Probability' is therefore a significant paper not only for those interested in the foundations of probability, but also for cognitive psychologists, economists, Bayesian statisticians and decision theorists. It is also of particular interest when one is studying Ramsey's own philosophy, because it is the first essay really imbued with the basic ideas of pragmatism which he came to develop in a number of related papers. For Ramsey it is a first and portentous step away from logic, mathematics and the philosophy of mathematics. This is why I have decided to devote Chapter 1 entirely to this outstanding essay (and to a number of notes related to it).

Two other philosophical pieces, written about the same time as 'Truth and Probability' or shortly afterwards, are closely connected with it. The paper 'Facts and Propositions', published in the *Aristotelian Society Supplementary Volume VII* in 1927, and the note 'Knowledge', written in the summer of 1929, are heavily influenced by the ideas developed in 'Truth and Probability'. In 'Truth and Probability' Ramsey develops a theory of partial belief: in 'Facts and Propositions' he uses the same philosophical apparatus to develop a corresponding theory of truth, which strikingly exemplifies the maxim that if we cannot answer a question, it has probably been badly put. In this case, Ramsey argues that the question, 'What is truth?' is elusive simply because it is the wrong question. According to Ramsey, it is obvious that 'It is true that Caesar was murdered' means no more than that Caesar was murdered. The only real question is what a belief – for example, the belief that Caesar was murdered – is. If we have analyzed belief, Ramsey says, we have solved the problem of truth. Ramsey's answer to that problem therefore is to define the meaning of a belief; 'by reference to the actions to which asserting it would lead', that is 'by reference to its possible causes and effects'. This is the essence of the subsequently so-called redundancy theory of truth. But Ramsey's theory and his intentions have been much misunderstood in later literature, partly because their connection with his work on partial belief has not been recognized. Ramsey's theory of belief and truth is discussed in Chapter 2.

In 'Knowledge' Ramsey uses his theories of probability and truth to analyze the concept of knowledge. In one and a half pages, he develops a superior alternative to the traditional analysis of knowledge as true justified belief: namely, that belief is knowledge if it is obtained by a reliable process, and if it always leads to success. Ramsey thus strikingly anticipates much of recent debate, and his theory has recently been advocated in various forms by several philosophers, who have not always given him credit for it. This short note on knowledge, another contribution to Ramsey's brand of pragmatist philosophy, is discussed in Chapter 3.

At the time of his death, Ramsey had been working on a book for some years. This manuscript (part of the *Frank Ramsey Collection*, the Archives of Scientific Philosophy in the Twentieth Century, University of Pittsburgh) is far from ready for publication; it is only a first draft of what might have been a unified and very interesting work on belief, truth and probability. Ramsey himself was not satisfied with it and was undoubtedly in the process of rewriting it. But the three papers above (and thus Chapters 1–3 of the present book) give us a clue to the kind of unified pragmatist theory Ramsey was looking for.

In his paper 'Theories', written in the summer of 1929, Ramsey develops a view of scientific theorizing which anticipates ideas widely discussed today. Ramsey argues that the so-called theoretical terms of a theory ought to be regarded as existentially quantified variables. The theoretical term 'electron' can be compared with the term 'prince' in a fairy tale. Of the latter, we say 'Once upon a time there was a prince . . .' and then proceed to tell the story. Of the former, we similarly say something like 'There are entities which we shall call electrons . . .' and then go on to say what properties these entities have.[3] This idea has been discussed a great deal but is often misinterpreted. Ramsey's aim was not, as some suppose, to *eliminate* theoretical predicates like 'electron'. He simply wanted to explain their functioning within a theory. In so doing, he also incidentally explains how different theories can give quite different meanings to theoretical concepts, thus generating the so-called problem of incommensurability. In explaining that problem – decades before it was even formulated – Ramsey came as far as we have come today. 'Theories' is discussed in Chapter 5.

By using existentially quantified variables to explain theoretical terms (i.e., by introducing the Ramsey sentences), Ramsey has been accused of introducing unacceptable ontological assumptions. Replacing theoretical terms with existentially quantified predicate variables expands our ontological commitments far beyond what can be accepted, at least by nominalists. But Ramsey had thought of that problem, too. In the paper 'Universals', first published in 1925 in *Mind*, he tackled the problem of universals in detail, and the brilliant metaphysical theory of that paper is all he needs to demolish the above criticism of Ramsey sentences. In 'Universals' Ramsey denies that there is any fundamental distinction between universals and particulars (arguing, for example, that predicates are essentially no more incomplete than subjects are). This metaphysical theory is one of Ramsey's most outstanding contributions to philosophy. It enables the realist about us to overcome the most serious objections to his position, and it enables all of us to dismiss several venerable metaphysical problems as nonsense. In short, those who have criticized Ramsey's work on theories for its apparently facile extension of a theory's ontology have failed to take account of Ramsey's own work on universals. The paper 'Universals', and a related paper 'Universals and the "Method of Analysis" ' (written in 1926 for a symposium with H. W. B. Joseph and R. B. Braithwaite), are discussed in Chapter 8.

In 'Theories' Ramsey also advocates a strongly instrumentalist view of science: for him theories have no truth-value. But Ramsey also believed in ontological instrumentalism: the theoretical terms of a theory – 'electron', for example – should be viewed instrumentalistically. But if a scientific theory lacks truth-value, in what way can it be right or wrong? Ramsey gives a pragmatic answer to this question. To him scientific theories or 'causal laws form the system with which the speaker meets the future'. Our scientific laws make up the map by which we find our future way. These laws are not to be regarded as objectively given facts, but as rules by which to plan our future conduct. This is the view developed by Ramsey in 'General Propositions and Causality', written in the summer of 1929, at the same time as he was working on 'Theories'. In 'Facts and Propositions' he had followed W. E. Johnson and Wittgenstein in analyzing the generalization 'For all x, fx' as the conjunction of all instances of 'fx'. But in 1929 he rejected this analysis along with the arguments he had formerly put forth in favour of it. Instead he developed a pragmatic analysis of general propositions. General propositions (or 'variable hypotheticals') are, as Ramsey puts it, not judgements but rules for judging. One should thus read this paper when 'Facts and Propositions' is still fresh in one's mind. According to Ramsey's theory of truth, a belief is true if it always results in success. If general propositions have no truth-value, this means merely that belief in them can have no success beyond the success of beliefs in their instances. This does not, of course, make them worthless as a basis for action: on the contrary, they are indispensable as generators of such beliefs in future instances. Once again we see how Ramsey's different papers and ideas knit together.

A year earlier, 1928, in 'Universals of Law and of Fact', Ramsey had developed a rather different theory of how laws differ from 'universals of fact' (accidental generalizations). This theory says that 'causal laws are consequences of those propositions which we would take as axioms if we knew everything and organized it as simply as possible in a deductive system'. It is thus more in line with some of the ideas defended in 'Facts and Propositions'. And we should also note that Ramsey's reasons for giving up the Johnson–Wittgenstein thesis about generalizations are connected with a change in his view of the foundations of mathematics. Ramsey's two papers on law and causality are discussed in Chapter 4.

Besides these major works on philosophy, Ramsey wrote several shorter articles, all wonderful to read, and a number of comments on previous papers (especially on 'Truth and Probability') which I will not explicitly mention here. Most of them, however, are discussed in the following chapters. But there is one other paper that should be mentioned before we turn to his work on economics: the short note entitled 'Philosophy', written in 1929. This essay, which says a good deal about Ramsey's view of philosophy, begins:

> Philosophy must be of some use and we must take it seriously; it must clear our thoughts and so our actions. Or else it is a disposition we have to check, and an inquiry to see that this is so; i.e. the chief proposition of philosophy is that philosophy is nonsense. And again we must then take seriously that it is nonsense, and not pretend, as Wittgenstein does, that it is important nonsense!

Economics. Keynes and one of his colleagues at Cambridge, Arthur Pigou, encouraged Ramsey to work on problems in economics. His work on the Douglas proposal must have proved to them that he had the talent to become an outstanding mathematical economist. And indeed, his two papers, 'A Contribution to the Theory of Taxation' and 'A Mathematical Theory of Saving', published in the *Economic Journal* 1927 and 1928, respectively, are remarkable achievements. They give the solution to two difficult problems of economics. The first paper answers the question 'How is a given revenue to be raised by proportionate taxes in order that the decrement of utility may be a minimum?' The second paper tells us how much of its income a nation should save. The solutions to these problems are given by a mathematician who knew his trade. Ramsey's solutions are not only beautiful in their mathematical elegance; the paper on optimal saving is the first to use the calculus of variations to solve a problem in economics. Both these papers have given rise to new and thriving schools of economic theory. The former essay is the point of departure for the theory of optimal taxation and the latter lays the foundations of the theory of optimal saving. Ramsey's contribution to economics can be appreciated if one notes that few Nobel laureates have founded equally important areas of economic research.

To Ramsey's contribution to economics may also be added his axiomatization of utility in 'Truth and Probability'. This axiomatization has several virtues compared with the much later theory, far better known to economists, of von Neumann and Morgenstern, which was presented in their *Theory of Games and Economic Behaviour*.[4] It is also noticeable that in Ramsey's two papers on economics, he relies on the existence of a fully developed theory of utility, a theory which he had developed only a year earlier.

Logic and mathematics. Ramsey is probably best known for his works on the foundations of mathematics. Especially famous is his reconstruction of the theory of *Principia Mathematica* in 'The Foundations of Mathematics', published in the *Proceedings of the London Mathematical Society* in 1925. As R. B. Braithwaite puts it in the introduction to *Foundations of Mathematics*, it is an attempt to reconstruct the theory so that 'its blemishes may be avoided but its excellencies retained'. What Ramsey does is to put forth an alternative theory to the ramified theory of types, introduced by Russell as a solution to the problem of the paradoxes. What is today known as the *Ramsey*fied theory of types avoids some of the worst defects of Whitehead's and Russell's theory, especially the axiom of reducibility. Ramsey's theory gives *Principia Mathematica* a new and considerably more solid foundation. But it has also been said that 'The Foundations of Mathematics' constitutes both the peak and also the end, of a tradition. For having got rid of the axiom of reducibility, Ramsey became increasingly unhappy with some of the other axioms of logicism, which he abandoned, at the end of his life, for a finitistic view of mathematics. But in 'The Foundations of Mathematics' and in 'Mathematical Logic' (published in *The Mathematical Gazette* in 1926), he is still defending logicism against the attacks of Hilbert's formalism and Brouwer's intuitionism. These works are discussed in Chapters 6 and 7.

Ramsey was a lecturer in mathematics at Cambridge and he was known as a clever and talented mathematician. But, as Braithwaite's introduction to *The Foundations of Mathematics* puts it, 'though mathematical teaching was Ramsey's profession, philosophy was his vocation', and what is today known as *Ramsey's theorem* is in fact his only contribution to pure mathematics. Ramsey's interest in the foundations of mathematics induced him to try to find a solution to the *Entscheidungsproblem*. In 'On a Problem of Formal Logic' published in *Proceedings of the London Mathematical Society* in 1928, he succeeds in solving a special case of the decision problem for first-order predicate logic with equality. But six years after Ramsey's death it was shown that the general problem is unsolvable. Thus, as D. H. Mellor has put it, 'Ramsey's enduring fame in mathematics, which was his job, rests on a theorem he didn't need, proved in the course of trying to do something we now know can't be done!'[5] But Ramsey's theorem is an exceedingly difficult and extremely beautiful and imaginative theorem of combinatorial analysis. It has given rise to a vigorous new branch of mathematics now called *Ramsey theory*. The theorem is presented in Chapter 7.

Unpublished papers. The *Ramsey Collection* at the University of Pittsburgh comprises an almost complete collection of autograph material by Ramsey, roughly 1,500 autograph pages in all. (This material is also available on microfilm in the University Library at Cambridge.) The collection contains the above-mentioned papers, unpublished manuscripts and papers, classroom notes and lecture notes. I have read all of

Ramsey's unpublished notes and manuscripts, some of which I use in the following chapters. (When I do so, I give the title of the paper, as well as its number in the collection.) However, I believe that Richard Braithwaite and Hugh Mellor have published all of Ramsey's papers that are in a publishable state. I doubt that Ramsey would have agreed to publish many of the other papers and notes in the collection. In some cases, it is unclear whether he is developing a theory he wants to defend, or simply trying out an idea. Nor can it be denied that many of these papers are below the standard of his published work. But those with a special interest in, for example, the foundations of mathematics, probability theory, or economics may well find gems among them – like the beautiful little note on the value of collecting evidence mentioned at the end of Chapter 1.

I hope that this volume will convey a feeling of the remarkable originality and depth of Ramsey's thought – its breadth of range and its versatility. The reader will find that, as Moore puts it, 'he was capable of apprehending clearly, and observing consistently, the subtlest distinctions' and that he had 'an exceptional power of drawing conclusions from a complicated set of facts: he could see what followed from them all taken together, or at least what might follow, in cases where others draw no conclusions whatever.' With unusual clarity, his agile mind always found rewarding and fruitful solutions to difficult problems.

Chapter 1

Philosophy of probability

Many earlier theories of probability focused upon concepts intimately connected with the possible outcomes of parlour games: e.g., what is the probability that the King and Queen of Spades will come up if five cards are drawn from a pack? Even today such questions can spark off heated arguments and feelings among card-players. But besides these trivialities, there were, broadly speaking, two main theories of probability discussed at Cambridge when Ramsey wrote his masterpiece 'Truth and Probability' in 1926: frequency theories and logical theories.[1]

Underlying frequency theories is the idea that the probability of an event is linked to the observed frequency of occurrences of this event. When a surgeon tells a patient that the probability of his recovery is .95, he means that this is the proportion of patients who have actually recovered from this operation. This is not to say that the patient can infer that the probability that he himself will recover is .95. Strictly speaking, the doctor has only stated the probability that a patient, randomly selected from those already operated on, would be one who had recovered. Probability theory is thus rooted in actual percentages; no subjective element is admitted.

Examples of this sort of reasoning may be found as early as the mid-sixteenth century in Cardano's works: but it was a hundred years before probability theory assumed a stricter logical form that made possible more precise discussions of the subject. Scholars who then contributed to its development included Pascal, Bernoulli, Bayes, and Huygens (who

11

wrote the first textbook of probability, in which he formulated the principle of mathematical expectation – a principle crucial to Ramsey's theory). But the first fully argued frequency theory is that of J. Venn's *The Logic of Chance;* and the whole frequency way of thinking may be said to culminate in R. von Mises' works.[2]

Ramsey deals briskly with the advantages and disadvantages of a frequency theory. He mentions that he believes it gains support from the way we use the concept of probability in everyday life, for example, in the surgeon's statement. But this by no means justifies accepting the whole theory. Ramsey does not attack the frequency theory in detail, and we can only speculate how he would have done so.

When our knowledge is very limited, and our knowledge of frequencies slight or non-existent, certain probability judgements are still more reasonable than others. Even a new-born baby would be considered irrational if he or she thought the probability of the King and the Queen of Spades both occurring in five cards drawn from a pack was .99. Ramsey gives an example which indicates he had something like this in mind when working out his own theory. Suppose you come to an unfamiliar crossroad where there is no signpost. You must decide whether to take the dirt road to the right, to walk straight ahead, or to take the major road to the left – and a wrong choice could easily be fatal. Your decision is clearly based on some idea of probability; and you can make at least a rough probability comparison without any frequency information relevant to your decision.

The rival concept of logical probability shares much of its terminology with the frequency concept. This is because both draw on a well-established mathematical structure, which had to be settled before philosophers could begin to take an interest in questions of interpretation. Just as we can find frequency ideas in very early literature, so we can trace aspects of the logical concept a long way back. But its authoritative exposition is found in J. M. Keynes's *A Treatise on Probability.*[3]

Roughly, Keynes argued that probability is an objective relation between propositions, which is capable of varying degrees. The probability of a proposition is thus always relative to a given set of propositions that constitute our evidence for it. For Keynes, these probability relations are a fundamental basis of many of our beliefs. However, it should then sometimes be possible to perceive these probability relations by introspection. And Ramsey's first criticism of Keynes's theory is that for almost no pair of propositions have we the remotest idea what their probability relation is. When asked to estimate a probability, says Ramsey, we do not introspect a probability relation: we just assume our evidence is true, and then assign a degree of belief to our hypothesis.

Ramsey's probability theory may be seen as an attempt to overcome the difficulties of both the frequency and the logical theories, while retaining as much as possible of their virtues. From Keynes, he takes the idea of degrees of belief, for which, however, unlike Keynes, he shows how to provide a quantitative measure. He also believes that Keynes's probability relations need justification, not as degrees of justified rational belief, but as degrees of belief qua basis for action. And for that, he recognises that frequencies play a major role in our assessments of probabilities. By thus focusing on the individual agent, Ramsey solves the problem very cleverly. Both the agent's state of belief and his known frequencies are decisive for the probability a person assigns to a given proposition. Ramsey abandons the ideal of logical theory in favour of one that is both subjectively and prescriptively oriented.

Ramsey's main aim in 'Truth and Probability' is to bring out the connection between the subjective degree of belief we have in a proposition p and the probability we assign it. More precisely, he shows how

i. we can measure the degree of belief an agent has in a given proposition;

13

ii. if the agent is to act reasonably in certain obvious respects, this 'degree of belief' will have a measure that satisfies the mathematical laws of probability.

A second goal is to justify induction in a pragmatic and rational way, repudiating Wittgenstein's position that induction is no more than a Humean habit.

The theory Ramsey presents in 'Truth and Probability' is fragmentary in many ways. It is evident that Ramsey preferred to emphasize the overall ideas rather than penetrate the formal items. The theory consists of four main parts. First, there is an operational method, a measuring rod or a ruler with which we can establish or 'measure' value distances, that is, in principle use it to establish how much better a person experiences that one event takes place rather than another. Second, the theory consists of a set of axioms, axioms which require rational conduct on the part of the agent. Third, the theory includes a couple of definitions that show how knowledge of the agent's utility assessments and conduct in betting situations uniquely discloses the degree of belief the person has in a proposition, and finally, a proof that this measure of degree of belief satisfies the laws of probability theory, in other words, that it is a probability measure. In the following sections we study more closely the structure of the operational methods and their advantages and disadvantages. We then formulate Ramsey's axioms and see how they lead to a utility scale or utility function; that is, we study Ramsey's 'unfinished' representation theorem. After that, we deal with the step from a given utility scale to precise (subjective) probabilities. We show that the measure representing the degree of belief that an agent has in a proposition satisfies the axioms of probability theory. Further, we establish that the conditions set out are necessary if the agent is not to be exposed to a betting situation in which he or she inevitably loses money. Finally, we examine what Ramsey meant by 'human logic' and its bearing on the question, 'To what degree is Ramsey's theory a subjective theory of probability?'

RAMSEY'S OPERATIONAL METHOD

Is there a reliable method by which one can measure an agent's degree of belief in an arbitrary proposition p, a method that really brings out the agent's or the subject's assessments? We want to avoid, for example, a random number between 0 and 1 being given or that a subject in an experiment is consciously or unconsciously trying to bring down or help the experimenter. The problem is tremendously complicated, and perhaps this occurs to us when we think of the great number of probability estimates unconsciously made every day, assessments which are necessary for our survival and which influence our actions. Our wishes and hopes affect our probability assessments whether they are conscious or unconscious. The probability assessments made by a war correspondent concerning the easing of tension in a regional conflict are, of course, affected by his own longing for peace. On a more workaday level, I always rate the likelihood of 'ice-cream for dessert' very high, simply because this is my favourite dessert. The method has to surmount difficulties like these, too.

It was a well-known fact when Ramsey wrote his essay that a betting method may be used for establishing the degree of belief an agent has in a proposition p. To get the feel of how this works, we assume that p is the proposition that the strawberries at the bottom of the basket are just as nice as those on top, and $-p$ is its negation. By examining the lowest odds that the agent is ready to lay on p, we can arrive at the required information concerning his partial beliefs. Assume that the person in question is willing to bet 3:1 that p is not true. This means that the degree of belief he or she assigns $-p$ equals $3/(3 + 1)$, that is, .75. This is because the individual in question has shown that in three cases out of four he thinks that the strawberry seller has put the rotten strawberries at the bottom of the basket. Thus it follows that the degree of belief in p is .25.

Although Ramsey appraised this betting method as being 'at bottom sound', it nevertheless contains certain weaknesses. Today it is considered an empirical fact that in situations like the one described above people's idiosyncrasies affect the odds they are prepared to accept. Two interesting groups of behaviour patterns emerge. We have on the one hand those who really accept worse odds than those they judge to be ideal in the situation but also those who are prepared to pay an inordinate sum to avoid taking part in the bet or to improve the odds. Neither the risk-prone nor the risk-aversive subjects will disclose their 'true' odds. The feeling of satisfaction or unease that a betting situation causes has as a result that it is impossible under such conditions to establish with any certainty the degree of belief the agent has in the proposition in question.

Ramsey wanted to side-step these problems but not at the cost of introspection. He did not accept the possibility of asking the agent directly what degree of belief he has in the proposition. It is Ramsey's basic pragmatic outlook that prevails here. He stresses that it is only from an agent's actions that we can gain a more or less exact idea of his partial beliefs. Ramsey seems to believe that the behaviour of subjects can be examined under controlled experimental conditions and that it should be a question of hypothetical alternatives of action. This approach is taken, of course, in order to avoid having the measurements upset by 'irrelevant' factors. One may imagine, for example, that in a carefully constructed experiment it would be feasible to check up on such variables as risk aversion and risk proneness and on the problem of the desirability of the outcome affecting the probability assessment.

As suggested, Ramsey tries to solve the above problems by more or less accepting the betting method, with the proviso that before the method is applied, the utility values of the outcomes used to construct the bet must be known. By gaining more knowledge of the risk-aversive individual's utility curve, we prevent it from affecting the desired measurement of degree of belief. Let us examine more closely the structure of the operational method and how Ramsey uses it to establish utility values.

ETHICALLY NEUTRAL PROPOSITIONS

Of decisive importance to Ramsey's operational method is the existence of *ethically neutral propositions*. But what is an ethically neutral proposition? Ramsey gives the following definition:

[A]n atomic proposition p is called ethically neutral if two possible worlds differing only in regard to the truth of p are always of equal value.[4]

What does it mean to say that two possible worlds differing in regard to p being true or false are of equal value? In order to understand what Ramsey means by this definition we must first distinguish between *worlds*, or what I call *outcomes* (without introducing the distinction acts, states and consequences – which is not present in Ramsey's text in a systematic way), here designated $a, b, c, \ldots$, and *propositions*. The former are introduced in order to obtain a reward system; the latter are the objects of partial beliefs. This is a rather artificial distinction, but since Ramsey used it, and I am not sure why, I am going to stick to it.

Now let a be the outcome 'It is going to rain tomorrow' and p the proposition that I'll remember to take my umbrella to work tomorrow. The proposition p is then ethically neutral according to the above definition if the following condition is satisfied:

i. $-(a\&p\mathbf{P}a)$ & $-(a\mathbf{P}a\&p)$,

where $\mathbf{P}$ denotes the preference relation 'is preferred to' or 'is better than'. Therefore, if the value of 'it is going to rain tomorrow and I will remember to take my umbrella to work' is equal to the value of 'it is going to rain tomorrow', then we say that p is an ethically neutral proposition. But those of us who, at one time or another, half-asleep have left our umbrellas at home and returned in the evening soaking wet and furious know that this is not true. The proposition p cannot therefore be regarded as an ethically neutral proposition.

Thus our first attempt to exemplify an ethically neutral proposition has been far from successful. It seems, however, that there is a type of proposition which is suitable for the present purpose. I am thinking primarily of the type we encountered in discussing the problem of the early probability theorists. We choose one of many variants and let p be the proposition that 1, 2 or 3 will come up at the next throw of the die which is in front of me on the table. Does this change of p mean that (i) is now satisfied; that is, is p an ethically neutral proposition? This depends on what will happen if the outcome of the throw of the die is 1, 2 or 3. If one is shot dead on the spot or exposed to different horrors, it is scarcely likely that p can fulfil its task. The fact is that the outcome need be neither diabolical nor divine to upset the applicability of p. Relatively common outcomes in a positive or negative direction are sufficient to restrict the use of the proposition. But if hypothetical outcomes can be constructed in such a way that they do not alter the agent's status quo, it is quite possible to take p as an ethically neutral proposition. This means, in principle, that we accept that it is impossible to find a universally useful p for experimental purposes but that for given experimental situations or subjects it is possible to find a useful p.

The examples show how difficult it can be to find an ethically neutral proposition p. In the following, however, we assume that there is (at least) one ethically neutral proposition and worry less about what that proposition is. It turns out that if such a proposition exists, it has a number of interesting characteristics.

One subtlety about an ethically neutral proposition is that it does not in any way affect an agent's preference ranking. Let a, b, c and d be four outcomes whose preference ranking is:

$a \textbf{ P } b \textbf{ P } c \textbf{ P } d;$

that is, *a* is preferred to *b* which in turn is preferred to *c*, and so on. But since *p* is assumed to be an ethically neutral proposition, we know in the light of (i) that *a&pSa, b&pSb, c&pSc* and *d&pSd*, where **S** stands for the relation 'neither better than nor worse than'.[5]

That this is the case permits us to substitute *a&p* for *a, b&p* for *b,* and so on. We thus arrive at the following preference ordering, equivalent to the one we began with:

a&p **P** *b&p* **P** *c&p* **P** *d&p.*

An example is in order. Let *a* be the outcome 'It is going to be sunny tomorrow' and *b* the outcome 'It is going to rain tomorrow'. We assume that 'sun' is preferred to 'rain'. If *p* is the proposition that 1, 2 or 3 will come up at the next throw of the die, we can presuppose that this is ethically neutral in the restricted sense we discussed above. This means that it is going to be sunny tomorrow and 1, 2 or 3 will turn up at the next throw of the die is to be preferred to it is going to rain tomorrow and 1, 2 or 3 will come up at the next throw of the die. The latter preference ordering also seems logical since only assumptions about obscure causal connections between the throw of the die and the weather conditions would affect this ordering.

By way of conclusion and somewhat parenthetically, a problem similar to the one Ramsey has in finding an ethically neutral proposition also exists in other, essentially different theories. For example, in Marxist economics a problem arises in transforming a quantity in abstract working time into money. The price of an article is defined as the sum of the barter value of the basket of goods and the transferred barter value, where the so-called profit quotient acts as a constant. But since these quantities in turn are based on the concept of abstract working time, what Marx calls a general equivalent is needed to serve the same purpose as money. Ramsey's ethically neutral proposition and this general equivalent are surrounded by largely the same problems.

AN ETHICALLY NEUTRAL PROPOSITION BELIEVED
TO DEGREE ½

Ramsey's next step towards a complete operational definition is to define what is meant by having a degree of belief ½ in an ethically neutral proposition.

Irrespective of whether p is ethically neutral, it would seem logical to say that an agent has the degree of belief ½ in the proposition in question if the following two bets are considered equally good:

ii. a if p is true, b if $-p$ is true,

iii. b if p is true, a if $-p$ is true.

The outcomes a and b could be anything we like, but to make the idea work we need to assume that either $a\mathbf{P}b$ or vice versa.

As usual, it is easier to understand the idea behind the definition by looking at an example. We let a be the outcome 'You will receive a dollar' and b 'You will lose a dollar'. For most of us, $a\mathbf{P}b$ holds. If p is an ethically neutral proposition, you have the degree of belief ½ in it if you consider (ii) and (iii) as equally attractive bets. Why? Assume that your degree of belief in p is somewhat greater than ½. Would you then still maintain that the two bets are equal in value? Hardly! Since your degree of belief in p is slightly greater than ½, it would be rational to choose (ii) rather than (iii), for then the chance of winning a dollar in cash increases. The reverse reasoning also applies, of course, if p is assessed a value less than ½: that is, in this case bet (iii) will be preferable.

Ramsey himself has the following to say about the definition:

> This comes roughly to defining belief of degree ½ as such a degree of belief as leads to indifference between betting one way and betting the other for the same stakes.[6]

Experimental psychologists have tried to find something which in experimental contexts can play the part that an ethically neutral proposition of degree of belief $\frac{1}{2}$ does in Ramsey's theory. In a series of experiments, Davidson, Suppes and Siegel used a specially constructed die. As a basis they were using Glaze's studies of the associative value of combinations of letters. As we have seen, it is essential that the ethically neutral proposition does not add anything to the outcomes contemplated. It turned out in Glaze's studies that the combinations of letters 'ZOJ' and 'ZEJ' lack associative value. Therefore a die was constructed with the inscription 'ZOJ' on three of the sides and 'ZEJ' on the other three sides. In this way the three had cunningly succeeded in constructing an experimentally useful device that largely fulfilled Ramsey's demand for an ethically neutral proposition.[7]

THE DEFINITION

For the sake of simplicity, let us introduce some new notations. Bets of the type included in the definition of an ethically neutral proposition with a degree of belief $\frac{1}{2}$, for example (ii), will be written $(a;p^{\frac{1}{2}};b)$, where $p^{\frac{1}{2}}$ denotes an ethically neutral proposition of degree of belief $\frac{1}{2}$. The condition that (ii) and (iii) are to be ranked equally can then be written more concisely as

iv. $(a;p^{\frac{1}{2}};b)\mathbf{S}(b;p^{\frac{1}{2}};a)$.

Having defined what is meant by an ethically neutral proposition, Ramsey shows how p can be used to study (measure) the relative size of the value distance between two arbitrary outcomes. As before, let a, b, c and d be four arbitrarily chosen outcomes and let $d(a,b)$ denote the value distance between a and b. Ramsey's operational definition may then be expressed as follows:

Definition R. The value distance between a and b is said to be the same as the value distance between c and d, $d(a,b) = d(c,d)$, if and only if $(a;p^{\frac{1}{2}};d)\mathbf{S}(b;p^{\frac{1}{2}};c)$.

In an experimental study I used the following four hypothetical outcomes: 'Receive a week's holiday at a resort of your own choice', 'Receive 100 pounds in cash', 'Receive 5 pence in cash', and 'Lose the nail of the little finger of your left hand'.[8] Let us refer to these four possible outcomes as a, b, c, and d, respectively. For one of the subjects participating in the experiment, the above presentation of the possible outcomes is in agreement with his ranking of them. The subject was invited to choose one of the following two bets:

B1. Receive a week's holiday at a resort of your own choice if p is true and lose the nail of the little finger of your left hand if $-p$ is true.

B2. Receive 100 pounds in cash if p and receive 5 pence if $-p$ is true.

No die was used as a substitute for p; instead the subject was given an account of the significance of the proposition which could play the part of p. In the choice between B1 and B2, the subject in question preferred to play B2. This choice, according to Ramsey's definition, means that the subject viewed the value distance between c and d as greater than the value distance between a and b. Expressed differently, it would be decidedly better to receive 5 pence in cash than to lose the nail of the little finger on his left hand, but it would not be such a striking improvement to receive a week's free holiday at a resort of his own choice instead of 100 pounds in cash.

The function of the definition will be seen most clearly if one assumes that a utility measure $u(.)$ exists, representing the utility or subjective value the agent assigns a given outcome. That the bet B2 is considered better than B1, given the assumption that we are utility maximizers, means that the expected utility of the bet B2 is greater than the corresponding value of bet B1. The expected utility of B2 is equal to the probability of receiving c, which is $\frac{1}{2}$, multiplied by the utility of c, that is, the utility of receiving 5 pence in cash, plus the corresponding product of b. We can express this more formally as $U(B2) = \frac{1}{2}u(c) + \frac{1}{2}u(b)$. If B2 is now preferred to B1, B2PB1, then $U(B2) > U(B1)$; that is, $\frac{1}{2}u(b) + \frac{1}{2}u(c) > \frac{1}{2}u(a) +$

$\frac{1}{2}u(d)$. Divide by $\frac{1}{2}$ on both sides and make some rearrangements and we have $u(c) - u(d) > u(a) - u(b)$ – that is, the qualitative relation $d(c,d) > d(a,b)$ expressed with the aid of a utility function, a relation which seems highly reasonable under the circumstances.

Definition R then expresses the gauge needed to gain information about the ordinal ranking not only of a number of outcomes or worlds but also of value distances between outcomes. As mentioned, however, def R is not capable on its own of assigning every outcome a definite utility value. For this purpose, a set of axioms is needed – more precisely, eight in all, in Ramsey's axiomatization. These axioms guarantee the existence of a utility function $u(.)$ and are worth studying in greater detail, but first let us look at one or two alternatives to Ramsey's definition.

ALTERNATIVE OPERATIONAL DEFINITIONS

Ramsey's definition is far from unproblematic. The doubtful assumption of the existence of an ethically neutral proposition has made many people recoil from the whole idea. At the same time, philosophers and psychologists alike have been interested in finding alternatives to Ramsey's operational method. Naturally they have sought an alternative which is not impaired by the problems discussed above. P. Suppes and M. Winet envisage a definition based on the concept of value distances.[9] In their theory, information is obtained about the value distances $d(a,b)$ and $d(c,d)$ by letting the subject be in possession of b and d and then investigating how much he or she is willing to pay to obtain a and c, respectively. If the subject pays x pence in order to exchange b for a and y pence to obtain c instead of d, and $x > y$, we know that the value distance between a and b is greater than the corresponding distance between c and d. If $x = y$, the value distance is to be considered equally great and we thus have a parallel with Ramsey's definition. The obvious problem of this definition is that it is based on a monetary scale. A linear relation between amounts of money and utility distances is not required. What has to be assumed is that the relation is monotonically increasing. Still, I believe that the individual's attitude to money has a far too great and uncontrolled impact and that even such a seemingly reasonable assumption does not hold for most situations. Ramsey's problem with the risk-aversive person has its equivalent here in the skinflint.

Another definition which like Suppes's and Winet's is based on value distances but which unlike theirs avoids the complications caused by a monetary scale has been proposed by S. Halldén.[10] The idea behind the definition is that strength of preference is revealed by one's second-order preferences. If I prefer to be able to prefer 'pea soup for lunch' to 'pea soup containing poison for lunch' to being able to prefer 'ice-cream for dessert' to 'fruit for dessert', then I have disclosed that the value distance between 'pea soup' and 'pea soup containing poison' is greater than the value distance between the latter pair. The choice of preferences thus gains decisive importance.

Our friend the science fiction writer is sitting in his room devising possible worlds. The earth becomes a place of exile of a diabolical kind for the dissidents of a remote planet. But in order for their stay on earth to be full of hardships, their possibilities of making second-order preferences must be restricted. Those in exile, however, are allowed to choose which preferences they can retain and thus which nerve paths are to be blocked. The choice of primary preferences is of vital importance for the dissidents, and a bad choice may lead to greater suffering.

The example may appear rather drastic. But it shows clearly how important it is to choose the 'correct' primary preferences. Choices of this type are made frequently, but most often they are made unconsciously. R. Jeffrey has found an excellent example of a second-order preference.[11] It is perhaps of the unconscious kind but one which can easily be raised to the conscious level. An individual may prefer smoking to not smoking but the second-order preference says something different. The same person prefers to prefer not smoking to smoking to preferring smoking to not smoking. A knotty problem for many smokers.

Jeffrey mentions that he has never been able to find a sign of a second-order preference in his old cat, and H. Frankfurth has taken the ability to make second-order preferences to be the feature distinguishing humans from other species of animals.[12]

If we let **B** stand for the second-order preference relation 'as good as' and assume that $a\mathbf{P}b$ and $c\mathbf{P}d$, we can express the definition put forward by Halldén as follows:

Definition H. The value distance between a and b is said to be as great as the value distance between c and d, $d(a,b) = d(c,d)$, if and only if $(a\mathbf{P}b)\mathbf{B}(c\mathbf{P}d)$.

Is it possible to show that def R and def H are equivalent? If this is not the case, it must be that one of the definitions does not give us the information about value distances sought but something else, which is still unknown. On the other hand, if both of them can be proved to be equivalent, theoretically and experimentally, then we have very strong support that we are getting information about the actual value distances. One possible approach is to assume that a choice of primary preferences can be represented as a choice of one bet rather than another. These bets can then in turn be assumed to be equivalent with more manageable disjunctions and, finally, these assumptions taken together can result in the type of bets on which Ramsey's definition is based. In his book *The Foundations of Decision Logic*, Halldén carries out a proof of this kind and in the previously mentioned experiment, I arrive at results showing that the value distances obtained do not depend on which of the two definitions is used.

Ramsey's definition thus gains support from an unexpected quarter. In the light of def H, def R stands out as a more reliable method, and vice versa. But it must be borne in mind that this does not mean that the problematic parts disappear when it comes to application of the definitions. We can only work on the assumption that under certain conditions the methods give us correct information about the agent's value distances.

A system of axioms, as those used, for example, by Ramsey, can be divided into two categories: *structure axioms* or *ontological axioms*, on the one hand; and *rationality* or *behavioural axioms*, on the other.[13] We shall use this distinction in studying Ramsey's theory since it allows us to pick out the empirically testable parts of the theory from its purely mathematical content.

The rationality axioms are axioms that a 'rational' person is supposed to satisfy when making decisions. A typical example of a rationality axiom is the transitivity principle. Stated in terms of outcomes, this principle says that for all outcomes a, b and c, if a is preferred to b and b is preferred to c, then a should be preferred to c. That is,

If aPb and bPc, then aPc.

The best-known argument in favour of this principle or axiom is the 'money pump' argument. Assume that you violate the transitivity principle: you prefer a to b and b to c, but you prefer c to a. Thus, given b, we would expect you to be willing to pay a small sum of money (as small as you like) to get a instead. Similarly, you would be willing to pay an amount of money to get c instead of a, since you prefer c to a, but also to pay money to get b back, since b is preferred to c. Thus you end up with what you had at the beginning, but with less money. If you do not correct your intransitive preferences, you can be used as a money-pump until you run dry. This and similar arguments are put forth in favour of most of the rationality axioms.

Nevertheless, it is not necessary under all conditions to accept the rational in the transitivity principle. If someone were to assert that a stochastic variant of the condition (i.e., that there is only a certain probability of the consequence being fulfilled) were the ideal axiom for a decision theory, it need not follow that the person is advocating anarchy and an irrational system. It should not be forgotten that in stipulating the transitivity axiom we assumed that the agent possesses extraordinary perceptual and mental capacities. To enable us to follow the axiom consistently in all conceivable situations, it is not only necessary to be infinitely sensitive to subtleties but also to have an overwhelming ability to store and process data. For this reason, other axioms will be relevant if one assumes the agent is not so completely ideal and these axioms are still to be designated rationality axioms. The rationality axioms are those axioms that tell us how an agent in a given state of knowledge should act to 'optimize' his behaviour, if feasible.

The other type of axiom on the other hand, the ontological or structural axiom, does not make any demand on the agent's actions. These axioms are primarily of mathematical or philosophical interest. They tell us, for example, what we can expect to exist, and provide us with the necessary mathematical tools to prove the desired representation theorems. A good example of an axiom of this kind is Ramsey's first axiom, which states:

(R1) There is an ethically neutral proposition p believed to degree $\frac{1}{2}$.

From an empirical point of view, it is thus the rationality axioms that are of interest. These are the axioms that can be empirically tested (the distinction between the two kinds of axioms is somewhat slippery; structural and ontological axioms can have behavioural significance, e.g., if we want to take cognitive limitations into account) and psychologists have thoroughly scrutinized them. An overwhelming majority of their experiments indicate that people are far from satisfying even the most common and acceptable rationality axioms.[14] This fact has led to a debate about whether people are rational or not. I would argue that these experiments do not tell us much about human rationality. What they do tell us is that we generally do not act in accordance with a number of, what we believe to be, reasonable principles of sound behaviour. The question of rationality can, I take it, only be answered within the framework of much more general psychological theories.[15]

We shall simply use the distinction to scrutinize Ramsey's axioms. This will, it is hoped, contribute to our understanding of the representation theorem which is one of the important links on the way to an amalgamation of the concepts probability and degree of belief.

THE AXIOMS

Ramsey's first axiom, axiom R1, is thus a purely ontological axiom and it is needed to make the operational definition function.

Axiom R2 states that if two ethically neutral propositions exist and both are believed to degree $\frac{1}{2}$, then def R will give the same result whichever of these two propositions is applied. Take the die inscribed ZOJ/ZEJ and assume that we have another die which satisfies the above conditions; the only difference is that we have engraved on that die the combinations WUH/XEQ.[16] Suppose that you receive 50 pounds if ZOJ comes up and lose 10 pounds if ZEJ comes up. If we exchange ZOJ for WUH and ZEJ for XEQ and nothing else is changed, it seems completely logical that you consider the two bets to be of equal value. This is also exactly what Ramsey's axiom states that you should do. Consequently the axiom is of the rational variety.

Axioms three and four (R3 and R4) are two transitivity axioms and thus remind us very much of the transitivity principle of preference theory we discussed previously. R3 states that if bets B1 and B2 are considered to be of equal value and the same is true of B2 and B3, then B1 and B3 are to be judged as equal. R4 is the corresponding axiom for value distances, which means that if the value distance between a and b is equal to the value distance between c and d and the latter in its turn is equal to the value distance between e and f, then the value distance between a and b should be the same as that between e and f; that is, $d(a,b) = d(c,d)$ and $d(c,d) = d(e,f)$, then $d(a,b) = d(e,f)$. These two axioms are thus each other's counterparts. The first requires rational behaviour when it comes to ranking bets of type $(a;p\frac{1}{2};b)$; the second axiom demands that the corresponding relation holds in ranking the value distances.[17]

The axiom R5 requires that for all outcomes a, b and d there is a unique outcome c such that $d(a,c) = d(b,d)$. Axiom R6 states that for all outcomes a and c there exists one and only one outcome b such that the value distance between a and b is equal to the corresponding distance between b and c; that is, $d(a,b) = d(b,c)$. In other words, there is always an outcome, the value of which is located exactly between two other arbitrarily selected outcomes.

Axiom R7 is a continuity axiom. The type of axiom Ramsey imagines here is quite obvious if we first recall some of the earlier elements we learned about the properties of real numbers. The axiom concerning an upper bound says that every non-empty set of real numbers with an upper bound has a least upper bound, and from this axiom it follows that every non-empty set of real numbers with a lower bound has a least lower bound. That this does not apply to the rational numbers is comparatively easy to see. Take the rational numbers greater than $\sqrt{2}$ but less than π. This is a set of numbers for which there is neither a greatest lower bound nor a smallest upper bound within the set. Ramsey needs axiom R7, among other things, in order to arrive at a well-defined set to which he can effectively apply his definition.

Finally, axiom R8 is the Archimedean axiom which is now common in the context of measurement theory. This is a forceful axiom and its strength will soon be evident. However, Ramsey does not mention how he thought this axiom ought to be formulated more precisely but only says that it is to be an Archimedean axiom. Nevertheless, it might be of interest to imagine how the axiom would probably have looked if Ramsey had written it out. Archimedean axioms got their name for the simple reason that they corresponded to one of the properties of real numbers, called the Archimedean property. For any positive number x, no matter how small this number is, and for any number y, no matter how large it is, there exists an integer n such that n times x is greater than or equal to y. To Ramsey it is important that the corresponding relation holds for value distances. No matter how small the value distance is between a and b, and no matter how large the value distance is between c and d, there exists an integer n such that n times $d(a,b)$ is greater than or equal to $d(c,d)$.

THE REPRESENTATION THEOREM

According to Ramsey, these eight axioms give us the possibility to assign every outcome a a definite utility value, that is, a real number $u(a)$ such that

$$d(a,b) = d(c,d) \text{ if and only if } u(a) - u(b) = u(c) - u(d).$$

This means that the agent's preferences may be represented by a utility function $u(.)$ which is determined up to a positive affine transformation.[18]

Ramsey, however, never gives the proof for this theorem and it might be interesting to try to reproduce his representation theorem in rough outline and see how these eight axioms in accordance with def R give the function $u(.)$ as a yield.

Let O be a set of outcomes. Let a and b be two outcomes in O such that $a\mathbf{P}b$. Axioms 1–4 guarantee both the existence of an ethically neutral proposition with a degree of belief $\frac{1}{2}$, and that the agent behaves rationally when it comes to ranking value distances and bets. We can thus assume that all the outcomes in O are ranked on an ordinal scale; that is, if a, b and c are three outcomes in O, either $a\mathbf{P}b\mathbf{P}c$ or some other permutation in terms of preferences of these three outcomes holds. But def R gives us more information than merely the agent's ordinal preferences between the possible outcomes. Each value distance between any two outcomes is ranked with respect to length. We know not only that the agent prefers coffee to tea after dinner, and tea to water, but also that he or she strongly prefers coffee to tea, but is rather indifferent to whether he or she gets tea or water. The strength of the agent's preferences, measured by employing def R, is important for the decision he or she intends to make. Both the ordinal and the cardinal preference ranking fulfil the demands for rationality that we made above. What worries us is how each of these outcomes included in the ranking is to be assigned a real number in the way that Ramsey claims is possible.

The high school student of today is faced with similar ranking problems when choosing a career. Considerations of labour market policy have to be weighed against personal inclinations. The safe labour market for clergymen has to be compared with the problems of earning a living for the theology graduate who is not ordained. These two professions must in turn be contrasted with more specific vocational training as a craftsman. To put it quite simply, there will be a choice between two alternatives in further education – one theoretical and one practical. But to be able to decide in favour of one of these two alternatives, the high school student must weigh the various components against each other. It must be possible to numerically compare the advantage of being a potter with the advantage of being a clergyman, and so on.

Let a be the outcome 'become a potter' and b the outcome 'become an unemployed theologian'. We assume, moreover, that a is better than b. Since a and b both belong to O, axiom R6 tells us that there is a proposition $a_{\frac{1}{2}}$ the value of which lies between a and b.[19] But as a reiteration of the same principle shows, there is a proposition $a_{\frac{1}{4}}$ which lies between $a_{\frac{1}{2}}$ and b, and a proposition $a_{\frac{3}{4}}$ the value of which lies between $a_{\frac{1}{2}}$ and a, the problem seems to be moving towards a solution. The information obtained so far can be illustrated heuristically as follows:

$$a - a_{\frac{3}{4}} - a_{\frac{1}{2}} - a_{\frac{1}{4}} - b.$$

We thus have a long way to go before getting the numerical utility assessments Ramsey's theorem claims. But axiom R6 also tells us that there are outcomes that lie in value between any two of these five outcomes. Thus we know there exists an outcome $a_{\frac{7}{8}}$ which in value is situated between a and $a_{\frac{3}{4}}$, and another $a_{\frac{3}{8}}$ which is situated between $a_{\frac{1}{2}}$ and $a_{\frac{1}{4}}$. These may in turn correspond to one or other alternative in the high school graduate's preference ranking; let us say becoming a doctor and becoming a bricklayer.

While axiom R6 fills in the holes in our scale so elegantly we have axiom R5 to fall back on when it is no longer sufficient. Axiom R5 states that for three arbitrary outcomes a, b and d, there exists an outcome c in O such that the value distance between a and c is identical with the distance between a and b. One could then imagine apportioning the numerical values in the following simple way: a is given the utility value 1, since the potter's profession is the one judged to be best and the value 0 to the outcome b, since being a theologian without any work would appear to be sheer punishment. Furthermore, we can let $a_{\frac{1}{2}}$ have the utility value $\frac{1}{2}$ – that is, $u(a_{\frac{1}{2}}) = \frac{1}{2}$ – and let $u(a_{\frac{1}{4}}) = \frac{1}{4}$, $u(a_{\frac{3}{4}}) = \frac{3}{4}$, and so on. In this way we assess the propositions in O utility values between 0 and 1.

But victories are seldom so easily won and the fact is that in this case, too, we have a good way to go. If we have not succeeded in deriving the utility measure Ramsey aimed at, this in turn must mean that an 'error' has arisen in our assessment of utilities. The thought that there is not perhaps just one but an infinite number of outcomes left in O may be annoying. However, the problem can be simplified somewhat by maintaining the validity of only two possibilities. One of these is that the outcome in question is definitely worse (better) than b (a). The high school graduate shrinks from his counsellor's suggestion of a career in administration. Becoming a civil servant is not an alternative in any circumstances. The other alternative is that the outcome lies in value somewhere between a and b but for one reason or another it has not been assigned a utility value according to our procedure above.

It is not possible that c is an outcome in O such that aPc and cPb but where c is not assigned a utility value between o and 1. R5 states quite definitely that given a, b and c there is an outcome d such that the value distance between a and d is equal to that between b and c. If d is assigned a utility value according to the above method, c will also have a utility value assigned to it. The only interesting variant is therefore to assume that there is an outcome c in O such that cPa or bPc.

For the sake of simplicity, consider the case in which b is better than c. Of course the following argument also holds for the case in which cPa. The hitherto unused axioms R7 and R8 now come into play. The student counsellor's answer to the high school pupil will be more or less a verbalization of axiom R7: 'All right! Maybe it does feel awful to be a civil servant but there must be some limit to the misery'. Axiom R7 says precisely that; it must be the case that the preference ordering is limited from both above and below. This now means that we do not constantly come across progressively worse alternatives, but only that these, in that case, converge on a lower limit, as it were.

We can now return to axioms R5 and R6 since these guarantee the existence of outcomes $c_{\frac{1}{2}}$, $c_{\frac{1}{4}}$, $c_{\frac{3}{4}}$, and so on. But we also need the Archimedean axiom R8 to solve the problems that arise because we allow continually worse outcomes. Furthermore, we are required to make the final adjustments to the system. Axiom R8 says that no matter which c we choose in this interminable order of preferences we can measure the distance between b and c by the concatenation of a selected standard value distance (say, $d(d,e)$). Since 'standard sequence' means a sequence of distances of nonzero and equal length (of a chosen unit length), axioms R7 and R8 say that every strictly bounded standard sequence is finite. Thus R7 and R8 guarantee avoiding an Achilles problem and they guarantee continuity. Furthermore, by using axioms R5 and R6, of course, we obtain a yardstick which we can insert n

times. The Archimedean axiom has thus appeared with full force.

To simplify somewhat, imagine that we have been working with a huge plank. We have taken care to ensure that it is neatly sawn off at either end. The plank has no marks on it but since we are interested in disposing of parts of it, we must be able to cut it up in an economically satisfying way. We take a piece of wood – let us call it a unit-stick – with the aid of which we can measure and divide the plank into required lengths. In Ramsey's system the plank is the equivalent of the complete preference ranking and the unit-stick is the equivalent of an arbitrarily small value distance between two outcomes.

We thus arrive at yet another of the objectives on the way to subjective probabilities. We – or rather Ramsey – have a utility scale to be used as a link in this theoretical chain. All the outcomes in O by repeated use of def R, together with the rationality axioms and certain logical assumptions (the ontological axioms), have been assigned a definite utility value. We shall now see how this scale of utilities may be used to establish the degree of probability an agent assigns to an arbitrary proposition.

FROM UTILITY COMPARISONS TO PROBABILITIES

The question now is how this utility scale may be utilized to obtain exact numerical information about the degree of belief an agent has in an arbitrary proposition. As explained earlier, Ramsey bases his theory on a refined version of the betting method as an operational method. The idea is that it should be possible to systematically compare preferences between bets of the type we have previously come across, but where the utility value for the outcomes included in the bet are known, in the hope of avoiding some of the problems we have touched on before, such as risk aversion.

Assume that our high school pupil is faced with the choice between b with certainty or a if p is true and c if p is false, where *b* stands for 'becoming a clergyman', *a* for 'becoming a potter' and *c* for 'becoming a civil servant'. We assume then that the order of preferences is the same as before, namely, *a***P***b***P***c*. The following two bets are offered to the high school student:

B1. *b* if *p* is true and *b* if −*p* is true, i.e., *b*, and
B2. *a* if *p* is true and *c* if −*p* is true.

If the pupil is indifferent to these two bets, then we define his or her degree of belief in *p* as the quotient between the value distance between *b* and *c* and the value distance between *a* and *c*. Ramsey says:

> This amounts roughly to defining the degree of belief in *p* by the odds at which the subject would bet on *p*, the bet being conducted in terms of differences of value as defined.[20]

In order to understand the meaning of this, it is perhaps easiest to tackle Ramsey's definition from the wrong end, as it were, that is, by taking for granted what we want to arrive at. Assume that we have a probability function *P*(.) defined over the propositions which are relevant. Provided that one accepts the principle that it is rational to maximize expected utility, it follows that B1 and B2 are considered equal in value if and only if the expected utility is the same for the two bets. The fact that $U(B1) = U(B2)$ thus means that $P(p)u(b) + P(-p)u(b) = P(p)u(a) + P(-p)u(c)$. Since B1 has *b* as the sole outcome, we can reduce this identity to $u(b) = P(p)u(a) + P(-p)u(c)$. From the assumption that *P*(.) is a probability measure, it follows that $P(p) = 1 - P(p)$, and after multiplying and transposing we obtain the following identity: $u(b) - u(c) = P(p)(u(a) - u(c))$. It is now easy to see that dividing both sides by $u(a) - u(c)$ exemplifies the definition drawn up by Ramsey. Expressed formally, the definition is as follows:

If *b***S**(*a*;*p*;*c*), then we say that

$$\frac{d(b,c)}{d(a,c)} = \frac{u(b) - u(c)}{u(a) - u(c)} = P(p).$$

35

If our pupil assigns a, b and c the utility values 20, 10 and 5, respectively, it thus follows that $P(p) = (10 - 5)/(20 - 5) = \frac{1}{3}$, where p may be an arbitrary proposition whose truth value has not yet been determined, for example, that the economic situation will improve by so many units. Put less elegantly, we know that the degree of belief that the high school pupil assigns to the proposition that the economic situation will improve is .33 because the outcome 'becoming a clergyman' is considered equal to a bet between 'becoming a potter' and 'becoming a civil servant', where the pupil's future in the latter case depends on how the country's economy will develop.[21]

But this definition is not sufficient to connect unambiguously the degree of belief in a proposition with the subjective probability of the same proposition. To do this, we also require a definition of conditional probabilities. We have to define what is meant by the degree of belief in a proposition p given the proposition q. Ramsey mentions in this connection:

> This does not mean the degree of belief in 'If p then q', or that in 'p entails q', or that which the subject would have in p if he knew q, or that which he ought to have. It roughly expresses the odds at which he would now bet on p, the bet only to be valid if q is true.[22]

Assume we want to establish the degree of belief in p, the economic situation will improve, given q, the government will devalue by at least 20 per cent. This knowledge can be arrived at, according to Ramsey, by means of two indifferent bets:

B3. a if q is true, b if $-q$ is true, and

B4. c if p is true and q is true, d if $-p$ is true and q is true, b if $-q$ is true.

In order to gain an insight into how this functions, we shall again assume that $P(.)$ is a function representing the degree of belief that an agent has in a proposition, and that this function satisfies the laws of probability theory. If B3 and B4 are equal in value, it follows that

$$P(q)u(a) + P(-q)u(b) = P(p\&q)u(c) + P(-p\&q)u(d) + P(-q)u(b).$$

Since $P(-q)u(b)$ can be dropped from both sides of the identity, the difference may be written

$$u(a) = \frac{P(p\ \&\ q)}{P(q)}\ u(c) + \frac{P(-p\ \&\ q)}{P(q)}\ u(d).$$

In addition, the assumption that $P(.)$ is a probability measure means that the formal definition of conditional probability is applicable; that is, we can use our knowledge that $P(p/q) =_{df} P(p\ \&\ q)/P(q)$. This gives

$$\frac{u(a) - u(d)}{u(c) - u(d)} = P(p/q)$$

or

[T]he degree of his belief in p given q is the ratio of the difference between [a] and [d] to that between [c] and [d], which we must suppose the same for any [a, b, c, d] which satisfy the given conditions.[23]

We have assumed that $P(.)$ is a measure representing the degree of belief the agent has in a proposition and that this measure satisfies the axioms of probability theory. However, Ramsey must prove this is the case. He has to prove that the axioms together with the given definitions as a yield give a probability measure $P(.)$ and only then will he have shown it is possible to link together partial beliefs and probability assessments in a reasonable way.

I shall deviate a trifle from the way in which Ramsey proves the measure obtained is a probability measure. The reason for this is that nowadays we are accustomed to seeing a probability measure as defined over a propositional field (i.e., over a number of propositions closed under certain logical operations), and where the measure satisfies the following three requirements:

P1. $P(p) \geq 0$
P2. $P(T) = 1$, and
P3. if p and q are incompatible, $P(p \vee q) = P(p) + P(q)$

('T' denoting an arbitrary tautology). By making use of these axioms, we also simplify Ramsey's presentation.

It is comparatively straightforward to see how condition (P1) follows from the above definitions and the way in which we have constructed our measuring rod; that is, one notes that $0 \leq u(b) - u(c) \leq u(a) - u(c)$. Condition (P2) follows if we note that, if p is equivalent to T, b must be equivalent to a, for b with certainty is to be assigned the same value as a bet where one receives a if p is true and c if $-p$ is true. This is because p is true from the agent's point of view and he therefore acts as if a will be the outcome. Thus, what remains is to prove that the measure obtained satisfies the third requirement.

We start by assuming that $P(p) = x$ and $P(q) = y$. To obtain a with certainty can then be written as a bet in accordance with the definition above:

$$aS(a + (1 - x)b; p; a - xb),$$

where b can be arbitrarily chosen. This rephrasing can be taken even further by rewriting the two constituents of the bet. We begin by rewriting the left-hand side. To receive $a + (1 - x)b$ if p is equivalent to receiving $a + (1 - x)b + (1 - y)c$ if p and q and $a + (1 - x)b - yc$ if p and $-q$. The corresponding change on the right-hand side means that obtaining $a - xb$ if $-p$ is equivalent to obtaining $a - xb + (1 - y)c$ if $-p$ and q, and $a - xb - yc$ if $-p$ and $-q$. We simplify by letting our arbitrary b equal c and by applying the assumption that p and q are incompatible. These operations give us the following indifference:

$$aS(a + (1 - x)b - yb; p \vee q; a - xb - yb).$$

Ramsey's first definition together with the principle of mathematical expectation gives

$$P(p \lor q) = \frac{u(a) - (u(a) - xu(b) - yu(b))}{(u(a) + (1 - x)u(b) - yu(b)) - (u(a) - xu(b) - yu(b))}.$$

After some transpositions, $(xu(b) + yu(b))/u(b)$ drops out and it is easy to see that $P(p \lor q) = x + y$.

We have thus proved that the obtained measure of the degree of belief an agent has in a proposition satisfies the third axiom of probability theory. However, since this measure also satisfies the two other axioms, it is a probability measure – a measure of subjective probability.[24]

THE APPLICABILITY OF THE DEFINITIONS

The above definitions provide a transition from comparisons of utility to subjective probabilities and are intended to replace the previously used betting method in order to obtain knowledge of the degree of belief an individual has in an arbitrary proposition. However, they are not only replacements for the earlier method but will also be improvements on this method. If we replace our old spectrograph with a new one, it should be technically superior to the first one. For what is the use of exchanging a measuring instrument that works for one that is identical but of a different make? But is Ramsey's method superior to the betting method and does it avoid the traps it is designed to avoid? The betting method and Ramsey's definitions are not essentially different. At bottom is the idea that an individual's behaviour in different betting situations gives us correct information about his or her probability assessments. Therefore we ought perhaps to begin by asking why Ramsey did not totally abandon the idea that betting situations can give us this information and, instead of rebuilding an already existing model, create a radically different method. Ramsey has the following to say about this:

> [I]t is based fundamentally on betting, but this will not seem unreasonable when it is seen that all our lives we are in a sense

betting. Whenever we go to the station we are betting that a train will really run, and if we had not a sufficient degree of belief in this we should decline the bet and stay at home.[25]

Ramsey's argument then is that we can see life as one big lottery. We buy or have forced upon us lottery tickets and sometimes we prefer the sure to the unsure and refuse to participate. This is true regardless of whether it is a question of going to the station, signing a business contract with England or buying a bottle of claret to take to our neighbour's dinner party. Ramsey's arguments are very tempting and weigh extremely heavily, but there are objections to be raised. D. H. Mellor for example, has argued that the drawback with a method such as Ramsey's is that some topics cannot be bet on. One requirement that has to be fulfilled is that the bet is settleable to the satisfaction of the respective parties and in a currency or benefit whose value can be assessed before the bet.[26] But these requirements, Mellor says, are not fulfilled if we are to make a bet on a life after death. If there is no life after death, this means that one of the people involved in the bet will not be possessed of the possibility to receive his possible winnings. On the other hand, if the assumption is true, it would seem reasonable to ask oneself what currency is negotiable, and if so what can I spend the money on? Mellor's example is neat and illuminating but I do not think that it seriously affects the validity of Ramsey's approach. I can well imagine that any winnings there happen to be will be distributed in a clearly specified way among those who outlive me. Our life insurance policies are a bet of this kind, a bet in which the relatives are the 'winners' and not the better himself.

It is possible, of course, to imagine certain reinforcements of Mellor's argument. Assume that we intend to take a bet on the extinction of the whole human race or the truth of different theories of physics where these theories, for example, are only distinguished from each other in the kind of numbers used. The problems arising here do not indicate a limitation in Ramsey's theory but rather the fact that we are not always able to decide in a meaningful way on the truth-value of a proposition.

Let us now return to our primary question, that is, whether Ramsey's definitions are better than our traditional betting methods. One of the problems with the traditional betting method is that the desirability of the outcomes in the bet influences the probability assessments. But this can scarcely be the problem for Ramsey. Ramsey's method builds on the idea that the consequences of a bet are not to be measured by the outcomes but in terms of utilities. Since these utility values, among other things, represent the desirability of the outcome, this disturbing factor is eliminated.

But what happens if we cannot establish the subject's utility curve? To apply the definitions, we must know the utility function up to a positive affine transformation; that is, all the utility values can be multiplied by a positive constant and be added to another constant without changing the informational content. Bruno de Finetti who independently and almost at the same time formulated a theory similar to Ramsey's on subjective probabilities must have had this problem in mind when he suggested that the classic betting method be used as an operational method, but with the qualification that the outcomes be monetary and very small.[27] Assume that you have a choice between two bets. The first gives x pence if p is true and z pence if neither p nor q is true. The second bet gives y pence if p is true, x pence if q is true and the same as before if neither p nor q is true. It is then easy to see that if you prefer the first bet you have a greater degree of belief in p than in q, because the choice of this bet gives:

$$P(p)x + P(q)y + P(-p\&-q)z \geq P(p)y + P(q)x + P(-p\&-q)z, \text{ i.e., } P(p) > P(q).$$

By applying de Finetti's definition, one of course avoids the complicated process of assessing all the utility values that are important. But a notable defect in this operational method is that it assumes the utility function is linear with money. It is not enough to assume that the relation between value distances and amounts of money is monotonically increasing. We realize now that one of the advantages of Ramsey's theory, despite the above criticism, is that it does not make use of an operational method based on an application of monetary units.

It remains to be seen how risk-aversive or risk-prone behaviour affects Ramsey's definitions. If we adopt the economist's definition of the concept of risk, risk-aversive behaviour occurs when one chooses the cash equivalent of a bet rather than taking the bet itself. Assume that the bet is (+1 pound; $p\frac{1}{2}$; 0 pounds). This bet has an expected value of 50 pence. If 50 pence is preferred to participating in the bet, the person in question is said to be risk-aversive. In principle this means the individual is risk-aversive if and only if the marginal utility is decreasing.[28] This in turn means risk aversion has been linked with a property of the utility curve. If this is a correct procedure, Ramsey has taken risk-aversive behaviour into account since, by knowing the curvature of the utility function, we know whether the individual is risk-aversive or risk-prone. But if, as I am inclined to do, one asserts that this method of establishing degree of risk aversion is far from satisfactory, then it follows that Ramsey's method has not taken different kinds of risk behaviour into account. The reason for this is that it seems reasonable to assume we have utility curves with marginally decreasing utility without being risk-aversive on that account. A pure saturation effect makes the phenomenon inclined to set in sooner or later. I enjoy a good piece of cake and maybe even two, but sooner or later the enjoyment wears off if I am pressed to have a third, a fourth, or a fifth. This means the risk-judgement factor may affect the indifference assessments and thus the probability assessments, although the utility values are fixed.[29]

In Ramsey's defence, the above counter-argument is forceful only if it is asserted that the theory has a descriptive intent. But Ramsey never thought of it as a descriptive theory. As a purely normative model, it is unimpeachable from these points of view. Ramsey assumes an ideal agent whose ability to make choices between bets is unlimited. Or, as Ramsey puts it, his theory requires that the subject is persuaded that the experimenter has the power of the Almighty; so that the outcomes of the bets, viewed as complete courses of the world, can be put in order of value. Nonetheless, it would seem the pragmatic outlook requires that the theory be descriptively applicable. We shall return to the problem of interpretation in a later section.

Another question that should be addressed is Ramsey's reliance on mathematical expectation. Many theorists, prior to and after Ramsey, have queried the applicability of mathematical expectation as a basis for a decision rule, particularly when it comes to different decisions that will never be repeated. Assume, for instance that you arrive at a remote spot where they sell Coca-Cola for 5 cents a bottle. The price of a bottle has risen to 6 cents recently but the machine only takes nickels. If every sixth bottle in the machine is empty in a random way, the expected price per bottle will be six cents. For the owner of the machine and those who often use it, this will be quite satisfactory, but for you the visitor passing through, the system is of doubtful value.[30]

In situations like this, are we to maximize the expected value or ought another decision rule be used? The idea that risk aversion is not taken into consideration is a commonly occurring criticism nowadays. Ramsey has the following to say about relying on the mathematical expectation:

> [I]t is based throughout on the idea of mathematical expectation; the dissatisfaction often felt with this idea is due mainly to the inaccurate measurement of goods. Clearly mathematical expectations in terms of money are not proper guides to conduct.[31]

This opinion has been championed by a whole generation of decision theorists after L. J. Savage had rediscovered Ramsey's works in the early fifties. We shall leave this question without going into the arguments for and against the assumption of expected value.[32]

CONSISTENCY AND COHERENCE

After having shown that the obtained measure of degree of belief is a probability measure, Ramsey continues:

> These are the laws of probability, which we have proved to be necessarily true of any consistent set of degrees of belief. Any definite set of degrees of belief which broke them would be inconsistent in the sense that it violated the laws of preference between options, . . .
>
> We find, therefore, that a precise account of the nature of partial belief reveals that the laws of probability are laws of consistency, an extension to partial beliefs of formal logic, the logic of consistency. . . .
>
> Having degrees of belief obeying the laws of probability implies a further measure of consistency, namely such a consistency between the odds acceptable on different propositions as shall prevent a book being made against you.[33]

Ramsey mentions almost in passing that the axioms of probability theory are necessary for a consistent set of probability assessments. At the same time, he points out that if the probability measure does not satisfy these laws, then the agent exposes himself to the possibility of inevitably making a net loss in a bet. To Ramsey, this fact is an interesting corollary, but many probability theorists after Ramsey have taken this as the decisive argument in favour of the fact that a set of partial beliefs has to be free of contradiction. To understand the extent and depth of the argument, we must be aware of what Ramsey means by a consistent set of degrees of belief and that one should try to avoid a 'book'.

According to what we can gather from the above quotation, Ramsey places consistency on a par with satisfying the axioms of probability theory. Ramsey's wording is perhaps rather unfortunate. A consistent system of partial beliefs must not be confused with a consistent logical system. If a logical system is inconsistent, we can deduce sentences of the type '$p \& -p$', which is not at all necessary for an inconsistent system of partial beliefs. The term used today, 'coherence', therefore says more about what is intended. The agent's probability assessments should be coherent and then with respect to what the requirements or axioms above state. A typical example of inconsistent behaviour is if I assess the probability of p as .6 while at the same time assessing that the probability of $-p$ is .2. According to our axiom, the sum of the probability of a proposition and the probability of its negation has to be 1.

What then is the reason for modelling our behaviour in accordance with these axioms? If such motivation is lacking, we might just as well retain our incoherent assessments. The very heart of the argument in favour of the axioms is that if we do not follow them, an experienced bookmaker will make use of our incoherent assessments and make a net profit whatever we do. The bookmaker makes what is called a 'Dutch book', or what Ramsey calls simply a 'book'.

Let p be the proposition that Pegasus will win the trotting race. Assume further that our player has made the in-coherent probability assessment $P(p) = .6$ and $P(-p) = .2$. The cunning bookmaker now offers the player two bets:

a. Receive 6 pounds if $-p$, lose 4 pounds if p,
b. Lose 8 pounds if $-p$, receive 2 pounds if p,

where (a) is valid for the assessment $P(p) = .6$ and (b) for the assessment $P(-p) = .2$. We can see why the bets are linked to a given assessment if we calculate the expected value for each of the bets. Since the bookmaker knows that the gambler assesses the probability of Pegasus winning to be .6, he also knows that the better is prepared to bet 4 pounds on p if he puts 6 pounds on $-p$. Bet (a) will thus have the expected value $-4 \times .6 + 6 \times .4 = 0$ pounds, which is a prerequisite for the bet to be valid. It follows that the expected value of bet (b) is 0 pounds if the bet is made in accordance with the rules given. In that case, the better is willing to bet 8 pounds in all on $-p$ if he gets 2 pounds plus his own stake if it turns out that $-p$ is the case. If we regard the two bets (a) and (b) as a pair, it is obvious the gambler will make a net loss whether Pegasus finishes first or not.

Provided that Pegasus wins the race, (a) will give a loss of 4 pounds and (b) a win of 2 pounds, that is, a total loss of 2 pounds. On the other hand, if Pegasus loses the race, which in itself seems improbable, (a) will mean a win of 6 pounds and (b) a loss of 8 pounds. Once again there is a net loss of 2 pounds. What is to be done?

A simple way for the gambler to avoid this unfortunate and precarious situation is to make sure the probability assessments are coherent. If our gambler is firmly convinced that the probability of Pegasus winning is .6, he cannot simultaneously assess $-p$ a probability of .2. The probability of the horse losing must in this case be equal to .4. On the other hand, if it is the probability of $-p$ he is certain of, he must adjust the probability of p to .8. The very low degree of belief in $-p$ makes it necessary for a high degree of belief in p. Of course it is possible to correct both assessments, but this should be done in a coherent way. $P(p) + P(-p)$ has to add up to 1. But let us assume that it is the probability assessment for $-p$ that is the reasonable one. In this case the gambler will no longer be willing to accept bet (a) since the expected value of that bet now is a loss of 3 pounds and 20 pence. If we correct the bet in such a way that the expected value is 0 pounds, it follows that the combination of (a) and (b) cannot enforce a net loss. It is also impossible to find other pairs of bets which could be used in this way to make a profit out of the agent's probability assessments. The moral is that if we want to avoid the unpleasantness that a Dutch book entails, we must make sure that our system of partial beliefs is coherent, or in Ramsey's terminology, consistent.

The assumption that it should be impossible to expose an agent to a Dutch book is based on a precondition of rationality. Relatively weak demands on rationality give the results that a system of partial beliefs can be represented by probabilities. But is this assumption of rationality reasonable? The question has both a descriptive and a normative side. Empirical investigations have shown more or less unambiguously that people lack the ability to follow the axioms of probability theory. Thus we cannot say that we are rational in everyday life in the accepted sense. Normatively speaking, it is more reasonable to uphold the condition. It seems there is no problem in stipulating that behaviour is to be considered irrational or unsound if we lose a sum of money whatever we do. We can also say that if we were aware that our system of partial beliefs is inconsistent, we would correct it so that it became coherent. As a basis for action, a coherent system is superior to an inconsistent one. If nature is the bookmaker, our only chance of coping tolerably is to see to it that our system of probability assessments is coherent. For there are no moral misgivings or charitable considerations – only the maximization principle counts; from an evolutionary perspective, only the most rational agent can be expected to survive.

However, one should note that incoherent probability assessments do not necessarily imply an incoherent set of partial beliefs. It may well be that our degrees of belief are not at all so precise or stable that a precise measurement of them can be obtained. By this I do not mean that the techniques of measurement are imprecise and thus that, although we have precise degrees of belief, we cannot measure them accurately. This is what Ramsey has in mind when in 'Truth and Probability' he says, 'I have not worked out the mathematical logic of this in detail, because this would, I think, be rather like working out to seven places of decimals a result only valid to two'.[34] What I have in mind is something different. Assume there is no definite real value representing the agent's degree of belief. Imprecise degrees of belief would then in a natural way lead to imprecise subjective probabilities. Thus an agent may very well be willing to bet on the least odds $x{:}y$ for p, but at the same time bet on the least odds of $w{:}z$ against p, where $x/(x + y)$ is not equal to $w/(w + z)$. One could thus say that the Dutch book assumption places too heavy a demand on people's willingness to make bets, but also on how precise the degree of belief we have in a proposition actually is. To me it seems reasonable to abandon Ramsey's assumption that the agent's state of belief can be represented by a *unique* probability measure. A much better alternative is to relax this assumption and instead argue that imprecise beliefs have to be represented by sets of probability measures.[35]

At the end of his paper, Ramsey tries to show that it is possible to develop a human logic, to give a justification of induction, which will not attempt to be reducible to formal logic. Here he turns against Wittgenstein's opinion that induction cannot be given a logical justification but only a psychological one. Ramsey says:

> From the other side it is contended that formal logic or the logic of consistency is the whole of logic, and inductive logic either nonsense or part of natural science. This contention, which would I suppose be made by Wittgenstein, I feel more difficulty in meeting. But I think it would be a pity, out of deference to authority, to give up trying to say anything useful about induction.[36]

Although Ramsey doesn't say so, it is clear from an earlier and unpublished paper of his ('Paper to the Society', Autumn 1922)[37] that there are three points in the *Tractatus* which caught Ramsey's attention. (In passing it should be mentioned that the aim of this unpublished paper is to defend Wittgenstein's thesis.) In 6.31, 6.363 and 6.3631, respectively, Wittgenstein states:

> 6.31   Das sogenannte Gesetz der Induktion kann jedenfalls kein logisches Gesetz sein, denn es ist offenbar ein sinnvoller Satz. - Und darum es auch kein Gesetz a priori sein.

> 6.363   Der Vorgang der Induktion besteht darin, daß wir das *einfachste* Gesetz annehmen, das mit unseren Erfahrungen in Einklang zu bringen ist.

6.3631   Dieser Vorgang hat aber keine logische,
sondern nur eine psychologische Begründung.
Es ist klar, daß kein Grund vorhanden
ist, zu glauben, es werde nun auch wirklich
der einfachste Fall eintreten.

Ramsey wanted to show that the inductive method can be justified from a pragmatic standpoint. Following what he took to be Peirce's view, he states that induction is 'a habit of the human mind'.[38] It is also a 'good habit' for 'it is better to be right sometimes than never'. Concealed in this last statement is also his idea about how a principle of induction can be justified. Our aim is to be 'right' more often than 'wrong'. To achieve this aim, a principle of induction is a vital instrument. The limits of the applicability of the instrument are determined by Ramsey's theory.

When we see a flash of lightning, we wait for the thunder. Similarly, we expect that what has been true in 99 cases will also be true the hundredth time. Two habits are the basis of the expectations. In the first case, the expectation is 'after a flash of lightning there will be thunder'. In the latter case, the habit is that from 99 similar cases one can generalize the fact that the hundredth, too, will agree with the previous ones. As a basis for further actions, this type of vague principle of induction is invaluable. In order to be able to decide among many possible alternatives of action, I must compare their value. This means in turn that relevant probability assessments must be made. There is no demand that in making them I am obliged to follow the inductive method, but if I believe in a principle of induction I will usually arrive at a better result than if I ignore it completely.

The angler has to decide if he is going out on the lake one day when dark clouds are beginning to threaten and the wind blows harder. If he can remember that these weather conditions are usually a sign of thunder, it would seem foolhardy to go out fishing. The probability of a storm coming up and the heightened risk of an accident are weighed against the probability of and value of fresh fish for dinner.

This alternative of action in turn is to be compared with the possibility of staying indoors and eating yesterday's left-overs, thus gaining greater protection against all the possible dangers of the storm. Experience is undoubtedly of decisive importance in our choice of actions. Those of us who rely on a principle of induction will manage better in the long run than those who do not, and according to Ramsey, it is a sufficient and good reason for making inductions that are not tautologous. So he has both dismissed Wittgenstein's doctrine and shown that it is not necessary, as Keynes believed, to justify the principle of induction logically and formally.

At the very end of the above-mentioned paper, Ramsey mentions that he just had what might prove a useful idea:

> [A] type of inference is reasonable or unreasonable according to the relative frequencies with which it leads to truth and falsehood. Induction is reasonable because it produces predictions which are generally verified not because of any logical relation between its premiss and conclusion. On this view we should establish by induction that induction was reasonable, and induction being reasonable this would be a reasonable argument.

And, as far as I can see, this is the idea being more fully developed four years later in 'Truth and Probability'. The idea that induction may be used to justify induction, I take to be the correct approach to the problem. What we get is a productive spiral of related inductive arguments, which is something different from a vicious circle.

Behind Ramsey's idea of a human logic and his justification of induction lies what might be called a well-articulated paradigm of philosophy (to use one of his own phrases), that is, a philosophical analysis of the related concepts 'belief' and 'action'. Most clearly, this view, his basic view, on this relation is stated in a few lines in 'Facts and Propositions', where he discusses what it means to say that a belief is true. Ramsey's answer to this question is roughly that a belief is true if it is useful. As an example he takes a chicken that believes a certain sort of caterpillar is poisonous. He says '[A]ny set of actions for whose utility p is a necessary and sufficient condition might be called a belief that p, and so would be true if p, i.e., if they are useful'.[39] In view of what has been said above, one might take exactly the same attitude towards a principle of induction. The principle is reasonable according to the relative frequencies with which it leads to truth or falsehood, that is, according to the relative frequency with which it is useful.

CHANCE

One question which has been the subject of long and occasionally lively discussion is how to interpret the axiom of probability theory. We have dealt with the frequency interpretation, the logical interpretation and a possible subjective interpretation. Generally the adherents of one interpretation have little patience with those who argue in favour of another interpretation. In recent years, however, several proposals for dualistic interpretations have emerged. One of those who realized early on that a double interpretation might be valuable and even necessary was Carnap. Carnap distinguishes between probabilities-1 (pr_1 = belief assessments) and probabilities-2 (pr_2 = frequencies). We shall see here that corresponding ideas were already present in Ramsey's texts.

Ramsey's aim was to show that we are able to measure the degree of belief an agent has in a proposition, and that provided the agent follows some principles of rationality, the measure by which we can represent this 'degree of belief' is a probability measure. He also believed that such a subjective probability measure was not open to the criticism levelled against, for example, the frequency theories or logical theories of probability. Ramsey does not, however, believe that subjective probabilities are the only probabilities there are. In 'Reasonable Degree of Belief', 'Statistics' and 'Chance' (written in 1928, two years after 'Truth and Probability' – the notes contain some reinforcements of earlier arguments and attempts to show the applicability of the original theory) Ramsey suggests that besides a subjective interpretation, we have an objective interpretation of probability theory – a chance interpretation.

Ramsey's ideas about the concept of chance remind us of what might be called objectified subjective probabilities, that is, subjective probabilities given a vast amount of information. Ramsey's concept of chance is based on degrees of belief:

> Chances are degrees of belief within a certain system of beliefs and degrees of beliefs; not those of any actual person, but in a simplified system to which those of actual people, especially the speaker, in part approximate.[40]

Why it is not a question of an actual person's degrees of belief is explained by Ramsey in the following passage:

> [B]ut they do not correspond to anyone's actual degrees of belief; the chances of 1,000 heads, and of 999 heads followed by a tail, are equal, but everyone expects the former more than the latter.[41]

Ramsey also excludes a frequency interpretation. The chance of the Queen of Spades being drawn from a well-shuffled pack of cards is not necessarily equal to the proportion of the number of times this has happened. 'Chances are in another sense objective, in that everyone agrees about them, as opposed e.g. to odds on horses.'[42] I believe that Ramsey's concept of chance is closely related to the concept of probability often used in the natural sciences. If we accept certain physical theories, and thus indirectly the experimental evidence for these theories, some probability assessments are more reasonable than others. Our theory may, for example, tell us that the probability of recording a given particle in a given state at a given time lies in a closed and narrow interval. I believe this is what Ramsey means by saying that chances are degrees of belief within a certain system of beliefs and degrees of belief. Ramsey seems to have taken objective probabilities for granted. He believed that Boltzmann's probabilities are a matter for physics, that is, definitely not for logic. He also thought that in order to apportion our belief to the probability, we must be able to measure our belief.

Thus it is important to note that Ramsey, in his stance towards objective probabilities, differs from others who have developed subjective theories of probability, for example, de Finetti, Savage and Jeffrey. Ramsey does not believe that the concept of chance is incoherent or that the objective concept of probability can be reduced to a subjective one. True, according to Ramsey chances are degrees of belief, but not those of any actual person. Chances are degrees of belief in a simplified system, degrees of belief given by a theory, to which actual people in part approximate (see the discussion in Chapter 4). Ramsey would thus have rejected de Finetti's famous dictum that 'Probability does not exist' – meaning that objective probability does not exist.

Another difference between Ramsey and other subjectivists is therefore that Ramsey would probably say that some probability assessments are not all that rational. If a person has a degree of belief which clearly differs from the chance given by an accepted theory, I believe Ramsey would have said that this degree of belief is not well calibrated; it is not a rational degree of belief. If, for example, you give 10 to 1 odds on the toss of a fair coin, it seems somewhat irrational behaviour. However, according to de Finetti's theory there are no grounds for criticism at all in this case. One assessment is as good as any other. For the extreme subjectivist, there are no objective probabilities to be taken into account. But in Ramsey's case, if we have a system of beliefs and degrees of belief, then we have a chance to evaluate subjective probability assessments.

DECISION THEORY

It is commonly thought that two main types of factors influence our decisions. One is our wants or desires. These determine the utilities of the possible outcome of a decision. The other is our beliefs about what the world is like and how our possible actions will influence the world. A decision theory is thought to provide a model for how we handle our wants and beliefs and provide an account of how they are to be combined into rational decisions.

Theories of this type are generally founded on four basic assumptions.[43] First, the values of the outcomes in a decision are determined by a utility measure which assigns numerical values to the outcomes. Second, when determining the value of a decision alternative, the only information about the agent's wants and desires that is used is the utilities of the possible outcomes of the alternative. Third, an agent's beliefs about what might happen in a given situation (about the states of the world) can be represented by a unique probability measure defined over the states. Fourth, for all states and all alternatives, the probability of the state is independent of the act chosen. Finally, it is argued that the fundamental decision rule is the principle of maximizing expected utility. In a given decision situation, the agent should choose the alternative with maximal expected utility.

We have seen that Ramsey's primary interest was to give a foundation to the third assumption. However, it should be pointed out that in doing so he also gives foundations to the three other points (and this is not often noted in the literature). Thus what might be called Ramsey's utility theory is a theory closely related to von Neumann and Morgenstern's theory, and what might be called Ramsey's decision theory is a theory closely related to Savage's theory. The latter two theories, for example, give almost identical results (except for some technicalities concerning 'null events'). This should be kept in mind when in Chapter 9 we turn to Ramsey's two papers on economics. The utility theory on which the results of these papers are based was developed a year before in 'Truth and Probability'.[44,45]

Chapter 2
Belief and truth

WHAT IS TRUTH?

And Pilate said unto him, What is truth?
And Echo answered – the prophet would not tell
His lips were sealed, no answer was forthcoming
The Nazarene descended into Hell.

But thank the Lord for all these wise professors
To whom the truth is there but to descry
Their number it is legion, there are many
Who've given the doubting Roman a reply.

But it's odd to me that truth the one and only
So magically changes shape and hue,
What's called the truth in Berlin or in Jena
In Heidelberg is anything but true.

It's like hearing young Prince Hamlet when he's teasing
Old Polonius 'bout the clouds up in the sky
'Methinks that cloud is like unto a weasel
– or is it like a camel passing by?'

Gustaf Fröding[1]

In two pages of the essay 'Facts and Propositions' (1927), Ramsey formulates a theory of truth which has caught the attention of quite a few philosophers. The aim of his essay is not, however, to discuss the concept of truth, taken by itself. Ramsey develops his theory in the course of discussing the notions of 'belief' and 'judgement'. But interestingly enough, it is these two pages, a parenthesis in a 20-page paper, that

55

have been taken to be its most valuable contribution. My view is that for Ramsey these two pages were no more than a statement of an obvious fact. What was of significance to him was to find an analysis of the concept of belief which did not presuppose the concept of truth.

THE REDUNDANCY THEORY

The basic idea of what has become known as Ramsey's redundancy theory of truth, that we can say without the help of a truth predicate whatever we can say with it – that is, that the truth predicate is redundant – has a longer history than one might expect. In *Metaphysics*, Aristotle already seems to have pondered over a similar idea and it has appeared in various forms throughout history ever since. A concise formulation of this line of thought can be found in a two-page note written around 1915 by Gottlob Frege. Frege writes:

> Wenn ich behaupte 'es ist wahr, dass das Meerwasser salzig ist', so behaupte ich dasselbe wie wenn ich behaupte 'das Meerwasser ist salzig'. Hierin ist zu erkennen, dass die Behauptung nicht in dem Worte 'wahr' liegt, sondern in der behauptetenden Kraft, mit der der Satz ausgesprochen wird. Danach könnte man meinen, das Wort 'wahr' habe überhaupt keinnen Sinn. Aber dann hätte auch ein Satz, in dem 'wahr' als Prädikat vorkäme, keinen Sinn. Man kann nur sagen: das Wort 'wahr' hat einen Sinn, der zum Sinne des ganzen Satzes, in dem es als Prädikat vorkommt, nichts beiträgt.[2]

Also W. E. Johnson in his *Logic* of 1921 discusses the eliminability of the predicate 'true'. According to Johnson, this predicate and its semantic import is best understood if it is compared with the functioning of the number '1' within arithmetic. Multiplying a number by 1 does not change anything, nor does adding 'it is true' to a sentence.

> Thus the assertion of p is equivalent to the assertion that p is true; though of course the *assertum* p is not the same as the

assertion that *p* is true. The adjective *true* has thus an obvious
analogy to the multiplier *one* in arithmetic: a number is un-
altered when multiplied by unity, and therefore in multiplication the factor *one* may be dropped; and in the same way the
introduction of the adjective *true* may be dropped without
altering the value or significance or the proposition taken as
asserted or considered.[3]

Thus, both Frege and Johnson muse on the idea that 'true' is
merely a linguistic token which does not alter the strength of
a sentence and which is therefore redundant. The truth
predicate can always be dropped without loss of assertional
content.

Ramsey does not say whether he got his idea from reading
Frege or Johnson. It is highly probable, however, that
Ramsey had not seen Frege's unpublished two-page note.
This note was published for the first time in 1969. On the
other hand, Ramsey knew the works of Johnson extremely
well (later on in his essay he does make a reference to Part II
of *Logic*). But since Ramsey was after all not trying to develop
a theory of truth, he might well have thought a reference to
Johnson here superfluous.[4]

Despite his lack of concern with truth, however, Ramsey's
remarks about it says something far more substantial than
the above quotations do. With a few examples he lays down
the broad outlines for a completely developed redundancy
theory; and that is why the redundancy theory is – rightly –
now associated with Ramsey rather than with Frege and
Johnson.

Ramsey presents his redundancy theory in a condensed
but lucid way. He says,

> But before we proceed further with the analysis of judgment,
> it is necessary to say something about truth and falsehood, in
> order to show that there is really no separate problem of truth
> but merely a linguistic muddle. Truth and falsity are ascribed
> primarily to propositions. The proposition to which they are
> ascribed may be either explicitly given or described. Suppose
> first that it is explicitly given; then it is evident that 'It is true

that Caesar was murdered' means no more than that Caesar was murdered, and 'It is false that Caesar was murdered' means that Caesar was not murdered. They are phrases which we sometimes use for emphasis or for stylistic reasons, or to indicate the position occupied by the statement in our argument. So also we can say 'It is a fact that he was murdered' or 'That he was murdered is contrary to fact'.[5]

This example shows how easily 'truth' can be eliminated from statements like 'It is true that Caesar was murdered'. But without too much mental effort one can construct more ticklish examples, examples which may indicate whatever weaknesses the theory might have. Ramsey himself mentions such an example.

How does one, within the framework of a redundancy theory, deal with statements of the type 'He is always right'. In this case the proposition is described rather than actually specified and we cannot straightforwardly eliminate 'truth' in this context. Not even if we rewrite the sentence 'He is always right' as 'Everything he says is true' is there a ready solution to the problem. Eliminating the word 'true' would just give us an elliptic sentence, 'Everything he says', which, if it tells us anything at all, does not say the same thing as our initial statement. Ramsey had of course thought about this problem, too, and gives us an astute solution to it.

> In the second case in which the proposition is described and not given explicitly we have perhaps more of a problem, for we get statements from which we cannot in ordinary language eliminate the words 'true' and 'false'. Thus if I say 'He is always right', I mean that the propositions he asserts are always true, and there does not seem to be any way of expressing this without using the word 'true'. But suppose we put it thus 'For all p, if he asserts p, p is true', then we see that the propositional function p is true is simply the same as p, as e.g. its value 'Caesar was murdered is true' is the same as 'Caesar was murdered'.[6]

Thus, Ramsey does not attempt to find a solution within ordinary English, but moves instead into a quasi-formalized language. This technique of introducing quantifiers in order to solve a philosophical problem is something that Ramsey makes use of in another of his essays. In 'Theories', written two years after 'Facts and Propositions', Ramsey uses more or less the same device in order to explain the functioning of a theory's so-called theoretical terms (see Chapter 5).

Ramsey's redundancy thesis benefits from his theory of universals – his view of what objects there are in the world and what type of 'logical constructions' propositions in fact are (see Chapter 8). Arthur Prior in his posthumously published *Objects of Thought*, a book in which some of Ramsey's ideas are developed in a masterly fashion, summarizes the thesis in the following way; ' "That grass is green is a true proposition" = "The proposition that grass is green is a true one" = "That grass is green is a truth" = "It is true that grass is green" = "It is the case that grass is green" = "That grass is green is a fact" = "It is a fact that grass is green" = the plain "Grass is green" '.[7] As Prior points out, this is not to say that this type of sentence is not to be used; it is to say what their meaning is. Furthermore, if ' "The proposition that the sun is hot is true" and "That the sun is hot is a fact" just mean "The sun is hot", they *must* be, precisely because of this, mind-independent and language-independent, for the sun's being hot in no way depends on anyone's thinking or saying that it is.'[8] I cannot see how anyone can reject this thesis, that is, when truth and falsehood are ascribed to propositions. To doubt it one would, I think, either be guided by a warped view of reality or be led to accepting the incredible position that, if there had been no beliefs, nothing would have been true.

But introducing quantifiers and thereby moving into a quasi-formalized language is not without its problems. After a few illuminating examples, we shall return to the philosophical problems connected with such a move.

SOME ADDITIONAL EXAMPLES

In a now classic essay, 'The Semantic Conception of Truth and the Foundations of Semantics',[9] Alfred Tarski discusses two examples which he takes to be impossible to analyse within the framework of a redundancy theory. His second example of a sentence from which the predicate 'true' cannot be eliminated is

The first sentence written by Plato is true.

It is hard to say that Tarski is mistaken on this point and that an elimination in fact is possible, since his objectives are rather different. Tarski is not worrying about the elimination of the predicate 'true'. He is primarily interested in the switch from sentences in a meta-language to sentences in an object language. However, I believe that Ramsey would have argued that Tarski's example is as easily dealt with as those discussed above, namely by introducing quantifiers. The example is then handled as follows:

There is a sentence p, such that Plato wrote p and for all other sentences q, if Plato wrote q then he wrote it after p, and p is true.[10]

Thus, from a redundancy theory point of view it is clear that 'the first sentence written by Plato is true' means no more than 'there is a sentence p, such that . . . , and p'.[11]

Tarski's example is thus to be considered as relatively unproblematic if we look at it in the right perspective. But we can, I think, get a far more difficult problem if we consider the sentence:

(p) p is true.

This sentence says of itself that it is true. To simply eliminate the predicate 'true' seems quite impossible. The statement that Caesar was murdered tells us something, we understand what it means, but is this also true for '(p) p'? Can one rewrite the sentence in a way which makes it less difficult to analyse? I do not think it is possible. How would Ramsey have handled this example or problem then?[12] It is of course impossible to answer this question, but one might get an idea by studying an example given by Prior. He discusses the proposition:

> There are facts and falsehoods as well as things that are neither.

Prior says,

> If this means 'For some p, it is the case that p, and for some p, it is not the case that p, and for some p, it neither is nor is not the case that p', it is false (because its last clause is). If it means 'For some x, x is a fact, and for some x, x is a falsehood, and for some x, x is neither a fact nor a falsehood', where 'x' is the kind of variable that can be replaced by the name of an object, it is nonsense.[13]

Maybe Ramsey would say that (p) is a nonsense sentence. It is not a meaningful assertion. I believe that Ramsey's treatment of The Liar might suggest such a solution. In Chapter 6 we note that (especially the quotation directly connected with footnote no. 15), Ramsey argues that the problem with this antinomy is that we do not have a definite meaning for *means*, and that the solution to the problem is to limit the order of 'p' in some way. Thus if the two 'p' are of the same order, the assertion is meaningless, but if they are of a different but adjacent order then it is meaningful, but then also the predicate 'true' can be eliminated.

Another line of thought is that the sentence is not meaningless but that it lacks a truth value, it is neither true nor false. Does the difficulty in eliminating 'true' in fact show this? The sentence (p) is what Kripke has called an 'ungrounded sentence'.[14] The example shows that a redundancy theory may need so-called truth-value gaps. But does a redundancy theory really presuppose truth-value gaps? Susan Haack asks this question and gives the answer 'yes'.[15] Since the redundancy theory argues that 'p is true' means no more than 'p', one may well, according to Haack, maintain that if it is neither true nor false that p, it is neither true nor false that it is true that p. This shows that Ramsey in no way committed himself to the denial of truth-value gaps, something which is, for example, the case with Tarski's semantic conception of truth.[16] Another, and maybe more obvious objection, is that if it is neither true nor false that p, it is false that it is true that p.

It would thus be possible to formulate Ramsey's redundancy idea as a test of truth. The test says that a proposition is truth-value bearing if and only if the predicate 'true' can be eliminated. If an elimination is impossible, we are dealing either with a nonsense sentence or an ungrounded sentence. But this is not at all what Ramsey had in mind. In his book manuscript he explicitly warns us not to confuse the questions of meaning with the search for a criterion of truth.

Susan Haack, who addresses Ramsey's redundancy theory in a number of essays, asks if the theory does not imply that a very important distinction is lost. Generally we make a distinction between the law of the excluded middle, that is, p or not p, and the metalinguistic principle that for all p, either p is true or p is false. But according to the redundancy theory, the latter principle can be written 'for all p, p or not p', which constitutes a reduction to the law of the excluded middle. I do not think that one could argue that this distinction must be kept for explanatory reasons. To me it seems as if Ramsey's theory clearly shows that this is a distinction of doubtful value, one which we had better do without.

Haack has also conveyed the related idea that the redundancy theory might force us into a position where we have to accept degrees of truth.[17] But, to be driven to accept that something is '$\frac{1}{3}$ true' or '$\frac{1}{4}$ true' is utterly unacceptable. The problem becomes very clear if one starts with a statement like 'It is possibly true that p' or 'It is certainly true that p'. Now it is evident that Ramsey does not accept such a concept of truth. This follows with crystal clearness from the well-known passage below in 'Truth and Probability':

Belief and truth

[I]f we believe pq to the extent of $\frac{1}{3}$, and $p-q$ to the extent of $\frac{1}{3}$, we are bound in consistency to believe $-p$ also to the extent of $\frac{1}{3}$. This is the ἀνάγκη λέγειν; but we cannot say that if pq is $\frac{1}{3}$ true and $p-q$ $\frac{1}{3}$ true, $-p$ also must be $\frac{1}{3}$ true, for such a statement would be sheer nonsense. There is no corresponding ἀνάγκη εἶναι.[18]

If, as Ramsey does, we carefully distinguish the proposition from our attitudes towards it, there is really no problem here. Adverbial modifiers of truth are used to express degrees of belief, not degrees of truth. Thus, 'It is certainly true that p' = 'I believe with certainty that it is true that p' = 'I have full belief in p' and 'It is possibly true that p' = 'I believe that it is true that p is possible' = 'I have a degree of belief in p' are then easily handled within the framework of Ramsey's theory of belief.

PROPOSITIONAL QUANTIFIERS

Ramsey's introduction of propositional quantifiers has been criticized by a number of philosophers. Introducing propositional quantifiers, it is argued, means that 'truth' is eliminated in letter rather than in spirit. In order to understand what the new sentences say, 'true' and 'false' have to be reintroduced. Thus an important question is whether the propositional quantifiers can be interpreted in such a way that these concepts are not forced upon us from behind. Ramsey was aware of the problem.

We have in English to add 'is true' to give the sentence a verb, forgetting that 'p' already contains a (variable) verb. This may perhaps be made clearer by supposing for a moment that only one form of proposition is in question, say the relational form aRb; then 'He is always right' could be expressed by 'For all a, R, b, if he asserts aRb, then aRb', to which 'is true' would be an obviously superfluous addition. When all forms of proposition are included the analysis is more complicated but not essentially different.[19]

63

Ramsey thus means that

For all p, if he asserts p, p,

is to be interpreted as if the final 'p' expresses a well-formed sentence containing a verb. If this can be done, we would not have to add 'is true' in order to have a grammatically correct sentence. If not, nothing has been eliminated.

In *From a Logical Point of View*,[20] Quine argues that introducing propositional quantifiers amounts to making serious ontological commitments. It is contended that a sentence like 'For all p, Xp' must be given the interpretation 'For all things or objects p, p has the property X'. Quantification is only allowed over things or objects. In the essay 'True to the Facts', Donald Davidson discusses the pros and cons of the redundancy theory. He says that 'Here, truth is not explained away as something that can be predicated of statements, but explained'.[21] But, says Davidson, the explanation presumes that we understand sentences of the type 'For all p, if he asserts p, p', but do we really? Once again the quantifiers make us suspicious.

The problem is the variable p and the illusory double meaning it appears to have. In the above sentence p occurs as a bound variable, as the name of an object, but also as a sentence of its own, which can be assigned a truth-value. What worries Davidson is that 'the range of variables must be entities that sentences may be construed as naming in both such uses'. Referring to Frege, he continues: 'But there are very strong reasons, as Frege pointed out, for supposing that if sentences, when standing alone or in truth-functional contexts, name anything, then all true sentences name the same thing'.

A possible answer to this type of criticism has been given by Prior:[22]

It is true, we may yet again admit, that forms like 'For some p, p' are not idiomatic English, perhaps even not idiomatic Indo-European, but it is not difficult to see the extensions of our ordinary verbal procedures which would yield equivalents of such forms.[23]

According to Prior the above difficulties are the result of weaknesses in our everyday language and not a defect of the redundancy theory. Everyday language beguiles us into a fallacious reading of the above-mentioned quantifiers, a reading which ostensibly demands that 'true' and 'false' are reintroduced. Therefore Prior suggests:

> So we could simply *concoct* the quantifiers 'anywhether', 'everywhether', and 'somewhether', and translate, say, 'For any *p*, if *p* hen *p'* as 'If anywhether then thether'.[24]

To say 'for all *p*, . . .' gives rise to misleading associations; we are tempted to expostulate the second '*p*' as the name of an object.

Prior exercises this insight to give a direct answer to some of the criticism directed against Ramsey's theory. We simply do not have to worry about what the '*p*' stands for. The variable merely occupies a position for a sentence, but it does not denote an object. There is no reason to let Frege's assumption that sentences must signify objects named True and False trouble us, since this assumption is fundamentally wrong. Sentences do not denote objects. Prior states his thesis very clearly on page 35 of his book:

> The question what it 'stands for' in the second sense, i.e. what would be designated by an expression of the sort for which it keeps place, is senseless, since the sort of expression for which it keeps a place is one which just hasn't the job of designating objects.

Prior's development of Ramsey's redundancy idea has a good deal of attraction, but I shall not spend more time on discussing these problems. Let us turn instead to what Ramsey thought to be the real problem of truth.

THE PROBLEM OF THE BELIEVING SUBJECT

We have seen that when truth and falsity are ascribed to propositions, and when propositions are pictured as logical constructions, there is really no problem of truth. But Ramsey's famous dictum 'that there really is no separate problem of truth but merely a linguistic muddle' should not be interpreted as saying that truth offers no problem. Ramsey has, however, far too often been interpreted that way. The reason for this is, I think, that people have been misled by only reading the two often-quoted pages about the redundancy idea. But, if one reads Ramsey's text carefully – that is, reads more than pp. 142–3 (in *The Foundations of Mathematics*), pp. 44–5 (in *Foundations*) or pp. 38–9 (in *Philosophical Papers*) – one finds that what he actually means is that truth presents no separate problem, that is, separate from the problem of belief. Actually Ramsey already makes this clear when he discusses the redundancy idea. He says,

> [F]or what is difficult to analyse in the above formulation is 'He asserts *aRb*'.[25]

Ramsey thus saw that the real problem of a redundancy theory is to say what a belief is without relying on the concept of truth. In particular, we do not want a belief ascription to give the content of a belief by referring to the truth-values of a sentence.

It is interesting to note that by emphasizing the agent, Ramsey takes a considerable step towards pragmatism, away from the influence of Wittgenstein. What has been said so far about the redundancy theory is closely related to the ideas discussed by Ramsey in his review of *Tractatus* in 1923. One point that particularly arrested his attention was

> 5.542   Es ist aber klar, daß "A glaubt, daß p", "A denkt p", "A sagt p" von der Form, "'p' sagt p" sind: Und hier handelt es sich nicht um eine Zuordnung von einer Tatsache

und einem Gegenstand, sondern um die Zuordnung
von Tatsachen durch Zuordnung ihrer Gegenstände.

In the review Ramsey says that '[t]his reduction seems to me
an important advance'.[26] However, four years later, having
read Peirce and written 'Truth and Probability', Ramsey is
not at all in sympathy with Wittgenstein's idea of eliminating
the subject. This, I believe, is but one of many examples that
show that 'Truth and Probability' is for Ramsey the beginning of something new – he rapidly becomes attuned to
pragmatism.

Except for the two pages of 'Facts and Propositions' discussed so far, the paper is concerned with an analysis of
belief ascriptions, such as 'He asserts that p'. Ramsey wants
to outline an answer to the question what it is to believe or
judge. However, to do so, he first has to give an outline of an
account of the logical form of a belief ascription.

So-called propositional verbs – such as 'believe', 'think',
'desire', 'hope' and 'wish' – are used to denote various mental states. These states are often referred to as propositional
attitudes. Among these different states of mind Ramsey was,
for reasons that will be obvious at the end of this chapter,
particularly interested in the states of mind called belief and
judgement. He argued that a belief ascription 'consists in the
holding of some relation or relations' between the believer
and the referents of the belief, that is, a relation or relations
between one's 'mind, or [one's] present mental state, or
words or images in [one's] mind' and 'the objective factor or
factors'. And the 'questions that arise are in regard to the
nature of the two sets of factors and of the relations between
them, the fundamental distinction between these elements
being hardly open to question'.[27]

The most straightforward view of the referents of belief is
that there is only one objective factor, a proposition. This
type of dyadic-relation theory has in one way or another
been advocated by numerous philosophers. Among the best
known are Bolzano, Meinong and Moore, but also Russell,

whose arguments for giving up the theory were later accepted by Ramsey. This type of theory forces upon us not only propositions and facts, but also an infinite number of objective falsehoods. This, as some people have put it, makes reality an overcrowded slum.[28] Ramsey exemplifies this by mentioning 'the incredibility of the existence of such objects as "that Caesar died in his bed", which could be described as objective falsehoods, and the mysterious nature of the difference, on this theory, between truth and falsehood'.[29]

Ramsey also puts forth an argument against two of Russell's later theories, that, unlike knowledge and perception, a belief or a judgement is not a relation between a believer and a fact and that one should view beliefs as either pointing towards or away from facts:

> Let us for simplicity take the case of perception and, assuming for the sake of argument that it is infallible, consider whether 'He perceives that the knife is to the left of the book' can really assert a dual relation between a person and a fact. Suppose that I who make the assertion cannot myself see the knife and book, that the knife is really to the right of the book, but that through some mistake I suppose that it is on the left and that he perceives it to be on the left, so that I assert falsely 'He perceives that the knife is to the left of the book'. Then my statement, though false, is significant, and has the same meaning as it would have if it were true; this meaning cannot therefore be that there is a dual relation between the person and something (a fact) of which 'that the knife is to the left of the book' is the name, because there is no such thing. The situation is the same as that with descriptions; 'The King of France is wise' is not nonsense, and so 'the King of France', as Mr Russell has shown, is not a name but an incomplete symbol, and the same must be true of 'the King of Italy'. So also 'that the knife is to the left of the book', whether it is true or false, cannot be the name of a fact.[30]

Ramsey thus went further than Russell in also rejecting facts as the objects of beliefs. However, he followed Russell in arguing that a judgement or a belief is a multiple relation of the mind, the mental factors or the believer to many objects, that is, to the objects that the belief is about.

As Brian Loar points out in his article 'Ramsey's Theory of Belief and Truth',[31] the multiple-relation theory of belief has been taken to lead to hopeless problems because of the proliferation of belief relations it results in. According to Loar, there are two different sources for this multiplicity of belief relations. The first source is that beliefs can have different numbers of referents. For example, the classical example, 'Othello believes that Desdemona loves Cassio', expresses a four-place relation, where 'Othello believes that Desdemona prefers Cassio to Iago' expresses a five-place relation. The second source of multiplicity is that to every distinct logical form in the 'that' clause there must correspond a distinct belief relation. Loar shows how both these problems can be eliminated by the use of more or less the same technical trick. First, the objects of belief are collected in ordered *n*-tuples. Second, we make use of so-called intentional abstractions to take care of the second source of multiplicity. Thus, 'Othello believes that Desdemona loves Cassio or Emilia detests Iago' could be written

B(Othello, $xyzw[x$ loves y or z detests $w]$, <Desdemona, Cas­sio, Emilia, Iago>).

The finesse is thus that the logical form of a belief ascription is always a three-placed relation, but one where the second and third argument may vary. How much of this idea can actually be found in Ramsey's text is a question of interpretation. Ramsey obviously had thought about the problem of multiplicity, but it did not worry him that much. However, in his unpublished book manuscript on belief and truth one finds an idea that can be considered similar to the ones above.[32] In this manuscript he talks about the necessity of introducing 'dispositional belief functions' and compares them with the propositional functions of *Principia Mathematica*. But the idea is not fully developed and it is thus far from certain how he intended to use the belief functions.

TRUE BELIEFS

Ramsey says that 'if we have analysed judgement we have solved the problem of truth'.[33] But in order to carry out such an analysis successfully we must make sure that it does not presuppose the concept of truth. We must say, or rather Ramsey must tell us, what the content of a belief is without falling into a regress by appealing to the meaning of sentences, understood as truth conditions. Concluding his essay, Ramsey briefly outlines the type of program he wanted to carry out:

> The essence of pragmatism I take to be this, that the meaning of a sentence is to be defined by reference to the actions to which asserting it would lead, or, more vaguely still, by its possible causes and effects.[34]

Ramsey thus clearly believes that when we have found a theory of truth we have also established a theory of meaning; they are one and the same. The program sketched reminds us of what Peirce has to say in 'The Fixation of Belief.' Peirce argues that '[e]very answer to a question that has any meaning is a decision as to how we would act under imagined circumstances, or how the world would be expected to react upon our senses'. And in 'How to Make Our Ideas Clear' he formulates the same idea in a slightly different way: 'what a thing means is simply what habits it involves'. Taken together with Peirce's thesis that a *belief* consists mainly in being deliberately prepared to adopt the formula believed in as a guide to action', we have a set of ideas closely related to the ones advocated by Ramsey.[35]

There is an important paragraph in 'Facts and Propositions' where Ramsey clearly indicates how he thinks that such an analysis can be carried out:

> [I]t is, for instance, possible to say that a chicken believes a certain sort of caterpillar to be poisonous, and mean by that merely that it abstains from eating such caterpillars on account

of unpleasant experiences connected with them. The mental factors in such a belief would be parts of the chicken's behaviour, which are somehow related to the objective factors, viz. the kind of caterpillar and poisonousness. An exact analysis of this relation would be very difficult, but it might well be held that in regard to this kind of belief the pragmatist view was correct, i.e. that the relation between the chicken's behaviour and the objective factors was that the actions were such as to be useful if, and only if, the caterpillars were actually poisonous. Thus any set of actions for whose utility p is a necessary and sufficient condition might be called a belief that p, and so would be true if p, i.e. if they are useful.[36]

In a note connected to this passage, Ramsey says:

> It is useful to believe aRb would mean that it is useful to do things which are useful if, and only if, aRb; which is evidently equivalent to aRb.

Ramsey says that he does not want to depreciate the importance of this kind of belief but that the beliefs he wants to discuss are the ones expressed in words or possibly images or other symbols, consciously asserted or denied.[37] But whatever we may think of the mental powers of chickens, the example is in fact excellent, and we may deflect irrelevant criticism by assuming the chicken to be both reflective and intelligent. Mother Nature now offers our chicken a choice between the following two actions:

a. Eat the caterpillar.
b. Refrain from eating the caterpillar.

If the chicken chooses to eat the caterpillar, this choice will lead to one of two consequences, depending on whether the caterpillar is poisonous or edible. If the caterpillar is poisonous, the chicken gets an upset stomach; if it is edible, the chicken gets a good dinner. If, on the other hand, the chicken refrains from eating the caterpillar, this means that it has either avoided an upset stomach or missed its dinner.

This information about the chicken's decision problem can be summarized in a decision matrix.

	Poisonous	Edible
Eat	Upset stomach	Excellent dinner
Refrain	Avoids upset stomach	Missed dinner

In Chapter 1, we saw how Ramsey developed a theory of probability and a theory of decision making which is of great value for any chicken trying to solve this problem. What 'Truth and Probability' teaches us is that if a chicken does not know whether the caterpillar is poisonous or not, he should act in a way that maximizes his expected utility. However, our present problem is not one of degrees of belief, but of full belief. We are not interested in measuring the chicken's degree of belief in the caterpillar being poisonous. Our concern is what is meant by saying that the chicken believes fully, that is, believes, that the caterpillar is poisonous. In the above example, this would definitely mean that the chicken refrains from eating the caterpillar: an action that is useful if and only if the caterpillar is poisonous. This general idea is, of course, reinforced if it is put into an evolutionary perspective. A chicken that eats poisonous caterpillars will not have that many offspring. If this behaviour is true of the whole species, it has a fair chance of rapidly becoming defunct.

This is basically the core of Ramsey's idea and presented in this way one sees clearly how dependent his sketch of a theory of truth and belief in 'Facts and Propositions' is on his 'Truth and Probability' written one year earlier. The same line of thought is also present in his unpublished and far from completed book manuscript on truth.[38]

But let us now look more closely at the type of beliefs that Ramsey explicitly says he prefers to discuss, that is, beliefs which are expressed in words, symbols or images. Discussing the logical form of belief ascriptions, we came across a number of examples which can now be used to exemplify Ramsey's analysis of belief. Othello believes that Desdemona loves Cassio by having names for the particulars Desdemona and Cassio and for the relation love. These mental factors, according to Ramsey, are connected in Othello's mind and accompanied by a feeling of belief.[39] If Othello believes that Desdemona loves Cassio, this means that Othello's mental state has certain causal properties, leading, for example, to the killing of Desdemona. Ramsey obviously thought that the logical form of a belief determined its causal properties. The difference between Othello's belief that Desdemona loves Cassio and his belief that Cassio loves Desdemona lies in their causal properties. The first mental state led to the killing of Desdemona, while the other could have led to the stabbing of Cassio.

One thing that Russell had difficulty in convincing his colleagues of was the existence of negative facts. In one of his papers on logical atomism Russell tells us that arguing for negative facts in a lecture at Harvard nearly produced a riot. But the problem was that regardless of what one thought of negative facts or general facts it was not that easy to produce a convincing alternative. Ramsey, however, saw a way out of the difficulty. In Chapter 4, we shall see how he removes general facts from our ontological commitments; in 'Facts and Propositions' he gives us a solution to the problem concerning negative facts. What Ramsey argues is that 'not' cannot name some element in a fact, 'for if it were, "not-not-*p*" would have to be about the object not and so different in meaning from "*p*" '.[40] He thinks it hard to 'believe that from one fact, e.g. that a thing is red, it should be possible to infer an infinite number of different facts, such as that it is not not-red, and that it is both red and not not-red'.[41] We are instead simply saying the same thing in a number of different ways. One should keep in mind, it is argued, that it is only an accident of our symbolism that we have the word 'not'. We could, as Ramsey points out, express negation by writing what is negated upside down. Double negation would then consist of first writing it upside down and then turning it the right way up again, and we would have eliminated the redundant 'not-not'.

Ramsey's contribution to this problem is based on his theory of universals (see Chapter 8). In 'Universals' he maintained that 'the whole theory of particulars and universals is due to mistaking for a fundamental characteristic of reality what is merely a characteristic of language'.[42] There are no negative or complex properties. To take a familiar example, there is no such property as grue. Negative facts, like complex properties, are superstition and lead to a distorted view of reality. For Ramsey the solution to the problem can be found in our attitudes of belief or disbelief. To believe that snow is white is the same as disbelieving that snow is not white.

> Suppose our thinker is considering a single atomic sentence, and that the progress of his meditation leads either to his believing it or his disbelieving it. These may be supposed to consist originally in two different feelings related to the atomic sentence, and in such a relation mutually exclusive; the difference between assertion and denial thus consisting in a difference of feeling and not in the absence or presence of a word like 'not'. . . .
>
> If this happens we can say that disbelieving 'p' and believing 'not-p' are equivalent occurrences, but to determine what we mean by this 'equivalent' is, to my mind, the central difficulty of the subject. The difficulty exists on any theory, but is particularly important on mine, which holds that the significance of 'not' consists not in a meaning relation to an object, but in this equivalence between disbelieving 'p' and believing 'not-p'.
>
> It seems to me that the equivalence between believing 'not-p' and disbelieving 'p' is to be defined in terms of causation, the two occurrences having in common many of their causes and many of their effects.[43]

Let us, for example, compare two possible mental states of our intelligent chicken. The first state expresses a feeling of belief towards 'the caterpillar is not poisonous', that is, towards 'the caterpillar is edible'; the second a disbelief towards 'the caterpillar is poisonous'. In the first case, the chicken would eat the caterpillar, but this is obviously true even in the second case. Having a full disbelief that the caterpillar is poisonous cannot mean anything else than that a rational and hungry chicken would eat the caterpillar. The two states of mind thus have the same causal properties. They express, as Ramsey puts it, really the same attitude.

But this causal property theory must also deal with more complex beliefs, for example, disjunctive or general beliefs. What precise differences are there between the various logical forms of a belief and its causes and effects? What about disjunctive beliefs?

> But when our thinker is concerned with several atomic propositions at once, the matter is more complicated, for we have to deal not only with completely definite attitudes, such as believing p and disbelieving q, but also with relatively indefinite attitudes, such as believing that either p or q is true but not knowing which. Any such attitude can, however, be defined in terms of the truth-possibilities of atomic propositions with which it agrees or disagrees. Thus, if we have n atomic propositions, with regard to their truth and falsity there are 2^n mutually exclusive possibilities, and a possible attitude is given by taking any set of these and saying that it is one of this set which is, in fact, realized, not one of the remainder. Thus, to believe p or q is to express agreement with the possibilities p true and q true, p false and q true, p true and q false, and disagreement with the remaining possibility p false and q false.[44]

Smith wants to talk to his friend Jones. He fully believes that Jones is either at work or at home. The causal properties of Smith's state of mind could then be that he decided to go and look for Smith at his work, at Smith's home, or (picking where to go first at random) both at Smith's work and at his home. But it would scarcely cause him to try to find Smith at Jim's Bar or at the tennis court.

So far, this causal properties theory works quite nicely. It is to a great degree an extension of Ramsey's theory of partial beliefs, or, if one prefers to see it the other way around, his theory of probability and partial beliefs is a generalization of this theory of beliefs. However, turning to general propositions, universal quantification introduces new problems which are not that easily resolved.

In 'Facts and Propositions' Ramsey follows Johnson and Wittgenstein and treats general propositions as the logical products and the logical sums of atomic propositions. 'All men are mortal' is to be interpreted as: *A* is mortal, *B* is mortal and *C* is mortal . . . And 'There is an *x* such that f*x*' consequently is equivalent to the logical sum of the values of 'f*x*'.[45]

With this analysis the causal properties theory is easily extended to cover also the case of general propositions:

> Thus general propositions, just like molecular ones, express agreement and disagreement with the truth-possibilities of atomic propositions, but they do this in a different and more complicated way. Feeling belief towards 'For all *x*, f*x*' has certain causal properties which we call its expressing agreement only with the possibility that all the values of f*x* are true.[46]

But, as Ramsey emphasises,

> this must not be regarded as an attempt to define 'all' and 'some', but only as a contribution to the analysis of 'I believe that all (or some)'.[47]

What causal properties has my feeling of belief towards 'All men are mortal'? According to Ramsey, this means that one expresses agreement with the possibilities '*A* is mortal', '*B* is mortal', '*C* is mortal', and so on. But, is this really true? Couldn't it be argued that the proposition 'All men are mortal' cannot be identified by a countable conjunction of atomic propositions each expressing a particular person's mortality, since we must add to the conjunction the rider 'and these are all the people there are'? This is basically Russell's argument against analysing general propositions in terms of logical products and sums and it led him to the acceptance of general facts. In his later writings, Ramsey followed Russell in rejecting the Johnson–Wittgenstein thesis (see Chapter 4).

Why, he asks in 'General Propositions and Causality' (1929), can, for example, 'All men are mortal' not be analysed as a conjunction? Ramsey believes there are four arguments for this. First, 'All men are mortal' cannot be written out as a conjunction. Second, it is never used as a conjunction. The statements are different as a basis for action. This is emphasised in the third argument which states that 'All men are mortal' exceeds by far what we know or have knowledge of. What we know is, to take another example, that a particular copper rod expands if it is heated, that a particular iron rod expands if it is heated, that a particular silver rod expands if it is heated, and so on. But this is quite different from stating 'All solid bodies expand if heated'. The latter sentence is a hypothesis which goes far beyond the experimental knowledge that may be the basis for the generalisation. Finally, he argues that what we can be certain about is the particular case, or a finite set of particular cases. Of an infinite set of particular cases we could not be certain at all.

Thus, 'All men are mortal'

> expresses an inference we are at any time prepared to make, not a belief of the primary sort.
>
> A belief of the primary sort is a map of neighbouring space by which we steer. It remains such a map however much we complicate it or fill in details. But if we professedly extend it to infinity, it is no longer a map; we cannot take it in or steer by it. Our journey is over before we need its remoter parts.[48]

Russell's analysis of general propositions resulted in his acceptance of general facts. General facts are needed as well as particular facts if general propositions are to be assigned any truth-value. Ramsey did not want to accept general facts. Wittgenstein was correct in stating that the world can be described entirely by using particular or atomic facts. But as conjunctions are constructed out of atomic propositions, propositions about atomic facts, we see that 'All men are mortal', not being a conjunction, cannot be a proposition. If it is not a conjunction and thus not a proposition, how then are we to look upon sentences of this type? What status do they have; in what way can they be right or wrong?

Ramsey gives a pragmatic answer to this question. The fact that general propositions are neither true nor false, that they carry no truth-value, does not imply that they are meaningless. In our day-to-day dealings, this type of sentence is the foundation of the expectations that direct our actions. If I accept that all men are mortal, this means that when I meet a man, I believe I have met a mortal. As Ramsey puts it, a general proposition *is not judgement but a rule for judging:* it cannot be negated but it can be disagreed with.

Ramsey's theory of truth and belief, as it is sketched in 'Facts and Propositions', is thus in this respect a somewhat different theory from the one we get if we also take account of his theory of general propositions in 'General Propositions and Causality'. Personally, I believe that the blended version is a much more interesting and accurate theory.

In terms of this theory we now see that Pilate's question is, if anything, a cry for help. The question 'What is truth?' should simply be equated with the question 'What shall I do?'[49]

MENTAL STATES

A belief is a mental state or a 'cognitive map' by which we steer. It is the primary beliefs that, taken together, form a cognitive map of reality. In the same way as a minor path can be marked or taken away from an ordinary map, a belief may be added or subtracted to a cognitive map. However, in the same way as some general principles are needed in drawing a regular map, general propositions or variable hypotheticals are essential when we build up our cognitive maps. They express inferences that we are at any time prepared to make; by being rules for judging, not judgements, they help us to extend the map. To draw further on this analogy, both ordinary and cognitive maps are judged by their causal properties. If a stone is marked on a map we assume that, if we go out and look for it, we will find it. If this is not the case, the map does not give us a true picture of reality. If the cognitive map says that someone is at home, we expect to find the person if we go there to meet him. If this is not the case, our cognitive map, our belief, is not true – the map has to be redrawn with some beliefs subtracted and others added.

Ramsey's theory of beliefs also has a number of other good features. First, as has been pointed out by D. M. Armstrong, it gives an answer to what could be called Hume's problem; that is, it tells us what the distinction is between believing something and merely entertaining that thought.[50] The answer of course is that a belief, but not a thought, is a map by which we steer, something *qua* basis for action. Second, Ramsey's theory avoids much of the criticism that has been directed against other theories of belief, for example, belief as mental acts or dispositional behaviour. To take but one example: equating belief with behaviour deprives a dispositional theory of belief of most of its explanatory power. It prevents one from explaining a person's actions by alluding to his or her beliefs and desires. However, Ramsey's theory, by keeping these two factors apart, clearly allows for such an explanation of our behaviour.[51]

Those interested in problems about mental images and mental representation may wonder what the essential difference is between Ramsey's theory, on the one hand, and some more recent theories of mental representation, on the other. Isn't Ramsey's theory closely related to various representational theories of mind?[52] Ramsey is advocating something like a 'language of thought', but he also has a well thought-out functionalistic theory. This, I think, is just another example of a research area in which it has taken us about half a century to catch up with him.

Finally, philosophers, psychologists and computer scientists developing normative, prescriptive or descriptive doctrines about the dynamics of beliefs can, I take it, learn a lot from Ramsey's theory. The theories so far developed are rather embryonic in that they primarily take an epistemic state to be a set of propositions closed under logical implication and then, from there, go on to define a number of operations over this set of propositions. These theories tell us, for example, how such a state of belief or epistemic state can consistently be expanded, revised or contracted.[53] However, in Ramsey we find the basis for a more sophisticated and realistic theory. What is indispensable for a theory of belief revision is the functionalistic basis on which Ramsey's theory is founded. It is, for example, obvious that an agent may have contradictory or conflicting beliefs, as long as they do not lead to conflicting behaviour. Most of us have contradictory or conflicting beliefs. However, it is not until we are in a state where we have to base our actions on them that we find it necessary to revise them. And what is important for the revision of our cognitive map or epistemic state is these causal properties or our beliefs. But Ramsey's theory tells us in addition that singular beliefs also have their dynamics. The logical form of a belief ascription I have discussed indicates that there are at least two obvious ways in which a singular belief may be revised. Othello may, for example, change his belief that Desdemona loves Cassio, B(Othello, $xy[x$ loves $y]$, <Desdemona, Cassio>), by realizing that Desdemona does not love Cassio, that is, B(Othello, $xy[x$ does not love $y]$, <Desdemona, Cassio>), or by coming to know that it is Iago that she really loves, that is, a change to B(Othello, $xy[x$ loves $y]$, <Desdemona, Iago>). How it is revised has to do with its causal properties. However, a full discussion of this topic would fall outside the scope of this book.

Chapter 3
Knowledge

What does it mean to say that we know something? Do we know anything at all? What is there to say that we are not brains floating in a glass tank in a laboratory? Flapping our ears – which have been left to us – we sail along in the glass tank. With our eyes which we have also been allowed to retain, we peer through the glass sides of the tank. The tank is placed in an even bigger tank on the inside of which is a screen. Onto this screen the laboratory staff project our reality. Smells and other sense perceptions are produced by electrodes inserted into our brains. At the same time as new slides are projected onto the white screen, a computer activates the electrodes in predetermined sequences. Would there be any noticeable difference between our actual life and life in such a tank? If the experiment were properly conducted, the brain would become just as hungry as we do and just as exhausted; it would fall in love now and again with one or other of the people projected on the screen; and so on. How then can we know that our life is not lived in such a tank? It is difficult to answer this sceptical question in a totally satisfactory way. Just as we have difficulty in convincing the solipsist of our existence, we have difficulty in convincing the sceptic that knowledge about a factual world is possible. From both we gain insight into how difficult the problem of knowledge really is.

But let us begin discussing the concept of knowledge in a more down-to-earth way, by trying to say what it means to have knowledge. A witness may say, for example, that he saw a blue car run a red light. Does this give us knowledge of the incident in question? When can we say that a doctor knows that a patient is ill? What conditions must be fulfilled for us to credit ourselves or someone else with any knowledge of anything? For a rewarding discussion of the evolutionary, psychological and/or dynamic aspects of knowledge it is crucial that we have a clear and reasonable definition which tells us what it means to possess knowledge under certain conditions.

In his 1929 note 'Knowledge', Ramsey gives us such conditions. On the surface, Ramsey's definition of knowledge agrees with the traditional view, but he adds components which make his theory extremely forceful and interesting, especially when compared with the theories of knowledge under discussion today. But before expounding his ideas, we should outline some of the advantages and disadvantages of the traditional theory of knowledge.

KNOWLEDGE AS TRUE JUSTIFIED BELIEF

The traditional theory equates knowledge with true justified or well-founded belief.[1] If I say that I know that Gustavus II Adolphus died in 1632 at the Battle of Lützen, this is said to mean that the king in question was actually killed that year and on that battlefield, that I believe that he was, and that this belief of mine is justified.

In general, the traditional theory says that a person X knows any proposition p, if and only if

a. p is true,
b. X believes that p, and
c. X is justified in believing that p.

It will be easier to remember these three conditions if we call them (a) *the truth condition*, (b) *the belief condition* and (c) *the condition of sufficient evidence*. These three conditions are supposed to give both necessary and sufficient conditions for knowledge. We shall discuss in most detail their sufficiency, but first a few words about their necessity.

Let us start by asking if the truth condition is really necessary for X to have knowledge of *p*. After all, our world is such that we seldom attain absolute certainty about anything. We inhabit a world of probabilities. Everything is more or less probable: nothing is absolutely certain. One need not be a devout believer in modern physics to embrace this proposition. It is extremely probable that Gustavus II Adolphus died at Lützen but it is not absolutely certain. Is this a criticism of the condition above? If I honestly believe that the monarch died at Lützen, I can of course honestly say that I know that that is the case. But it may be that I am wrong. Suppose it was not Gustavus II Adolphus who was hit by the fatal bullet, it was Carl Persson, a farmhand from Blädinge in Småland. At the last minute this corpulent soldier had been disguised as the king and rode out in the mist. (The king himself had died of overeating a couple of hours before the battle, but a heroic king is not supposed to die like that!) Carl Persson was seen to sacrifice his life and the corpses were exchanged. Do these fresh historical facts alter anything? Yes: they show that my belief was justified, my opinion probable, and shared by many. But still my belief failed in its fundamental object – that of being true. That is why we should not call false belief knowledge, however sincere and justified it may be. The truth condition is necessary.

The belief condition is equally compelling. If I do not even believe that the king died at Lützen, how can I be said to know that he did? There must be some such connection between knowledge and belief. But could we not imagine situations when this connection failed? Let us imagine that one afternoon in the early 1980s, the phone rings at the home of Italo Calvino. Lars Gyllensten (secretary of the Swedish Academy at that time) is phoning to tell Calvino that he has been awarded the Nobel Prize for Literature. 'I don't believe it', says Calvino – even though (indeed because) he seems to know that it is true. But this is not really a counterexample. Calvino does not really know that he has won the Nobel Prize. Gyllensten's message is, of course, correct and conclusive, but our author cannot at first take it in. When his initial bewilderment has passed off, his belief will change and the apparent conflict be dissolved.

How about (c)? A person testifies on oath that he saw a man with a bushy black beard and a noticeable scar on his brow murdering a young blonde and burying her body in a wood. The witness is convinced that what he saw actually happened. The incident did happen but the witness was never present at the scene of the crime. He dreamt it all. The dream was so vivid and realistic that he is quite convinced that he actually experienced the murder. There is no question of perjury. In a case like this would we say that the witness knows that the bearded man murdered the woman? Hardly. The witness is not justified in believing that the incident occurred; the condition of sufficient evidence has not been met. Another example will illustrate how important the condition of sufficient evidence is. Assume that I believe that the person sitting opposite me on the train home from Stockholm has a name beginning with the letter 'M'. I scarcely have any direct evidence for thinking this. On the spur of the moment I think that he is a typical Mats, Michael or Malte. Let us now assume that there really is a Michael sitting in front of me. Do I know that the person sitting opposite me is called Michael? The truth condition is satisfied. The same thing holds for the belief condition, but what about the condition of sufficient evidence? My belief is not based on available evidentiary facts. There are no such evidentiary facts available at all. Few would credit me with knowledge; rather they would say that I attach far too much importance to my intuition and am outrageously lucky.[2] Thus condition (c) is necessary, too.

The condition of truth, the condition of belief and the condition of sufficient evidence can be formulated in slightly different ways. Instead of requiring that X believes that p, one might maintain that X must accept p or that X must be certain that p is true. A change like this in the second condition naturally requires a corresponding change in the phrasing of the third condition. The classical theory, however, is epitomized by the three conditions we have chosen to discuss. In the following section, we shall refer to a famous essay by Edmund Gettier as a criticism of the adequacy of these three conditions. But let us first conclude this section by posing a question which seems unavoidable in trying to define knowledge.

Is it really possible to define knowledge in the way that we have done? One scholar who has claimed that the question 'What is knowledge?' is impossible to answer, that it is impossible to define knowledge, is J. C. Wilson. Wilson, who was professor of logic at Oxford at the beginning of this century, maintained that knowledge is to be considered a primitive, indefinable concept. Any attempt to define the concept would inevitably lead to creating a circular definition. Knowledge, according to Wilson, can only be exemplified. A classic example of knowledge in its purest form is mathematics. Wilson's argument for the circular definition idea drew on the fact that knowledge cannot be traced back to beliefs since every belief is in itself based on knowledge. According to Wilson, a belief demands that a particular piece of evidence is known and that we know that the evidence is inadequate. If I say that I believe that I have left my umbrella at work, this is because I have knowledge of some facts that support my statement but these facts are not sufficient grounds for me to be able to say that I know that I have left my umbrella at work.

There are several problems in Wilson's position. I mention this position chiefly to point out that definitions of the type on which this chapter focuses have not always been regarded as reasonable from a philosophical point of view. First, arguing against Wilson, one might say that the conceptual atoms of any philosophical or scientific system are relatively arbitrary. Usually we have historical or psychological reasons for choosing primitive terms in one way rather than another; rarely are the reasons purely logical. Second,

Wilson seems to assume a fairly strict form of evidentiary logic. A given piece of evidence is connected with a given state of knowledge. But is it not so that different individuals may evaluate the same amount of evidence in different ways and thus arrive at quite different states of knowledge? Third, one should remember that not all circles are vicious circles. For example, to base induction on induction or knowledge on knowledge may be the only fruitful way to approach the problem. We have to be careful not to confuse vicious circles with productive spirals.[3]

We have found that the three conditions above are necessary, but are they sufficient?

RUSSELL–GETTIER EXAMPLES

In a keenly debated essay of the early 1960s, Edmund Gettier, giving two examples, tries to show that the truth condition, the belief condition and the condition of sufficient evidence are not sufficient for knowledge. It is often forgotten that essentially the same argument was put forward by Russell 50 years earlier in *The Problems of Philosophy*.[4] We consider here one or two examples that differ from Russell's and Gettier's own examples in content but whose logical form is the same.

At a trial John Smith testifies that he has seen a blue car run a red light and cause a serious accident. The judge thinks he has evidence for believing Smith. Smith makes a trustworthy impression. He is calm and collected and also gives a business-like and careful account of what happened. He is also well-dressed, a not unimportant point in inspiring trust. The judge considers that he has evidence that (1) Smith saw the accident. From (1) the judge derives the more general proposition (2) that someone saw the accident. If Smith saw what happened, someone saw the accident. If the judge has evidence in favour of (1), then of course he has evidence in favour of (2). However, it turns out that Smith did not see the accident after all. He wasn't even present at the scene. His wife saw it all. But she refused point blank to testify and asked her husband to do so instead. Thus it is true that someone saw the accident. The judge has evidence that justifies him in believing that this really was the case and he thinks that someone saw a blue car run a red light. The truth condition, the belief condition and the condition of sufficient evidence are all satisfied, but would we say that the judge knows that someone saw the accident? Scarcely. The unusual circumstances mean that these three conditions are satisfied but quite independently of each other. A further example might be in order.

A doctor uses a sophisticated piece of equipment to make a certain type of diagnosis. The doctor decides whether the patient is ill or healthy by studying the figures displayed in a little window in the apparatus. Knowledge of the machine and its reliability give the doctor great confidence in the result and justify his confidence. In the present case, the machine indicates that the patient is ill. The doctor has evidence for assuming that (3) the patient is ill because the figures recorded indicate this. From (3) he derives (4) that the patient is ill and initiates the usual treatment. But it turns out that the machine was not working at all but the patient is ill despite this fact. Owing to the invisible hand of chance, the malfunctioning machine produced the 'right' combination of figures. An improbable incident, but the improbable does happen.

The patient is ill, the doctor believes the patient is ill and he has evidence for believing this, but would we say that the doctor knows that the patient is ill? Once more, unfortunate circumstances have resulted in the truth condition, the belief condition and the condition of sufficient evidence being simultaneously but independently satisfied. The doctor and the judge are in the same boat; their knowledge is an illusion. They possess no actual knowledge.

It is comparatively easy to see why Russell–Gettier examples create problems. The traditional analysis of 'X knows that p' assumes that X knows that p if and only if (a) p is true, (b) X believes that p and (c) X is justified in believing that p.

But these conditions can be satisfied independently of each other. Take, for example, the case in which adequate evidence exists but this evidence has nothing to do with the present case. A witness who was not present at the scene of the crime gives an exact account of the crime but this account is a complete fabrication; it just happens to be true.

Many alternative solutions to Russell–Gettier problems have been suggested in the literature. Usually their aim is to incorporate a fourth condition, a condition designed to eliminate the possibility that (a), (b) and (c) are simultaneously but independently satisfied. It has been pointed out, for example, that it is propositions (2) and (4) that cause the problem. These two propositions are derived from (1) and (3), respectively. But observe that (1) and (3) are false. It might be said that our belief in a Russell–Gettier example is based on a delusion. Therefore, if we require that the basis of our belief be true, if p is derived from q and X believes that q and has evidence in favour of q, and both p and q are true, then we undermine the very foundation of the Russell–Gettier problem.

We shall now adopt a quite different approach in proposing a solution to the problem. We shall see that the theory of knowledge propounded by Ramsey over 40 years ago ingeniously avoids problems of the type raised by Russell and Gettier.

RAMSEY'S THEORY OF KNOWLEDGE

The essay entitled 'Knowledge' (1929) is only one and a half pages long. The essay was unpublished at the time of Ramsey's death and is one of those written shortly before he died. 'Knowledge' is an essay of the condensed kind; superfluous words and sentences, perhaps even whole pages, have been omitted to great effect, leaving only what Ramsey considered essential. To me, the first paragraph of this essay stands out as being particularly significant:

I have always said that a belief was knowledge if it was (i) true, (ii) certain, (iii) obtained by a reliable process. But the word 'process' is very unsatisfactory; we can call inference a process, but even then unreliable seems to refer only to a fallacious method not to a false premiss as it is supposed to do. Can we say that a memory is obtained by a reliable process? I think perhaps we can if we mean the causal process connecting what happens with my remembering it. We might then say, a belief obtained by a reliable process must be caused by what are not beliefs in a way or with accompaniments that can be more or less relied on to give true beliefs, and if in this train of causation occur other intermediary beliefs these must all be true ones.[5]

On the surface, Ramsey's definition of knowledge reminds us of the traditional, true-justified-belief theory, but working out the details of his theory we will find that it departs considerably from the true-justified-belief account of knowledge. Let us therefore begin by considering his truth condition somewhat more closely. This condition has a rather different content in Ramsey's theory, a change of meaning which is worth noting. Assuming Ramsey adheres to his own theory of truth, the predicates 'true' and 'false' are superfluous linguistic markers. This means that condition (a) ((i) in the above quotation), p is true, in Ramsey's theory, can be reduced to (a') p. But, to understand what this means for Ramsey's theory of knowledge, we must return briefly to the discussion in Chapter 2 of the essay 'Facts and Propositions'. According to Ramsey, a belief is true if the action in which it results always leads to success. Remember that he argues that 'any set of actions for whose utility p is a necessary and sufficient condition might be called a belief that p, and so would be true if p, that is, if they are useful'.[6] If this interpretation of the truth condition is in agreement with Ramsey's own intentions (which I see no reason to doubt), we have here a major difference with the traditional theory, which usually seems to assume some type of coherence or correspondence theory of truth.

The belief condition is not needed in Ramsey's theory since he explicitly says that 'a belief is knowledge'. Instead the question is how to interpret his second condition, what he means by saying that in order to be knowledge a belief has to be certain. Let us call this second assumption of Ramsey's *the certainty condition*. One way to interpret this condition is to identify it to some extent with condition (c) above, the condition of sufficient evidence. A *belief* is knowledge if, among other things, it is certain, that is, backed up by a sufficient amount of reliable evidence. I strongly believe that this interpretation is false. This is, I believe, obvious if we note that, if it is interpreted in this way, the second condition will be redundant given his third condition. What the certainty condition says is simply that the belief must be *full* belief, that is, the agent is certain that *p*.

Ramsey must have been influenced by what Russell writes about knowledge in *The Problems of Philosophy*. In the latter part of this book, Russell takes up the probability aspect regarding knowledge:

> What we firmly believe, if it is true, is called *knowledge*, provided it is either intuitive or inferred (logically or psychologically) from intuitive knowledge from which it follows logically. What we firmly believe, if it is not true, is called *error*. What we firmly believe, if it is neither knowledge nor error, and also what we believe hesitatingly, because it is, or is derived from, something which has not the highest degree of self-evidence, may be called *probable opinion*.[7]

One reason for interpreting (ii) as 'X has full belief in *p*' is that the whole of Ramsey's philosophy is largely derived from a conviction that it is important to formulate a human logic, a logic of rational action. His philosophy of probability is only one example of the importance he attaches to understanding the rational elements of individual decision making. If X states that he knows that the bank is open until six o'clock today, Thursday, he does not need to telephone the bank to have this confirmed. If he believes that the bank is open until six o'clock and this belief is to be considered knowledge, he might just as well go to the bank after work as rush there during the lunch hour, and thus we could expect him to act accordingly. In this case, it means that he ought to act as if the proposition, the bank is open until six o'clock today, Thursday, has a probability of 1 (or sufficiently close to 1). A phone call would be quite unnecessary, a sheer waste of time and money. Such a phone call is therefore to be interpreted as meaning that X does not assign probability 1 to the proposition in question, that X is after all not certain that p. Perhaps X does not know that the bank is open in the evening; he is only expressing a probable opinion. In concluding the paragraph quoted above, Russell states something of importance to this example:

> Thus the greater part of what would commonly pass as knowledge is more or less probable opinion.

Ramsey's third condition is extremely interesting. His first two conditions of knowledge have some resemblances with the traditional analysis. But his third condition deviates considerably from the three conditions of the true-justified-belief approach. Ramsey requires X's belief (that p) has been obtained by a reliable process. It is not sufficient that X has evidence for believing that p; the actual belief must reproduce a reliable process between evidence and the object of knowledge – the way in which we acquire our beliefs should be reliable. We see the importance of Ramsey's view if we again imagine a situation in which a reliable witness who has not seen a particular incident manages all the same to pull off the feat of recounting the correct sequence of events. Probably one can then say, according to the classical analysis, that the judge has knowledge of the incident, that is, on the condition that he thinks he has evidence for accepting the witness's account. But this would seem to be unacceptable from another point of view. It is doubtful whether the judge can be considered to have any actual knowledge. The witness's account admittedly reflects reality, but it has no connection with the actual sequence of events. Something more is needed. The witness's account – which, if he is lying, is based on his belief – ought to keep track of reality. The process leading to the witness's memory of the incident and thus also to the judge's attitude must be reliable. Similar examples can be found in *The Problems of Philosophy* and they must have influenced Ramsey.[8]

Thus, I think it may be roughly in this way that Ramsey arrived at the importance of the reliable process. His brief discussion of memory and how our memories may be obtained by means of reliable processes speaks in favour of this. Ramsey's idea that such a process perhaps ought to be specified as a causal chain is extremely important.

It is also interesting to note that for Ramsey the certainty condition and his third condition of a reliable process are connected.

We say 'I know', however, whenever we are certain, without reflecting on reliability. But if we did reflect then we should remain certain if, and only if, we thought our way reliable.[9]

First, this means that the certainty condition and the condition of a reliable process are not allowed to be simultaneously but independently satisfied. Whatever number of favourable and concurring pieces of evidence we might have, they are worthless if they are not obtained by a reliable process. Second, full belief in p, to avoid some theoretical problems connected with the updating and dynamics of probabilities, should be interpreted as ascribing p a probability sufficiently close to 1. The evidentiary value model, discussed in the next section, tells us that in a reliable process the evidence does always raise the probability of the thesis if and only if the thesis is not impossible or certain. Thus, if by "reflecting on reliability" we should be able to change our view about the certainty of p, p has to have a probability less than 1 (it is enough if the difference is infinitesimal). We shall now see that this valuable insight into the importance of, what Ramsey calls, trains of causation for knowledge simply and effectively blocks all types of Russell–Gettier problems.

Let us start by reflecting on how Ramsey's theory functions in the case of the witness recounting his story. It is comparatively simple to note that what makes (2) true is the fact that there really was a witness to the accident. But the fact that it happened to be the witness's wife who observed the accident was no reason for the judge to believe that someone saw the accident. Obviously we have a case in which the causal connection between the wife's observation and the judge's belief is lacking. Things would have been different had the judge known that yet another witness had seen the accident, but for one reason or another she has not been found. The reliable process which is necessary for knowledge has not worked in this case. The judge does not know that somebody saw the accident.

A corresponding analysis can be carried out on the second of our two cases. The problem here again is the absence of a causal process at work. By chance, the machine has managed to indicate that the patient is ill. The process has not been in operation, however. Ramsey's theory again excludes such cases from being counted as knowledge. The doctor does not know that the patient is ill; in order to know that, he must be sure that his diagnostic methods are working satisfactorily – his belief must be obtained by a reliable process. The doctor's belief concerning the patient's condition must track an actual condition. Causal chains may not be broken.

Thus we see that Russell–Gettier examples are no problem to a theory of knowledge like Ramsey's. Ramsey's theory as it is presented here may be considered to give both necessary and sufficient conditions for knowledge. The theory constitutes a superior alternative to the traditional model of knowledge and to the variations on that theme. Knowledge is simply not true justified belief but rather *a belief is knowledge if it is obtained by a reliable process and if it always leads to success.*

In the next section I take the liberty of departing slightly from Ramsey's text. I say something more about how important the type of processes Ramsey mentions are for theories of evidence. I hope this will contribute to an understanding of his theory and to an awareness of its originality.

RELIABLE PROCESSES

By emphasizing that a reliable process is necessary for knowledge (a belief being knowledge if it is obtained by such a process and is true, that is, always leads to success), Ramsey side-steps many of the difficulties of the traditional theory. Richard Grandy, in discussing Ramsey's theory, has shown that the reliability idea can be found in theories of knowledge of later date. Armstrong, Unger and Watling all develop theories that bring to mind Ramsey's ideas about knowledge to some extent.[10]

Another theory that deserves mention in this context is Alvin Goldman's causal theory of knowledge.[11] Goldman suggests that there is a causal connection between what we have knowledge of and our beliefs. More precisely, he argues that a person X knows that p if and only if the fact p is causally connected in an 'appropriate' way with X's believing p. Goldman gives the following list of 'appropriate' knowledge-producing causal processes: (1) perception, (2) memory, (3) some types of causal chains. This idea ought to be compared with the following lines from 'Knowledge':

> Can we say that a memory is obtained by a reliable process? I think perhaps we can if we mean the causal process connecting what happens with my remembering it.[12]

Ramsey explicitly mentions (2) and (3) as examples of knowledge-producing reliable processes. Why he prefers to discuss memory instead of the more obvious alternative, perception, I cannot say. Neither do I know why Goldman does not compare his theory with Ramsey's (he does not even mention it), since there are, at least on the surface, clear resemblances. However, there are also obvious and essential differences between the two theories. Goldman has excluded the truth condition from his theory, as well as the certainty condition. I mention Goldman's theory in this context because I believe it shows that the reliable processes Ramsey mentions may prove difficult to interpret exclusively in terms of causality, although one may be tempted to do so. Why such an interpretation may be useful on occasion is evident, but it may result in unnecessary complications. Let me briefly mention one of the major ones.[13]

There are propositions that do not fit into Goldman's analysis, and thus raise questions about its generality. Most of us would, for example, say that we know that all men are mortal. But exactly how is our belief in this universal proposition connected with the fact that all men are mortal? Can the fact that all men are mortal be the cause of anything? Goldman's solution to the problem is to argue that logical and inferential connections should be included as parts of the appropriate causal chains. Since Goldman's aim is to give a causal analysis of 'X knows that p', this solution is not convincing at all, but rather ad hoc. For Ramsey's theory, this type of example causes no problem since among the reliable processes we can count causal as well as inferential processes. Thus mathematical knowledge can easily be handled. However, for quite a different reason (see Chapter 4), I believe Ramsey would have argued that we do not know that all men are mortal. In his later theory of law and causality, he argues that general (universal) propositions carry no truth-value. Thus the truth condition cannot be satisfied; we cannot be sure that our belief that all men are mortal will always lead to success.

One person who may be said to have developed Ramsey's idea that a concept of reliable process is important for a definition of knowledge is Robert Nozick. Nozick, however, does not seem to be aware of Ramsey's theory. In *Philosophical Explanations*, Nozick proposes the following analysis of the concept of knowledge.[14]

X knows that p if the following four conditions are all fulfilled:

a. p is true,
b. X believes that p is true,
c. If p were not true, X would not believe that p,
d. If p were true, X would believe that p and it is not the case that X believes that $-p$.

A straightforward example will clarify the meaning of these conditions. Assume that a witness has observed a traffic accident and firmly asserts that one of the cars involved, the green car, ran a red light. The first two of the above conditions appear obvious. If we want to say that the witness knows that the green car ran the red light, the green car must have run the red light, and the witness must believe that this actually took place, ignoring any philosophical worries regarding the question 'What is truth?' The third condition says that if the car did not run the red light, the witness would not believe that it did so, and the fourth condition says that if the car did run the red light, the witness would believe that it did, and it is not the case that the witness believes that the car did not run the red light. These two conditions are both introduced in order to eliminate some of the crucial examples directed against those theories which take knowledge simply as true justified belief (Russell–Gettier examples are, for instance, avoided by the third condition).

If a person X believes p, which is true, and condition (c) and (d) are satisfied, then according to Nozick's theory, the person's belief *tracks* the truth that p. This means that to know, in Nozick's sense, is to have a belief that tracks the truth. We know the past, for example, by following its tracks. The difference between a historian writing a book on Samuel Pepys and an author writing a short story based on a seventeenth-century theme is simply that the historian has to find the tracks of the past, whereas the author is in no way committed to this; he or she is free to use his or her own imagination.

I think one might say that conditions (c) and (d) in this theory amount to a way in which Ramsey's idea about a reliable process can be specified. If our beliefs track reality, they have been obtained by a reliable process. One question arising, however, is whether the conditions totally cover all the types of processes we would be prepared to include under the term 'reliable'.

Theories of knowledge and theories of evidence are intimately related. The question of how our beliefs relate to the object of our knowledge are linked with the question of how a given piece of evidence relates to a corresponding hypothesis or thesis. For this reason it seems natural for Nozick to transfer his intuitively appealing idea of 'tracking' to the field of evidence.

Evidence, or rather the connection between the evidence and a thesis, can be viewed as subjunctive. Some evidentiary situations are such that we are justified in saying that, if the thesis were true, the evidentiary fact would have been received. But also that if the thesis were not true, we would not have received the evidentiary fact. If the green car ran the red light, the witness would have so testified, but if the green car did not run the red light, the witness would not have told us that it did. We are merely using two conditionals in order to assert the strength of the evidence, and a much better evidentiary situation could hardly be hoped for. Nozick says that we have *strong evidence* if the two subjunctives above are both satisfied, that is, if the following two conditions are both fulfilled:

E1. If the thesis were true, the evidentiary fact would hold.

E2. If the thesis were not true, the evidentiary fact would not hold.

Observe that both these conditions constitute a direct parallel with conditions (c) and (d) above. In the same way as knowledge tracks truth, strong evidence tracks that which it is evidence of. If there is strong evidence that the green car ran the red light, there is no doubt that the car actually caused the accident; the evidence tracks reality. In Ramsey's terms, this could be expressed by saying that an absolutely reliable process exists. Strong evidence can be seen as an absolutely reliable process.

Unfortunately, there are few absolutely reliable processes; strong evidence is rare. We are often confronted with situations in which the thesis may be true although the evidentiary fact states the contrary. Negative evidentiary facts may hold because there is a missing link in the process. A judge knows all too well that it is extremely rare for a witness to supply strong evidence. The empirical researcher knows that a negative evidentiary fact does not demolish a theory. Too much may have been broken down in the chain of information leading from the thesis to the evidentiary fact. The witness, consciously or unconsciously, may have made a mistake. An extremely complicated measuring instrument may have ceased to function for a split second and chance instead has produced the negative piece of evidence we have before us. It is important, then, that condition E2 be replaced by a weaker condition.

E2'. If the thesis were false, the evidentiary fact might still be true.

E2' says that if the thesis is false, we might obtain a positive piece of evidence all the same, that is, one that speaks in favour of the thesis. For some reason or other, the witness may assert that the green car ran the red light although this was not the case.

Nozick says that if conditions E1 and E2' are satisfied we have *weak evidence*. Just as strong evidence can be seen as a perfectly reliable process, weak evidence can be compared with a process which on occasion does not function.

It is easily seen that the inference of the thesis from weak evidence does not track the truth of the hypothesis. If we know that the evidence is weak, we cannot draw the conclusion that the car ran the red light; the witness may have been wrong. Yet, although we cannot make this inference, we must be able to say something about how strong or weak the support for the evidence is. Nozick believes that we can get round the problem by taking the probability of the evidentiary fact given the thesis as a measure of the strength of the evidence. What, for example, is the probability of the witness saying that the green car ran the red light, given that the car really did so? If this probability is high, the evidence is considerably stronger than if the probability is low.

There are strong arguments against this type of thesis-oriented theory of evidence. Assume that the witness invents his testimony for some reason. As it turns out, the invented testimony agrees to the letter with the true state of affairs. Testimonies of this type cause problems (cf. the example in the preceding section). For this reason it is important to ask ourselves instead if the process connecting the thesis and the evidentiary fact has worked. Thus I shall not discuss Nozick's theory further but instead mention a theory much more interesting, a theory which emphasizes the importance of reliable processes in evaluating evidence.

Martin Edman and Sören Halldén have developed an interesting formal model of evidentiary value on the basis of Per Olof Ekelöf's informal theory of evidence. Edman and Halldén are of the opinion that, in order to avoid problems of the kind we have been discussing, one ought to put the main stress on evidentiary mechanisms. These mechanisms tell us something about the connection between the evidentiary fact and the thesis.[15]

These mechanisms may be compared with what Ramsey calls a reliable process. It is important that the witness has perceived, registered and reported the accident in a correct fashion. The process that leads us from the witness's registering of the accident to the witness's reporting of the accident must have been in operation – the evidentiary mechanism must have functioned properly. Edman and Halldén propose that as the evidentiary value we should take the probability of this mechanism or process having functioned in the light of the evidentiary fact. How probable is it that the witness has seen, registered and reported the accident correctly given the testimony before us?

It turns out that the probability of the thesis given the evidentiary fact is always greater than this evidentiary value.

Making assessments of the evidentiary value in the light of evidentiary mechanisms thus prompts us to avoid making decisions based on wrong connections between evidentiary facts and theses. This theory may be said to embody Ramsey's idea that in epistemological contexts, we have to pay regard to certain processes and their reliability.

We have come to the conclusion, then, that a person X's belief, that p, is knowledge if it is obtained by a satisfactorily reliable evidentiary mechanism and if this belief is true (i.e., if it always leads to success). Thus, we follow Ramsey by assuming that our beliefs are 'obtained by a reliable process', but we specify these processes in terms of evidentiary mechanisms. But, since few processes or evidentiary mechanisms are absolutely reliable, an attenuation of his third condition would seem to be called for. What counts for knowledge is that it is sufficiently probable that the mechanism has functioned. This is a weakening that I believe Ramsey would not have dismissed out of hand. The concept 'reliable process' seems to include this uncertainty; it is not the absolutely infallible process which is meant, but the sufficiently reliable one. The level we choose as a satisfactory level for knowledge will depend on the context in which a decision about the person X's knowledge must be made. If X testifies, for instance, that he saw Y murdering Z, we obviously want to be as sure as we can be that the relevant mechanism or process has worked. But if X says that Y is taller than Z, the same infallibility is not required as regards X's sensory mechanisms for us to be able to ascribe knowledge to X. Making the concept of knowledge context-dependent has clear advantages in my opinion, and also has interesting applications for this theory of knowledge.

The observant reader will have noted that Ramsey's theory of knowledge takes us towards a theory of evidentiary value which differs from the one Ramsey himself presents in 'Truth and Probability'. Ramsey's probability theory is strictly thesis-oriented. Such a theory of probability assumes rather that a theory of knowledge of the classical kind is to be advocated. Ramsey's theory of reliable processes, however, requires us to ignore the probability of the thesis and instead judge how probable it is that the underlying process functioned.[16] Whether Ramsey was aware of this unexpected result of his theory of knowledge we do not know.

Chapter 4
General propositions and causality

Ramsey abandoned logicism in 1929 for a finitistic view of mathematics (see Chapter 6). Behind this conversion lay his dissatisfaction with the axiom of infinity of set theory. However, it was not only Ramsey's view of mathematics that evolved during the period between 1926 and 1929 but his whole philosophical outlook. The advances in logic led the majority of British philosophers into fresh fields of research. The inter-war years were characterized by a more pragmatically biased philosophy. Ramsey was not unaffected by these currents. He read Peirce, was influenced by Johnson and turned increasingly toward pragmatism. The first sign of this change in Ramsey's philosophy is to be seen in 'Truth and Probability' (1926). This essay is imbued with the pragmatism of Peirce, although Wittgenstein's strong impact is still very noticeable and the mathematical elegance is there as always.

In this section we discuss some of the problems Ramsey was pondering during the period 1926–9. In some cases he presented complete solutions to a philosophical problem, but very often he only sketched a proposal for a solution. Things would have turned out quite differently had Ramsey lived longer than he did. Some of the ideas which Ramsey had and which proved extremely rewarding were only mentioned by him in passing.

General propositions and causality

[W]e must now say something about general propositions such as are expressed in English by means of the words 'all' and 'some', or in the notation of *Principia Mathematica* by apparent variables. About these I adopt the view of Mr. Wittgenstein that 'For all x, $[f]x'$ is to be regarded as equivalent to the logical product of all the values of '$[f]x'$, i.e. to the combination of $[f]x_1$ and $[f]x_2$ and $[f]x_3$ and . . . , and that 'There is an x such that $[f]x'$ is similarly their logical sum.[1]

This was Ramsey's position in 1927 in discussing the problem of so-called general propositions in the essay entitled 'Facts and Propositions'. 'All men are mortal' is to be interpreted from this standpoint as: A is mortal, B is mortal and C is mortal. . . . In discussing the axiom of infinity in 'The Foundations of Mathematics', he also assumes that this analysis is reasonable. Ramsey argues that 'There is an x such that x is identical with x' is to be interpreted as having the same meaning as the logical sum of all tautologies $x = x$; that is, $a = a$ or $b = b$ or $c = c$. . . . Besides being propounded by Wittgenstein in the *Tractatus*, the idea was advocated by Johnson in Part II of *Logic*, and Ramsey was of course greatly influenced by these theories.[2]

Russell's position, however, was the diametrically opposite one. In the articles in *The Monist* (1918–19) he asserts that propositions of the type

 i. For all x, fx

cannot be analyzed in terms of a conjunction. Russell's argument is that 'For all x, fx' states something more than that all x have the quality f – namely, that the particular individuals constitute all possible x. The proposition 'All men are mortal' cannot be identified by a countable conjunction of atomic propositions, each expressing a particular person's mortality, since we must add to the conjunction the rider 'and these are all the people there are'. Russell therefore felt obliged to accept the existence of general facts side by side with particular facts. 'All *A* are *B*' ('All men are mortal') can be a fact just as the observation that a certain *A* is *B* is a particular fact (e.g., that the Duke of Wellington was mortal).[3]

Familiar as he was with Russell's work, Ramsey takes up the theory as a possible criticism of the Johnson–Wittgenstein thesis (but without explicitly mentioning Russell. Probably he takes it for granted that we all know who proposes the erroneous theory). But, he says,

> To this Mr Wittgenstein would reply '*a, b* . . . *z* are everything' is nonsense, and could not be written at all in his improved symbolism for identity.[4]

Russell's analysis of general propositions is not to be dismissed so lightly, however. Critics only need to take into account the case in which we do not say anything about a finite or countable set of individuals. Take all mathematical statements of the type 'For all *x*, *fx*', where we are dealing with uncountable sets. How are general propositions of this type to be expressed reasonably as conjunctions?

Two years after publishing 'Facts and Propositions' Ramsey gave up the Johnson–Wittgenstein thesis. Probably Ramsey had second thoughts about Russell's theory. But he did not want to accept Russell's standpoint all the way. Instead he tried to find a theory that embraced both Russell's and Wittgenstein's arguments. Once again we notice how Ramsey's thinking starts out from the work of Russell and Wittgenstein and how, as it were, he discovers the rewarding synthesis of their frequently conflicting doctrines.

Why, Ramsey asks in 'General Propositions and Causality' (1929), can (i) not be analyzed as a conjunction? He believes there are four reasons for this. First, (i) cannot be written out as a conjunction. Second, (i) is never used as a conjunction. If, in the general case when *x* varies over a non-finite set, we state that '(*x*).*fx*', we are saying something more than '*fa* and *fb* and *fc* . . .'. The statements are different as a basis for action. This is emphasised in the third point which states that (i) exceeds by far what we know or have knowledge of. What we know is that a copper rod expands if it is heated, that an iron rod expands if it is heated, that a silver rod expands if it is heated . . . , etc. But this is quite different from stating that 'All solid bodies expand if heated'. The latter sentence is a hypothesis which goes far beyond the experimental knowledge that may be the basis for the generalization. The difference becomes even more striking if we switch to the theoretical plane.

Fourth, it is valid that

[t]he relevant degree of certainty is the certainty of the particular case, or of a finite set of particular cases; not of an infinite number which we never use, and of which we couldn't be certain at all.[5]

What we can be certain of are the particular cases, for example, particular experimental results or a finite number of such results. What Ramsey is alluding to is his new stand on the problem of infinity (see Chapter 6). One interesting question which I am unable to answer is, whether it was Ramsey's conversion to a view of mathematics of Hilbert's type which prompted a new theory for general propositions, or whether it was an altered view of the concept of propositions which led him to dismiss the axiom of infinity.[6]

Despite everything, we are enticed into analysing (i) as a conjunction because the sentence resembles a conjunction. From $(x).fx$ follows, as we know, fa, fb, fc, and so on, but also $fa\&fb$, $fa\&fb\&fc$, and so on. That is, (i) implies all finite conjunctions.

But we are also tempted into analyzing (i) in terms of a conjunctions because

[w]hen we ask what would make it true, we inevitably answer that it is true if and only if every x has $[f]$; i.e. when we regard it as a proposition capable of the two cases truth and falsity, we are forced to make it a conjunction, and to have a theory of conjunctions which we cannot express for lack of symbolic power.[7]

It is Wittgenstein's theory in the *Tractatus* that tempts us into falsely analysing (i) as a conjunction. Or as Ramsey, with the final words of the *Tractatus* in mind ('Wovon man nicht sprechen kann, darüber muß man schweigen'), succinctly and aptly puts it:

> But what we can't say we can't say, and we can't whistle it either.[8]

Russell's analysis of general propositions of type (i) resulted in his acceptance of general facts. General facts are needed as well as particular facts if general propositions are to be assigned any truth value. Ramsey did not want to accept general facts. Wittgenstein was correct in stating that the world can be described entirely using particular or atomic facts. But as conjunctions are constructed out of atomic propositions (propositions about atomic facts), we see that (i), not being a conjunction, cannot be a proposition. If (i) is not a conjunction and thus not a proposition, how then are we to look upon sentences of this type – what status do they have? Or as Ramsey phrases the question: '[I]n what way can it be right or wrong?'[9]

Ramsey gives a pragmatic answer to this question. The fact that general propositions are neither true nor false, that they carry no truth value, does not imply that they are meaningless. In our day-to-day dealings, this type of sentence is the foundation of the expectations that direct our actions. If I accept that all *A* are *B*, this means that if I were to come across an *A*, I know I have come across a *B*. Many of us believe, for instance, that all car salesmen deliberately try to deceive us. If the car salesman Mr. Jones speaks highly of a car we are interested in, then we assume that he is a swindler and out to con us – a judgement that affects our actions, of course. As Ramsey puts it, these propositions form the system with which the speaker meets the future. They are not judgements, but rules for judging; they cannot be negated, but they can be disagreed with.

Once again, we can understand Ramsey's idea rather better if we relate them to his truth theory. To simplify, in his view, a belief is true if it always results in success. If general propositions carry no truth-value, this means merely that we do not have any guarantee that they invariably result in success. However, this does not mean that they are worthless as a basis for action.

UNIVERSALS OF LAW VERSUS UNIVERSALS OF FACT

One of the numerous philosophical questions that have been endlessly discussed back and forth is whether there is any substantial difference between what are called *universals of law* and what are called *universals of fact* or *accidental generalizations*. Does the law, 'Copper always expands when heated', state anything more than the ordinary general statement, 'All the essays on this desk are about philosophy'?

It has been asserted that it must imply a good deal more to state 'For all *x*, if *x* is copper and *x* is heated, *x* expands' than to state 'For all *x*, if *x* is an essay and *x* is lying on this desk, *x* is an essay on philosophy'. Is it not so that the former statement expresses a significantly stronger link between the 'if' and the 'so', between the assumption and the consequence? It would be extremely irritating if a scientific law had the same status as a simple generalisation. Or is it not like that? Are we quite simply attempting to draw a line where no line can be drawn? When will the fresh water of Mälaren become salt water?

Ramsey's discussion of general propositions and the relation between universals and conjunctions led him into the set of problems mentioned above. The distinction between scientific laws and accidental generalisations was also keenly debated at Cambridge in the 1920s. Johnson maintained that what characterises universals of law is that they have a greater scope of validity than accidental generalisations (universals of fact). Laws are more widely applicable.

Johnson's idea is that an accidental generalisation may be

expressed as 'Any substantive PQ in the universe of reality is q if p', whereas a law should be formulated as 'Any substantive PQ in the universe of reality would be q if p', a distinction that Johnson attributes to Mill. This distinction, according to Johnson, shows that an accidental generalization only states something about what is a fact. On the other hand, a law takes us beyond what we know – a law states something about what is possible. If we word laws in the way that they ought to be worded, that is, by using subjunctive (or counterfactual) sentences, the distinction becomes clear. Physical laws, to take just one example, describe actual phenomena but also tell us something about what is possible. Using different laws, we can conclude what would happen if there were no friction or what a total vacuum would entail. Accidental generalizations, on the other hand, are wholly limited by our experience.[10]

Braithwaite preferred to sort out accidental generalizations by asserting that the difference is that laws are accepted on grounds that are evidentially correct.[11] When in his unpublished note 'Universals of Law and of Fact' of 1928 Ramsey put forward his theory on law and causality, he was inspired by Johnson's and Braithwaite's theories. To Ramsey's way of thinking, Johnson's thesis is impossible since it would mean that universals of law would apply over a wider range than accidental generalizations, but as he puts it, this would mean that they would apply over a wider range than everything, which appears to be impossible. Braithwaite's theory, on the other hand, is fallacious since we also believe some accidental generalizations on grounds that are not demonstrably correct; we do not believe certain laws of nature (because we quite simply do not know them) and we believe some laws on demonstrable grounds. Unfortunately, Ramsey does not give any examples of his criticism of Braithwaite.

In Ramsey's view, we should not try to find a space–time difference between laws and accidental generalizations. Likewise, we should give up the idea that our beliefs are of any importance to the distinction sought. The difference lies quite simply in the fact that a true law would exist even though we knew everything. If we were omniscient and organised our knowledge into a simple deductive system, true laws would remain unchanged. On the other hand, it is most plausible that the accidental generalizations that we accept today will be rejected by an omniscient being. Newton's second law is an example of a generalization that has been refuted and it is to be supposed that the great majority of today's physical laws will be refuted by an omniscient being.

The axioms in a deductive system of this kind are 'the ultimate laws of nature'. The theorems of the system, that is, general propositions that can be derived from the axioms, are 'derivative laws of nature'. We assign to this category what we normally call laws. A member of this category could be the law, 'All solid bodies expand when heated'. With the aid of particular facts we can derive from these general laws 'what are called laws in a loose sense'. The existence of copper allows us to derive the 'law', 'Copper expands when heated'. Finally, we have the accidental generalizations.

According to Ramsey, it is difficult to draw the line between real laws (axioms) and derivative laws of nature, on the one hand, and between accidental generalizations and what we sometimes erroneously call laws, on the other. Ramsey himself does not give any examples in this connection. One instance of a true law is probably the second law of thermodynamics. But I am not certain that Ramsey would accept this example unconditionally. (In a later essay he makes the following ingenious comment on this law: 'what is peculiar is that it seems to result merely from absence of law (i.e. chance), *but there might be a law of shuffling*'; my italics.)[12]

That there is no clear-cut line between the first two categories of laws is obvious to Ramsey:

The choice of axioms is bound to some extent to be arbitrary, but what is less likely to be arbitrary if any simplicity is to be preserved is a body of fundamental generalizations, some to be taken as axioms and others deduced.[13]

When we axiomatise a theory we will often be obliged to choose between different sets of axioms. Our reason for choosing one set rather than another may be purely historical (they are in good agreement with old X's theory), educational (they are easy to teach and work with), or purely logical (they are far from easy but they quickly yield interesting theorems). Which axioms we choose, however, is relatively arbitrary. Ramsey recommends that we choose one that is simple from the infinitely many equivalent systems of axioms. It is something of a surprise that a criterion of simplicity will to some extent determine which laws are to be considered basic laws of nature and which are to be considered deduced.

An objection to Ramsey's theory might be that we are hardly omniscient. Nor does there seem to be much hope of our ever being so, which we ought to be grateful for. Ramsey answers this type of critique by stating:

> [B]ut what we do know we tend to organise as a deductive system and call its axioms laws, and we consider how that system would go if we knew a little more and call the further axioms or deductions there would then be, laws (we think there would be ones of a certain kind but don't know exactly what).[14]

According to Ramsey, we do not need to know everything. What is needed is a reasonable systematisation of the accumulated knowledge we possess and a little creativity. A realistic view of science and a belief in scientific development does the rest and leads us on to the true laws.

Ramsey's theory has many advantages. It explains why the choice of scientific laws is not only a question of generality or universality. Some sufficiently general laws quite simply do not fit into the axiomatic system. The theory also explains the difference between the statements we regard as laws and true laws. There is most certainly a set of laws of nature which we are ignorant of today. Once these laws, or some of them, have been discovered, some of the statements that elevate them to the status of laws at present will be rejected as accidental generalizations. The laws and theories accepted at present are in all probability only close approximations.

Someone who has found Ramsey's theory about laws and causality acceptable for these and other reasons is David Lewis. In *Counterfactuals* Lewis advances the many positive sides of the theory. Ramsey himself abandoned the theory. In 'General Propositions and Causality', which was written in 1929, a year after 'Universals of Law and of Fact', he says that

it is impossible to know everything and organise it in a deductive system

and in this way undermines his theory.[15] The criticism Ramsey had waved aside a year before is now taken seriously. It is impossible to know everything, and if we did know everything it would probably be impossible to express the deductive model desired.

To Ramsey, the causal laws no longer distinguish themselves by their simplicity, but because we believe them. We consider ourselves to have sufficiently strong evidence to allow us to make the generalizations that a particular law implies. Ramsey leaves realism for pragmatism and thus approaches Braithwaite. But he only accepts certain general features of Braithwaite's theory.

Underlying this change of view on the theoretical status of causal laws is Ramsey's changed attitude to Johnson's and Wittgenstein's analysis of propositions containing the quantifiers 'all' and 'some'. If these general propositions really are conjunctions and hence express genuine propositions, an axiomatic viewpoint is the obvious one. In the end, hopefully we have expressed the true universals, that is, the true conjunctions. Laws are the true propositions that we would take to be axioms if we knew everything and organised it in a simple way. But if these propositions can no longer be identified as conjunctions and thus do not carry truth-value,

Ramsey's first theory collapses. A new method of attack is needed.

Ramsey's later analysis of general propositions took him away from Russell's logical atomism in the direction of a more pragmatic solution to the problem. Corresponding solutions ought to be directly applicable when it comes to causal laws:

[C]ausal laws form the system with which the speaker meets the future.[16]

For these laws it is valid that

[they] are not judgements but rules for judging 'If I meet a [*f*], I shall regard it as a [*g*]'. This cannot be *negated* but it can be *disagreed* with by one who does not adopt it.[17]

Our scientific laws make up the map by which we find our way into the future. These laws are not to be regarded as objectively given but as rules by which we plan our future conduct. However, they are neither, as Ramsey emphasizes, subjective in the sense that the mere enunciation of a law says something about ourselves or about our personal idiosyncrasies which can be passed by others. If we accept as a law 'All solid bodies expand when heated', and if we are rational, we ought to expect a solid copper rod to expand if we heat it. For the cross-country runner, the topography guides his choice of route; for the scientist, it is the laws. For both these activities it is of vital importance that we meet the future with a correct system of laws or with a correct map. Disagreeing about which system of laws or which map to use means that in the end the view that one of us takes will be proven to be wrong, and whether we choose sports or science as our activity, the outcome of a misguided belief can be anything between death and a loss of credibility.

One way of looking at Ramsey's theory is to regard the causal laws as limiting our alternatives of action. Two people who both accept the same system of laws ought to be expected to act in similar ways in a great number of choice situations. Viewed in this way, Ramsey's second theory of law and causality forms an interesting superstructure to his theory of probability. We note that Ramsey's theory of probability does not question the agent's beliefs, on the condition that they are coherent. The agent is completely free to assign an event whatever probability he likes. But if Ramsey's theory of law and causality is added on to his probability theory, the situation becomes rather different. What is now a rational assessment of probability is delimited by the laws the agent accepts.

If these laws are of a statistical type – that is, if they contain the notion of chance – the number of rational probability assessments will be severely limited. A combination of theories of this kind takes Ramsey's probability theory still further towards objective Bayesianism.

One problem for Ramsey is to explain what it means to claim that there are unknown laws. In the case of the axiomatic theory, such laws do not cause any problems. It is fairly obvious that we do not know everything and have not succeeded in drawing up the correct system of axioms – unknown laws exist. Regarding the second theory, a good deal of explaining is required. It is no longer a matter of an undiscovered truth, of an undiscovered axiom.

Claiming that there is a hitherto unknown law, in Ramsey's view, means the same thing as claiming a set of particular facts which if we knew them would prompt us to formulate this law. Perhaps a physicist might say: 'There must be a law explaining these subatomic phenomena but unfortunately we do not know it'. According to Ramsey, this is the same as claiming that there are a number of experimental facts which, if we knew them, would lead us to the law we sought. To clarify this point in his theory, Ramsey gives us an analogy. If we have a finitistic view of mathematics, unknown mathematical truths would be suggestive of unknown laws. Maintaining that there is an unknown mathematical truth means that one is stating that there is a theorem which is provable from certain principles. Laws distinguish themselves from mathematical theorems in that we do not put forward logical evidence in favour of them but collect empirical facts, but these empirical facts produce a chain of evidence which is strongly reminiscent of the formal proof of mathematics.

It may be questioned whether Ramsey's answer does not have a bitter flavour: Is it not circular? We say that there are facts such that if we knew them we would formulate the unknown law. To assert this is to accept a conditional proposition and we may ask by which laws acceptance of this sentence is supported.

> [A]nd here it may be urged that this means that they would lead us in virtue of one possibly unknown causal law to form a habit which would be constituted by another unknown causal law.[18]

Ramsey denies that there is any circularity in his argument:

> To this we answer, first, that the causal law in virtue of which the facts would lead us to the generalization must not be any unknown law, e.g. one by which knowledge of the facts would first drive us mad and so to the mad generalization, but the known laws expressing our methods of inductive reasoning; and, secondly, that the unknown variable hypothetical must here be taken to mean an unknown statement (whose syntax will of course be known but not its terms or their meanings), which would, of course, lead to a habit in virtue of a known psychological law.[19]

There is a set of laws, psychological laws and laws of inductive logic which put a stop to the circularity. It is from these laws that we systematise new facts and with the aid of which we arrive at new (causal) laws. If it is accepted that these laws are independent of the experimental facts that we want to systematise, no problem arises, but if this is not so one may query Ramsey's way of arguing. If Ramsey had had the opportunity to study the conflicting writings of present-day inductive logicians, he would probably have expressed some reservations. Quite simply it seems as if whichever system of laws we get in the end greatly depends on which system of inductive rules we accept.

Another problem Ramsey has is that in this latter theory the laws lose the objective status they had in his previous theory, a status that many want to ascribe to them. But for Ramsey this is hardly considered a real problem. Causal laws carry no truth-value as a consequence of general facts not existing; all mention of objectivity is meaningless.

Ramsey did not believe that we would meet the future with just any system of laws, however. From Peirce he took over the idea of 'the true scientific system':

> We do, however, believe that the system is uniquely determined and that long enough investigation will lead us all to it. This is Peirce's notion of truth as what everyone will believe in the end; it does not apply to the truthful statement of matters of fact, but to the 'true scientific system'.[20]

Many questions arise from this viewpoint.[21] One usually raised is: What guarantee is there that in the end we will reach the 'true scientific system'? A gambler is in no way guaranteed that he will break even if he gambles long enough. Things being what they are, he may go to his grave with a huge deficit. In a similar way, Nature may lead us towards a fallacious but usable theory. Another problem is that we cannot be sure that there is one and only one true scientific system. These questions have been much discussed in connection with the debate on Peirce's philosophy of science and we shall not discuss them in detail here. Peirce himself was aware of these difficulties and thus one might question if he really endorsed what Ramsey calls 'Peirce's notion of truth'.

But it has been maintained that from these problems it can be shown that there is no substantial difference between Ramsey's two theories. Jonathan Cohen points out that the above problems force Ramsey into idealized pragmatism, which assumes omniscience.[22] The demand for omniscience means that there are no essential differences between the two theories. However, it should be obvious from what has been said above, and even more obvious from reading Ramsey's own texts, that in order to be able to uphold a standpoint like Cohen's, Ramsey must have been either misunderstood or misinterpreted on a number of important points. As regards Ramsey's latter theory, for instance, any mention of truth is forbidden. Nor are we trying to set up a true axiomatic system, but we are looking for laws that can help us get through life. If we are omniscient, we can act on the basis of an axiomatic scientific system in such a way that we are always successful; if we are omniscient, we draw up axioms for the true system. But, if we are not omniscient, our goal is to find a map with which we can find our way into the future; and if this scientific map has been drawn by using general propositions, there is no absolute guarantee of success. The best we can hope for in the latter case is that our scientific system or map is as free from error as possible – that is, hopefully, it guides us towards success more often than failure. To me there is an obvious difference between a true map, a map that is drawn with the aid of a completely reliable process and that always leads to success, and a map that is drawn in perspective, by a more or less reliable procedure, and that is not always successful. There is an obvious difference between a chicken that always knows whether the caterpillar is poisonous or not and the chicken that has a firm and well-supported belief about the matter. There is a difference in degree between knowing and not knowing if this is my last supper.

Thus, to claim that there is no essential difference between the two theories is about the same as arguing that an instrumentalist and a realist take the same view of scientific theories, or that there is no difference between Brouwer's and Hilbert's views on mathematics.

CONDITIONALS AND THE RAMSEY TEST

I am quite sure that most of us have at one time or another heard someone say something like

i. If Germany had won the war, Sweden would have been occupied.

Many of us are also inclined to agree with this. Germany would not have been satisfied with just Norway and Denmark. Some of us might go so far as to say that proposition (i) is true. But there are certainly others who claim the opposite: Germany would never have occupied Sweden, not even if it had won the war. At all events, Sweden would be almost totally dependent on the new great power. The conditional proposition (i) is false. Now the question is, which is correct? If it is the truth of the proposition we are quarrelling about, the answer should not depend on our personal idiosyncrasies.

The problem is that (i) cannot be interpreted as an ordinary material implication, that is, as an ordinary if-then sentence. We know that Germany did not win the war. The antecedent of the proposition is false and according to traditional propositional logic the proposition is therefore true. But this is not what we mean by saying that it is true that if Germany had won the war Sweden would have been occupied. Conditionals of this type, so-called counterfactuals, require a logical analysis different from that of the traditional if–then propositions.

Logicians and philosophers who believed it necessary to give counterfactuals and other more general 'ifs' a logic have tried to develop different semantic systems by means of which we can assign various types of conditionals a truth value. It is interesting to find that Ramsey (though without having any intention of doing so) has contributed to the formation of these theories in an important way.[23]

Ramsey was aware that one of the differences between laws and accidental generalizations is that a law supports a counterfactual whereas an accidental generalization does not do so. Let us take our earlier example: Copper expands when heated. This law supports the following counterfactual sentence: 'If we had heated the copper rod, it would have expanded'. Let us assume that we have destroyed the rod and so in reality it is impossible to heat the rod. But the accidental generalization 'All the essays on this desk are about philosophy' does not support the corresponding counterfactual, 'If this essay had been on the desk, it would have been about philosophy'. The subjunctive conditional sentence, 'If we were to heat this copper rod, it would expand', likewise gets support from the law. The accidental generalization, on the other hand, does not uphold the corresponding subjunctive conditional sentence. Sometimes this is an insight attributed to Nelson Goodman, but besides Ramsey it would seem that Johnson (and several other philosophers), too, worked with it in mind.

In Ramsey's opinion, general propositions do not bear truth-value. But since conditional propositions such as (i) play a decisive part in our everyday life, we ought to be familiar with the conditions under which it may be considered reasonable to assert such propositions. What criteria of acceptability are applicable to general conditional propositions? In 'General Propositions and Causality' we find a hint of an interesting answer to this question.

[S]uppose that he has a cake and decides not to eat it, because he thinks it will upset him, and suppose that we consider his conduct and decide that he is mistaken. Now the belief on which the man acts is that if he eats the cake he will be ill, taken according to our above account as a material implication. We cannot contradict this proposition either before or after the event, for it is true provided the man doesn't eat the cake, and before the event we have no reason to think he will eat it, and after the event we know he hasn't. Since he thinks nothing false, why do we dispute him or condemn him?

Before the event we do differ from him in a quite clear way: it is not that he believes p, we $-p$; but he has a different degree of belief in q given p from ours; and we can obviously try to convert him to our view.[1] But after the event we both know that he did not eat the cake and that he was not ill; the difference between us is that he thinks that if he had eaten it he would have been ill, whereas we think he would not.[24]

In the footnote included in the text Ramsey makes the following comment:

> If two people are arguing 'If p will q?' and are both in doubt as to p, they are adding p hypothetically to their stock of knowledge and arguing on that basis about q; so that in a sense 'If p, q' and 'If p, $-q$' are contradictories. We can say they are fixing their degrees of belief in q given p. If p turns out false, these degrees of belief are rendered *void*. If either party believes $-p$ for certain, the question ceases to mean anything to him except as a question about what follows from certain laws or hypotheses.

Once again it should be emphasised that what Ramsey is discussing in this quotation, the gist of what has become known as the Ramsey test for conditionals, is, from his point of view, not at all a general test for conditional propositions, but rather the traditional theory for conditional probabilities. But there is in Ramsey's footnote an obvious suggestion of such a test for open conditionals, where the agent does not know whether the if clause holds or not ('If two people are arguing "If p will q?" and are both in doubt as to p, . . .'). However, it is doubtful whether or not the final sentence of the footnote can be read as a rudiment of a test for closed conditionals. But, there is so much substance in it that a person pondering on these problems may have got a hint of how to solve them.

A proposal for evaluating conditional propositions, to a degree associated with Ramsey's name, can be summarised in the following way. In order to determine whether a conditional proposition is acceptable in a given state of belief, one, first, adds the antecedent of the conditional hypothetically to the given stock of beliefs. Second, if the acceptance of the antecedent leads to a contradiction, because it conflicts with formerly accepted propositions, one makes adjustments, as small as possible and without changing the hypothetical belief in the antecedent, so that consistency is maintained. (What Ramsey says in the final sentence of the footnote is important here.) Finally, one asks oneself whether or not the consequent of the conditional is accepted in the revised state of belief. The conditional, 'If this copper rod were heated, it would expand', may be used to exemplify Ramsey's idea. Should we accept this sentence? In order to answer that question, we make use of Ramsey's three-step test. We begin by enriching the knowledge we have already by adding the antecedent, 'The copper rod is heated', hypothetically to our stock of belief. We change our state of belief by adding yet another proposition and at the same time we take into account all the consequences the change leads to. Then we ask ourselves if, in the light of this new state of belief, we can accept the consequent of the conditional, that is, 'the copper rod expands'. If we accept the consequent, we accept the conditional as a whole, while if we reject it we also reject the conditional.

A counterfactual of the type 'If Germany had won the war, Sweden would have been occupied' may be analyzed in much the same way as the conjunctive sentence above. But the analysis is complicated somewhat by the fact that we are now assuming that Germany was not victorious in the war. If, then, we add hypothetically to our state of belief 'Germany won the war', we will believe the contradiction, 'Germany won the war and Germany lost the war'. Since contradictions of this kind cannot be accepted, we have to change our initial state of belief in such a way that it is possible for us to accept the proposition, 'Germany won the war'. Ramsey does not state how this hypothetical change is to be made, but with today's thinking the state of belief should be revised 'as little' as possible. Only what is absolutely necessary for the antecedent to be accepted is to be changed. The final step in the test is identical with that used for conjunctive sentences. If we in our revised and hypothetical state of belief accept the consequent, 'Sweden is occupied', we accept the conditional. If on the other hand we reject the consequent of the counterfactual, we reject the sentence as a whole.

The so-called Ramsey test for conditionals has been keenly discussed in connection with attempts to develop a logic for this type of sentence. One of the leading advocates is Robert Stalnaker.[25] All the same, it is important to remember that, unlike many philosophers and logicians today (e.g., Stalnaker), Ramsey did not consider it reasonable to assign general conditional sentences truth-values. Ramsey's theory, again on the condition that there is such a theory, is of the pragmatic or cognitive kind. The test answers the question: How are we to look upon a certain conditional: should we accept it and thus let it affect our conduct? Or should we reject it? Accepting something does not mean that you take it to be true, or even that you accept that some truth conditions can be laid down.

One point of interest is that one could use the ideas in Ramsey's second paper on law and causality to outline a semantics of conditionals of a cognitive kind. In an analysis of conditionals along these lines the agent's state of belief is crucial. This down-to-earth theory is in sharp contrast to the semantic 'dream children' of the 1960s and 1970s. There is no need for possible worlds strategically placed at a suitable distance from each other in a universe for the analysis of conditionals.

There are many interesting things to say about conditionals, about their logic and about more or less imaginative semantics, but here I shall only mention one result which throws an interesting light on what has become known as the Ramsey test.

More stringently, the Ramsey test can be formulated in the following way:

(R) Accept a proposition of the form 'If p, then q' in a state of belief K if and only if the minimal change required to make p acceptable also requires accepting q.

This principle could be compared with a similar one which recurs in the subjective theory of probability, that is, in the tradition of probability of which Ramsey himself laid the foundation. A subjectivist or a Bayesian claims that our assessments of degree of belief ought to be updated by means of conditionalization (see Chapter 1). The very heart of the argument in favour of this standpoint may be expressed as follows:

(B) If a proposition q is accepted in a state of belief K and the proposition p does not contradict any proposition in K, then q is still to be accepted after K has been revised minimally so that p can be accepted.

The idea behind this principle is that knowledge should not be surrendered unnecessarily. If you learn that Mattias Fremling was professor of philosophy at Lund University ..t the end of the eighteenth century and the beginning of the nineteenth century, this newly acquired knowledge should not make you reject anything you already know, that is, as long as this knowledge does not contradict any of your old beliefs.

Peter Gärdenfors has recently shown that under certain elementary conditions the Ramsey test and the Bayesian principle are at odds.[26] We cannot work with both (R) and (B) at the same time; they are inconsistent with each other. This result is extremely curious since the principles appear equally acceptable. However, there are a number of objections to the assumptions Gärdenfors uses for his proof. One may question, for example, whether the equivalence assumed in (R) really constitutes a reasonable assumption. As we have noted, it seems reasonable to accept the proposition, 'If the metal rod is heated, it expands', provided the conditions of the Ramsey test are fulfilled. But is it reasonable to insist that if the test conditions are satisfied for two arbitrary propositions the conditional that can be constructed on the basis of these propositions be accepted? I would like to claim that the test condition is necessary but not sufficient for acceptance of a conditional. If (R) is expressed as an implication, one cannot prove that (R) and (B) are inconsistent with each other.

Let us assume, for example, that my initial state of belief is altered in such a way that I hypothetically accept the antecedent, 'The copper rod is heated'. In this revised state of belief it turns out that I believe I know that the price of petrol will rise by 50 pence. Are we prepared to assert that I must also accept the conditional, 'If the copper rod is heated, the price of petrol would rise 50 pence'? Hardly! The conditional sentence would tell us more than that a certain static state of belief exists. By accepting a conditional one shows that certain *changes* of belief are considered to be more reasonable than others.[27]

We may also imagine a situation in which two people have identical states of knowledge initially. After having made a minimal revision of their states of belief so that both believe that the copper rod was heated, it turns out that both of them also accept the consequent, 'The copper rod expands.' But despite these similarities, only one of them accepts the conditional, 'If the copper rod is heated, it would expand'. The reason is that for one of them the link between the heating of the copper rod and its expansion is just as tenuous as the link between the heating of the rod and the increase in the price of petrol. For such a link to exist, something over and above what a particular state of knowledge gives us is needed. To return to Ramsey's theory of general propositions, it can be said that what is required is a set of general propositions, a set of (causal) laws (see the final sentence of the footnote quoted above).

But, following Ramsey's theory, general propositions carry no truth-value. With this theory as a base, it would be possible to claim that a state of belief does not contain any general propositions. A state of belief (or knowledge) is generally considered to consist only of true propositions. A state of knowledge should be based on facts. If we develop Ramsey's thoughts in this way, the superstructure of laws gives us the interesting dynamic effects which are so important to an analysis of conditionals. To a great extent, it is these laws that tell us how to make minimal changes of belief. This means that just from a description of a state of belief we cannot decide whether a conditional is to be regarded as acceptable or not. Ramsey's theory also shows us how wrong most of the 'possible world' semantics are. The similarity relation that, according to these theories, exists between different possible worlds is assumed to be quite disconnected from whichever general proposition we accept for the moment. But the above reasoning suggests that to obtain a reasonable system this similarity relation must be linked with a system of laws. Thus it seems even more unreasonable to try – as some have done – to analyze the concept of causality by making use of this similarity relation and 'possible world' semantics.

Another objection which may be raised and which also leads to the result that Gärdenfors' theorem cannot be proved is directed to principle (B). Is this principle in fact too strong? Does the Bayesian theory of probability simply demand too much of its user? A more reasonable variant seems to be to require q to be compatible with the new state of belief rather than to require that it be accepted. But if the principle is expressed in this way, new methods are needed for conditionalisation and the question is whether the true believers in Bayesianism are willing to accept such a drastic change in their theory as this would involve. If we merely require q to be compatible with the new state of belief, this means, on the level of probability theory, that given some information there are a number of acceptable changes in our old measure of degree of belief and consequently no unambiguous change, as the subjectivists claim. If we assess the probability of rain tomorrow to be .7 but after having made that assessment find out that the trough of low pressure we have been expecting has been delayed in the Atlantic, then, according to the Bayesian theory, we should be able to work out a new point probability of rain tomorrow, on the basis of this new information. We would probably be less certain that it will rain and put the probability at .4. But, what I am saying is that this piece of information may instead lead to an interval assessment of the probability (or, better, to an assessment of a set of epistemically reliable probability measures); that is, after having found out that the trough of low pressure has been delayed, we believe that the likelihood of rain is somewhere between, say, .2 and .5.[28]

Chapter 5

Philosophy of science

It is probably no exaggeration to say that at the turn of this century we knew in broad outline as much about the philosophical foundations of science as we know today. The contribution of this century, as far as it goes, seems to be the formalisation of what was common knowledge among philosophers and historians of science some hundred years ago. The question thus remains to be answered if more or less heavy logic really has taught us anything of value.

The latter half of the nineteenth century offers up a mine of information for anyone who wants to see how a scientific era comes to an end and is replaced by a totally new way of thinking about the world. A deterministic view of physics and the world was no longer fruitful. Maxwell's electromagnetic theories could not, for example, be formulated within a mechanistic or deterministic conceptual framework. One of the physicists and philosophers who was influential at this time, and whose *Die Analyse der Empfindungen* may have had an unforeseen influence on Ramsey,[1] was Ernst Mach. Taking what Nagel calls a descriptive view of science, Mach strongly argued against so-called theoretical terms,[2] that is, against entities like 'electron', 'gene', 'risk-aversive' and 'introvert'. In his view such entities are justified only if they help us in systematising the empirical observations we have made. If not, they must be considered metaphysical terms and should be banished from science. Mach and others strongly believed that we have to distinguish strictly between things that are observable with our senses (or, to take a less phenomenalistic view of the matter, with one instrument or another), on the one hand, and things that are not observable, on the other hand. The object of science is 'the economy of thought'. But Mach, and with him several other influential figures around that time, did not put forth an instrumentalistic view of science. A theory is characterizable as true or false insofar as it is translatable into statements about what are considered to be observable phenomena.

The philosophers and historians of science of Mach's generation also taught us a great deal about the verifiability and falsifiability of theories. They gave us insights into the incommensurability of theories and about what has become known as 'theory-loaded' terms and about a great many other things, that is, insights that some of us tend to associate with philosophers of our own generation. Pierre Duhem and Henri Poincaré, for example, taught us that there are no evidentiary facts which allow us to falsify a sufficiently general scientific theory once and for all. Such a falsification depends on too many other theories. We are thus only allowed to say that the theory, or some of the theories, used in the process of falsification is false – not that the theory itself is false. That theories cannot be completely verified was well-known at the time. Thus, at the turn of the century, there were strong arguments in favour of some form of an instrumentalist's view of science; that is, scientific theories are instruments or tools and, as with hammers, screwdrivers, monkey-wrenches, our choice of them is to a large extent conventional. In the same way that the size of the nails, screws and nuts determines which tools we use, the experimental results determine which theories we choose. We need simple and usable tools as well as theories.

But whether we advocate a descriptive or instrumentalist view of theories, whether we take them literally as true or false, or as intellectual tools, will to some extent depend on whether we believe that theoretical entities really exist or whether we believe them to be logical constructions, simplifying notations of complexes of observable events or intellectual tools. Mach and those other philosophers with a descriptive view of science, whom history has named positivists, share with the logical positivist an instrumentalistic view of theoretical entities and a more or less realistic view of theories. I say more or less because to them theories are not literally true or false, as they are to the classical realist, but bear truth-value only insofar as they are translatable into statements about observable entities. But in order to be able to discuss how our view of a theory's terms affects how we handle some of the basic problems in the philosophy of science, and how Ramsey's work in this connection is of particular interest, a common point of departure is required. A rapid sketch of some of the classical concepts in the philosophy of science may thus be in order. We need a rough picture of the subject at the end of the 1920s. The picture I give borrows some well-known examples from the literature of logical positivism. But it should be kept in mind from the start that Ramsey was *not* a positivist or a logical positivist, as should already be obvious from the discussion in Chapter 4. It is rather so that he, like some other important and independent philosophers of science, has been kidnapped and had some of his ideas distorted by the logical positivist camp. Ramsey's philosophy of science is some sort of synthesis between classical positivism and pragmatism.

THE CLASSICAL PROBLEM OF OBSERVABILITY

When we sit on the beach in summer and idly throw things into the water, we notice sticks float but stones inevitably sink. We make the same type of observation as must have provided the basis for Archimedes' hydrostatics. But where does one draw a line for what is observable? Is everything beyond perception by our senses non-observable? Is it permissible to use a magnifying glass or binoculars? For scientists today the problem is a serious one. Modern scientific theories abound in concepts or terms that are not directly observable. We can see that a stone sinks to the bottom but we cannot see how an electron dances round the nucleus of an atom.

Many of us recall how our physics teacher tried assiduously to convince us that the 'tracks' we observed by means of the bubble chamber were tracks made by electrons. Few of us went along with this fact. We quite simply observed a mass of streaks that reminded us of a scratched spectacle glass.

An economist says that a person who prefers certainty to fair uncertainty is risk-aversive. How can we observe risk-aversive behaviour outside the framework of econometric models? What instruments do we have at our disposal? Neither a magnifying glass nor binoculars are any use here. For example, is the lady who buys fish over the counter instead of frozen fish risk-aversive?

In order to understand the structure of a scientific theory, the traditional philosophy of science distinguishes between two types of terms – *theoretical* and *observable*.[3] This division follows, for example, from Mach's phenomenalistic epistemology as it is developed in *Die Analyse der Empfindungen*, and it is adopted in a more or less radical form by all positivists or logical positivists, although only some of them subscribe to a phenomenalistic conception of knowledge. We have already noted how difficult it is to draw the line for what is observable and thus classify terms used in different sciences. The problem of drawing such a line stands out more clearly if we relate it to a criterion of testability. To the logical positivists and to those devoted to 'physicalism', observable concepts were as essential as they were to Mach. Trying to avoid phenomenalism, however, they argued that theoretical statements are, without loss of meaning, translatable into an *observational language* or a *physicalistic thing-language*. Their hope was actually that all theoretical terms should be *explicitly* definable in terms of basic observable concepts.

The reason for positivism, or logical positivists, showing disapproval of theoretical terms is easy to understand. The goal of science is to give us increased knowledge of our nature, our society and ourselves. Theories are constructed to explain what happened and to predict future events, events which are of the observable kind. An overall economic theory should preferably predict what will happen if a certain political decision is implemented. The theoretical term 'inflation' is in itself uninteresting. It is the observable and tangible consequences of a state of inflation that are interesting.

The positivists and logical positivists were non-realists. To them, theoretical terms only had structural importance; electrons did not exist. They restricted reality to the observable. The realists contest this point of view, claiming that electrons really exist even though they are not observable in the ordinary sense. To understand how Ramsey's analysis of scientific theories can be a useful weapon in this continual war between realists and instrumentalists, we need to know something about empirical and theoretical laws.

EMPIRICAL AND THEORETICAL LAWS

Duhem distinguishes between various strata of a scientific theory, and similar thoughts can be found in the works of many other philosophers of science, such as Poincaré and Campbell. Classical examples of empirical laws are found in the sphere of physics; let us borrow one of Carnap's many examples.

In our physics classes many of us have measured the length of a metal bar before and after heating. With moderate enthusiasm we noted that the bar was a few millimeters longer when it was hot. 'This is true for all metals', the teacher preached from the other side of the desk, a generalization we did not question. Another bar would ruin all our chances of having an early lunch. But to say 'All metals expand if they are heated' is to formulate a general law, a law that can be confirmed or rejected.

If the experiment had never been carried out before, we would probably have taken the trouble to continue our investigation, first using metals we had access to, and then using those that took time to obtain. When we had exhausted our supply, we certainly would have proposed extending the experiments. A generalization would be desired. Other materials could be tested. We would undoubtedly have run into some setbacks, but in the end we would perhaps have been able to formulate a really general empirical law: 'All solid bodies expand on heating'.

The researcher in other fields works in a similar way. As an illustration, we can take the experimental psychologist. In the discussion of Ramsey's probability theory (Chapter 1) we noted the importance of some rationality axioms.

The transitivity axiom was given as an example. If one prefers meat-balls to black pudding and black pudding to fried herring, one ought to prefer meat-balls to fried herring. If we exchange *ought* for *do* we enter into the world of experimental psychology. Let us assume that a psychologist discovers that his friends have transitive preferences. A more thorough study results in the generalization, 'A person's preferences are transitive under the given conditions'. This empirical law may in turn be generalized further.

But the philosophers of science of Ramsey's generation tell us that there is a limit beyond which further empirical generalizations become pointless. However, the child's incessant question 'Why?' takes us further. Nevertheless, it cannot be answered by more empirical generalizations – a new type of law is needed.

Unlike an empirical law, a theoretical law is not an empirical generalization. A theoretical law deals, among other things, with the non-observable whereas, as we have seen, an empirical law is expressed exclusively in the observational language. A theoretical law telling us something about how solid bodies expand when heated would have to refer to the behaviour of molecules, thus being formulated within the framework of one atomic theory of matter or another. A theoretical law about people's behaviour, on the other hand, might best be formulated within the framework of some general psychological theory or of neurophysiology. In both cases, non-observable concepts will be applied.

The philosophers of science teach us that theoretical laws are not the last link in a chain of empirical generalization.

The relation between the two types of laws is rather that the former help us to explain the latter. If we aim to gain an overall understanding and structure, then the theoretical laws are valuable. These laws indicate the similarities and differences between classes of empirical generalizations found. The theoretical laws are general hypotheses about how the world works.

It is said that a good theory and its laws yield empirical laws as a dividend. Some of these are well-known and tested. Others perhaps stand out as surprising and require further investigation. Consequently, it is conceivable that the empirical laws in some sense can be derived from the theoretical laws. In the same way, we can derive empirical facts from the empirical laws.

We now see clearly a problem in the philosophy of science of the tricky kind. How can empirical laws be derived from theoretical ones? The latter contain theoretical terms while the former contain purely observable concepts. If only the concepts that fulfil our testability criterion are to be permitted to occur in science and one requirement is that things are to be expressed in an observational language using observable terms, shouldn't all theoretical terms be eliminated from scientific jargon?

THE THEORETICIAN'S DILEMMA

Carl Hempel has formulated the requirement as follows:

[I]f the terms and the general principles of a scientific theory serve their purpose, i.e., if they establish definite connections among observable phenomena, then they can be dispensed with since any chain of laws and interpretative statements establishing such a connection should then be replaceable by a law which directly links observational antecedents to observational consequents.[4]

Let us agree that the theoretical terms are either meaningful or not meaningful. If the latter is the case, if the theory can

131

manage just as well without them, we can quite simply exclude them from all connections in which they occur. On the other hand, if they are meaningful, in that they have a part to play in the construction of the theory, according to Hempel they establish such connections between observable phenomena. But if they establish such connections, the same relations and laws can be expressed without theoretical terms. The conclusion is then that theoretical terms are superfluous.

Some philosophers of science hoped it was possible to define *explicitly* all the theoretical concepts in terms of concepts taken from a basic observational language. The concept 'risk aversion' can be given a strict definition in everyday terms from this point of view. A person X is said to be risk-aversive if and only if, in a situation where the choice is a lottery ticket or a bonus that one is certain to receive, and where the expected value of the lottery ticket is equal to the value of the bonus, the person chooses the bonus.

One well-known problem with this type of definition of theoretical terms is that if the antecedent of the definiens is false, if the conditions for a study of risk-aversive behaviour are not fulfilled, the definiens as a whole is still true and we can thus say that the person is risk-aversive. If the lottery ticket and the bonus do not have the same value, the antecedent of the definiens is false. Despite this, it follows that one can say that X is risk-aversive, a result scarcely to be desired.

THE PROBLEM OF EXPLICIT DEFINITIONS

The philosophers of science rapidly abandoned the idea of all theoretical terms being explicitly definable. But at the end of the 1920s, when Ramsey was working on the essay 'Theories' (1929), the philosophers of science were still advocating this type of definition. Or at least they still dreamt that it would be possible and reasonable to conjure away theoretical concepts by means of explicit definitions. Ramsey himself mentions a number of the best-known philosophers of the day whom he considered to be advocating this type of strategy. We have Russell, Whitehead, Nicod, but also Carnap. As is well-known, Carnap gave up the idea of explicit definitions. The arguments given by him against explicit definitions in his essay 'Testability and Meaning' are classic today. Instead of explicit definitions, *implicit definitions* were called for as well as *correspondence rules* and *bridge principles*.

In 'Theories' Ramsey tries to show by using a simple deductive system that it is possible in principle to formulate definitions of the type wanted. But if this is done, then the theory will lose all its vitality. Ramsey's argument is that a theory reformulated using explicit definitions becomes static and uninteresting.

It is mainly through Richard Braithwaite that Ramsey's esoteric essay has received the attention that it well deserves. In his book *Scientific Explanation*,[5] Braithwaite recapitulates some of Ramsey's ideas. Braithwaite's presentation of Ramsey's ideas is an educational exercise of an admirable kind. But since this is a book about Ramsey, I try to keep to his own text. I also deviate somewhat from Braithwaite's presentation in that I refrain completely from a detailed discussion of the formal content of Ramsey's essay.

RAMSEY'S EXAMPLES

Ramsey distinguishes between 'the primary system' and 'the secondary system'. The primary system can with some modification be identified as the logical positivists' observational language and the secondary system as the corresponding theoretical language. Or the distinction may be compared with what Campbell calls the hypothesis of the theory and the laws and consequences which it aims to explain. It is in the secondary system that we formulate the theoretical laws (axioms, in Ramsey's terminology) using theoretical concepts. It is here we shall look for Maxwell's laws, wave functions and so on. In the primary system we find purely empirical facts (consequences) and empirical generalizations, or laws. However, we should bear in mind that Ramsey's theory is open to other interpretations. In principle, it discusses only two languages and their mutual relations.

In order to link the theoretical terms of the secondary system with the 'observational' terms of the primary system, we need a dictionary. Campbell says that a theory is a connected set of propositions which are divided into groups. The first group is the hypothesis, the axioms; the second group is the 'dictionary'. According to Campbell, the ideas which are related by means of the dictionary to the ideas of the hypothesis are such that we know something about them apart from the theory. For every theory we can imagine such a dictionary. The common view of such a 'book' is that we can work out the meaning of the theoretical terms using the definitions listed therein. If we are wondering about the term 'electron', we simply look up the letter 'E' in the dictionary and find the word 'electron'. Since the dictionary is assumed to contain purely explicit definitions, the definitions give us an exhaustive and complete description of electrons in terms of the 'observational' language. Ramsey does exactly the opposite. He uses the dictionary to 'define' the observational terms of the primary language in terms of the theoretical terms of the secondary language. Thus an observational term would be defined in terms of the terms 'electron', 'spin', 'quark' and their logical relation, not the other way around.[6]

What we expect to find if we look up the term 'risk-aversive' in the dictionary of theoretical terms for modern utility theory is

risk-aversive $=$ $_{def}$ . . . A person who under conditions . . . chooses . . . instead of . . .

But what Ramsey's dictionary tells us is the opposite:

A person who under conditions . . . chooses . . . instead of . . . $=$ $_{def}$ probability . . . utility . . . risk-aversive . . .

By formulating axioms and a dictionary in this ingenious way, Ramsey is able, without begging the question, to answer a number of questions about the status of the theoretical terms. Two of these questions are:

Can we say anything in the language of this theory that we could not say without it?[7]

Can we reproduce the structure of our theory by means of explicit definitions within the primary system?[8]

To be able to give a satisfactory answer to these questions Ramsey has to show if and how one can invert the sentences of the dictionary of a theory in such a way that we get what we want, namely, a definition of the theoreticals using the observationals. It is not too difficult to see that there is no unique solution to this problem. The problem is that the laws and consequences of the primary system can be made true by various sets of facts, corresponding to different definitions. There is one possible solution to this problem. If we want to invert the sentences by using the dictionary alone, then we take the disjunction of the set of all possible definitions. However, as Ramsey swiftly points out, this is not too good a solution. One reason is that the secondary system has 'more degrees of freedom' or 'a higher multiplicity' than the primary system.

> Since, therefore, the dictionary alone does not suffice, the next hopeful method is to use both dictionary and axioms in a way which is referred to in many popular discussions of theories when it is said that the meaning of a proposition about the external world is what we should ordinarily regard as the *criterion* or *test* of its truth. This suggests that we should define propositions in the secondary system by their criteria in the primary.[9]

Ramsey now shows that it is always in principle possible to define the meaning of the theoretical terms by explicit definitions. However, such definitions will be so complicated that they are as unmanageable as the disjunctive definitions that were our reason for trying this line of thought.

Having shown that we actually can reproduce the structure of a theory by means of (explicit) definitions the obvious
question is: Are explicit definitions necessary?

ARE EXPLICIT DEFINITIONS NECESSARY?

For the type of simple theories Ramsey discusses in his essay, the structure of the theory can be reproduced – albeit at
the cost of crucial complexity – by using such definitions.
But Ramsey 'the mathematician' should have known how
this formally simple system could be extended so that the
argument would even apply to more general types of theories. A generalization of this kind seems unnecessary, in
part. If the explicit definitions necessary for similarity of
structure for relatively simple systems reach a degree of complexity of the arcane kind, it is easy to imagine that for more
general systems these definitions are totally incomprehen-
sible.

Is it not necessary then for us to be able to reproduce the
structure with the aid of this kind of definition in order to be
able to use the theory in an adequate way?

> To this the answer seems clear that it cannot be necessary, or a
> theory would be no use at all. Rather than give all these defini-
> tions it would be simpler to leave the facts, laws and conse-
> quences in the language of the primary system. Also the ar-
> bitrariness of the definitions makes it impossible for them to be
> adequate to the theory as something in process of growth.[10]

Over the centuries, scientists have used their theories without reflecting on the problem of theoretical terms. They have
successfully applied their formulae although no explicit definitions were available. Consequently, it would appear that
such definitions are not necessary for the application of a
theory.

In the above quotation, Ramsey apparently considers that
explicit definitions complicate the evolution of a theory.

Whether we prefer reading Kuhn or Popper, the question of the dynamic properties of theories is an interesting one. Even during a period of normal sciences, dynamic theories are required. We should be able to find new fields of application for our theories, and so on. Ramsey now asserts that a certain measure of arbitrariness in the choice of explicit definitions makes the theory static.

I shall let Braithwaite explain Ramsey's (and indeed his own) thesis:

> It is only in theories which are not intended to have any function except that of systematizing empirical generalizations already known that the theoretical terms can harmlessly be explicitly defined. A theory which it is hoped may be expanded in the future to explain more generalizations than it was originally designed to explain must allow more freedom to its theoretical terms than would be given them were they to be logical constructions out of observable entities. A scientific theory which, like all good scientific theories, is capable of growth must be more than an alternative way of describing the generalizations upon which it is based, which is all it would be if its theoretical terms were limited by being explicitly defined.[11]

At the end of the nineteenth century, the physicist J. J. Thomson showed that cathode rays consist of subatomic particles and he chose the term 'corpuscle' for these particles. One of Thomson's contributions to physics was to determine the mass of these corpuscles. Today we do not talk about corpuscles but about electrons, and an early theory was drawn up by Lorentz. Let us assume that Lorentz's theory settled once and for all the theoretical concept 'electron' by use of explicit definitions. According to Ramsey and Braithwaite, this would mean that the theory would lose all its dynamic force and could not possibly be applied to new phenomena. If new experiments demonstrated that the concept of the electron had to be revised, a full-scale revolution would be needed to bring about the change. All the old definitions would have to be discarded and new ones launched. But history teaches us that neither Thomson nor

Lorentz had any intention of settling the term 'electron' once and for all, but left the door open for the changes in definitions required so that Bohr, for example, could arrive at his theory.[12]

To illustrate further this important objection to explicitly defining theoretical terms, let us consider Ramsey's own definition of the theoretical term 'utility'. To measure the utility a person ascribes to a given object or outcome, he makes use of an operational method based on comparisons between 50–50 games. With this kind of game it is possible to establish utility values fairly straightforwardly. The utility of having coffee after dinner is much greater than the corresponding utility of tea. But if this were the only method by which utility values could be established, we would soon run into trouble when the theory and its laws were applied. Under some conditions, as we have seen in Chapter 1, Ramsey's method scarcely seems to be applicable. The method quite simply does not function adequately. In such situations, it is reasonable to look for an alternative method. But if the term 'utility' has been explicitly defined in terms of an individual's gambling behaviour, we have cancelled out any such expansion of the theory. The sphere of application of the theory has been fixed once and for all, its potential explanatory power severely pruned.

If Ramsey's and Braithwaite's arguments against explicit definitions are correct, there are two possible ways out. Either we throw overboard the idea that one of the most important tasks of a theory is to predict new phenomena, new empirical laws, or we abandon the idea of explicit definitions. Among philosophers of science, the choice is relatively straightforward. Carnap, for instance, maintained that the crucial value of a new theory lay in its dynamics. It can predict new empirical laws and consequences. The ability of the theory to also explain previously known laws is of subordinate importance.

> If a scientist proposes a new theoretical system, from which no new laws can be derived, then it is logically equivalent to the

set of all known empirical laws. The theory may have a certain elegance, and it may simplify to some degree the set of all known laws, although it is not likely that there would be an essential simplification. On the other hand, every new theory in physics that has led to a great leap forward has been a theory from which new empirical laws could be derived. If Einstein had done no more than propose his theory of relativity as an elegant new theory that would embrace certain known laws – perhaps also simplify them to a certain degree – then his theory would not have had such a revolutionary effect.[13]

Another illustration of the importance of new theories predicting new and unknown empirical laws is found if we consider the wave model for light. The theory gained its first great success by explaining a couple of new phenomena. As is well-known, Newton regarded light as a substance composed of corpuscles and these atoms of light were accompanied by waves in the ether. Actually we have here a suggestion for two competing conceptions of the nature of light – one corpuscular view and one wave model. Regarding light as a wave phenomenon, however, won no great following and the prevailing corpuscular view asserted itself fairly well. But at the start of the nineteenth century, when Thomas Young and Augustin Fresnel, in developing a wave theory proposed by Christian Huygens, succeeded in explaining a number of startling phenomena in terms of wave theory, phenomena that the corpuscular view could not explain, wave theory rapidly became popular. What happened was that Poisson, the French mathematician and advocate of the corpuscular view, showed that wave theory had a number of strange consequences. If the theory were true, then at a certain distance, the shadow cast by a perfectly circular disc should have a dot of light at its very centre, the result of light waves, arriving in phase, reinforcing one another. Contrary to all expectations, Fresnel succeeded in showing experimentally that this really was the case. But it was not only this event that decided the fate of the corpuscular conception. In 1850, Leon Focault showed that light travels faster in air than in water, a result that was predicted by wave theory. The corpuscular conception of light, on the other hand, led to the opposite conclusions.[14]

But it cannot be said that Ramsey, or Braithwaite either, has really shown that explicit definitions lead to static theories. The simple theories they used as examples differ considerably from the extremely complex theories of modern physics. The theories contain no laws based on probabilities. On the other hand, there is no convincing evidence (or counter-example) of the opposite, as far as I know. The majority of counter-examples against the Ramsey–Braithwaite thesis assume that new definitions are introduced, and this in turn leads to a reinterpretation of the theory, something which is unacceptable to Ramsey.

> That is to say, if we proceed by explicit definition we cannot add to our theory without changing the definitions, and so the meaning of the whole.[15]

Thus, I believe that Ramsey's answer to the 'theoretician's dilemma' would be that it is based on false premises. Theoretical terms can serve their purposes without establishing definite connections among observables, there is no need to try to define them away and such an attempt would anyway run into insurmountable difficulties. It should also be noted that one of the reasons why Ramsey's paper has been misinterpreted to such a large extent is that one tends to confuse what he has said so far about the attempts of others to define theoretical terms and his own theoretical suggestions, which we now turn to.[16]

RAMSEY SENTENCES

Having rejected the idea of the necessity of (explicit) definitions, Ramsey asks how the function of a theory can be explained without them. What do we do about the theoretical terms when we cannot get rid of them by means of definitions? Ramsey's answer is to introduce what have come to be known as *Ramsey sentences*.

The best way to write our theory seems to be this ($\exists \alpha, \beta, \gamma$): dictionary . axioms.[17]

Perhaps this idea, based on a logical artifice we have seen him use before (see Chapter 2), should be elucidated somewhat. A theory T's axioms introduce a set of theoretical terms: $t_1, t_2, \ldots, t_n$. These terms are also to be found in the dictionary. The dictionary links the theoretical terms with a number of terms in the primary language. A theory T can therefore be written as a conjunction of all axioms (theoretical laws) and the dictionary; that is, $A_1 \& A_2 \& \ldots \& A_m \& D$. But when the dictionary in turn is a conjunction of a set of 'definitions' (non-explicit), $d_1, d_2, \ldots, d_k$, the theory can be formulated as $A_1 \& A_2 \& \ldots \& A_m \& d_1 \& d_2 \& \ldots \& d_k$.

Ramsey proposes that in this sentence all the occurrences of theoretical terms should be replaced by corresponding variables and that the open-sentence formula obtained by this process is closed by adding a set of existential quantifiers, one for each variable. The result will be a sentence of the type found in the quotation above. This is a reproduction of the theory T but without any occurrence at all of theoretical terms and where the Ramsey sentence and the theory have the same empirical consequences.

Presented in this way, Ramsey sentences appear to be some kind of abstract conjuring trick, and their importance for the question of the status of theoretical terms seems farfetched. What we need is a didactic example explaining Ramsey's line of thought. One of those who has succeeded in giving such an example is Carnap, and instead of inventing an artificial example of my own, I borrow Carnap's copybook example.[18] However, I use his example in a way which I believe is more in line with Ramsey's original idea.

Carnap's theory T is a simplified gas theory. The theory contains a number of theoretical terms, among them the terms 'Mol' and 'Hymol'. The first of these two terms refers to the class of molecules, and the second to the class of hydrogen molecules. Expressed differently, 'Mol' is a one-place predicate, the extension of which is all molecules. 'Hymol' is also a one-place predicate, but with a different extension – the class of hydrogen molecules.

We also assume that a space–time coordinate system has been fixed. This means that a point somewhere in space and time can be identified with the aid of the four coordinates x, y, z and t. The system of coordinates permits us to introduce yet another set of theoretical terms, this time of a more complex variety. We let 'Temp' stand for 'temperature' and we can then write 'the body B's temperature at time t is 37 degrees' as 'Temp(B,t) = 37'. Similarly, 'B's pressure at t' can be written as 'Press(B,t)', if we introduce the term 'Press'. The mass of a body is designated 'Mass' and its velocity 'Vel'. Thus, 'the body B's mass is 150 grams' can be written 'Mass(B) = 150' and similarly for the concept of velocity. 'Temp', 'Press', 'Mass' and 'Vel' differ from 'Mol' and 'Hymol' in that the former are two-place theoretical predicates or relations.

As Carnap points out, a theory of this kind will contain a variety of laws – laws, for example, from the kinetic theory of gases, telling us something about molecules' motions, velocities, collisions, and the like. But also macro-gas-theory laws concerning, for example, the temperature and pressure of a gas body. Finally, more specialized axioms or laws about hydrogen will also undoubtedly be introduced into the theory.

If we now reformulate the theory in accordance with Ramsey's ideas, we obtain something which initially looks like one half of a theory.

(T) . . . Mol . . . Hymol . . . Temp . . . Press . . . Mass . . .
Vel. . . .

Here the axioms or laws of the theory and their interdependency are only indicated by writing out the theoretical terms and connecting them by dots.

But the other half of the theory is missing – a dictionary has to be formulated. According to Carnap, a complete theory needs to contain partial definitions or reduction sentences for only some of its theoretical terms, a point with which Ramsey would agree, although he would not use the word 'definition' in exactly the same way. Ramsey's view of the dictionary, I believe, is more like Campbell's (although I believe that he does not commit himself to the one or the other interpretation). The dictionary is to be understood as in some way relating theoretical terms with observationals in such a way that a theoretical sentence (e.g., containing the term 'Temp') is true if and only if a corresponding empirical sentence is true, that is, relates the unfamiliar with the familiar. The dictionary consists of rules of translation which make verification or falsification possible, rather than of 'definitions'. However, one or another type of 'definition' is not excluded from the dictionary. Thus, notice that if by 'Vel' we mean an individual molecule's velocity, the kinetic theory of gases lacks a rule of translation for this term. But we can choose, for instance, to give rules or definitions for the theoretical terms 'Temp' and 'Press'. A rule of translation for 'Temp' would tell us how we are to measure the temperature of a gas. If we come across the word 'Temp' in our dictionary, the 'definition' must give us a clear operational account of how to set about establishing the temperature, which methods are permissible. Perhaps it is only permissible to use a mercury thermometer – the new electronic measuring instruments are not considered suitable. Likewise, we have to be told how to construct and use a manometer in order to be able to measure the pressure of a gas.

The rules of translation thus relate the set of theoretical sentences of the theory with sets of empirical sentences. Let us denote the latter set of sentences O_{Temp}, O_{Press}, O_{Mass}, $\cdots$ Our dictionary can now be written as

(D) (. . . Temp . . . O_{Temp} . . .) & (. . . Press . . . O_{Press} . . .) &
(. . . Mass . . . O_{Mass} . . .) & . . . ,

if we choose to make the dictionary contain rules of translations for sentences containing the theoretical terms 'Temp', 'Press' and 'Mass'.

If we form the conjunction of the two sentences T and D, we get a symbolization of the complete theory TD.

(TD) (. . . Mol . . . Hymol . . . Temp . . . Press . . . Mass . . .
Vel . . .) & [(. . . Temp . . . O_{Temp} . . .) & (. . . Press . . .
O_{Press} . . .) & (. . . Mass . . . O_{Mass} . . .) & . . .].

But TD is not a Ramsey sentence but only a rather unusual way of formulating our theory. Ramsey's idea is that all theoretical terms are replaced by bound variables. Since Carnap's theory TD contains both class terms and relations, we have to choose variables in a corresponding way. Wherever the theoretical term 'Mol' occurs in the theory it is substituted by the variable 'C_1' and wherever 'Hymol' occurs in the theory we exchange it for the variable 'C_2'. The relation terms 'Temp', 'Press', 'Mass' and 'Vel' are replaced throughout by the relation variables 'R_1', 'R_2', 'R_3' and 'R_4'. If we replace all the theoretical terms consistently with class and relation variables, respectively, we will obtain an open sentence formula. To proceed from this sentence formula into a Ramsey sentence we add one existential quantifier for each one of the variables. The result of transforming TD into a Ramsey sentence will thus be

(TD^R) ($\exists C_1$)($\exists C_2$)($\exists R_1$)($\exists R_2$)($\exists R_3$)($\exists R_4$)[(. . C_1 . . C_2 . . R_1 . . R_2
. . R_3 . . R_4 . . .) & ((. . . R_1 . . . O_{R1} . . .) &
(. . . R_2 . . . O_{R2} . . .) & (. . . R_3 . . . O_{R3} . . .) & . . .))].

This sentence states that there is a class C_1, a class C_2, a relation R_1, a relation R_2, and so on, connected in a way specified by the axioms of the theory and such that the relation terms are connected with the observational terms, as specified by the dictionary. Or expressed differently: There exists a property C_1 (the property of being a molecule) which is such that from the axioms of the theory (stating something about this property) and the dictionary, we can derive empirically testable consequences (and similarly for C_2, R_1, etc).

Another, and somewhat different, example of a Ramsey sentence is obtained if we take Ramsey's theory of probability as a theory of human behaviour and rewrite this theory as a Ramsey sentence. The theory contains theoretical concepts such as 'Utility', 'Probability' and 'Ethically neutral proposition'. We also have a set of operational rules telling us, for example, how utilities and probabilities can be measured. These rules are part of the dictionary of this theory. It connects the theoretical concepts of the theory with things that are observable, in this case human actions and choices. Thus the first step in the transformation of this probability (or decision) theory (let us call it P, with dictionary D) into a Ramsey sentence would look something like this:

(PD) (. . . Ethic . . . Prob . . . Util . . . Risk) & [(. . . Prob . . . O_{Prob} . . .) & (. . . Util . . . O_{Util} . . .) & (. . . Risk . . . O_{Risk} . . .) & . . .],

and the complete Ramsey sentence would look very similar to the Ramsey sentence above. However, it asserts the existence of totally different entities.

Ramsey's theory is thus not a theory of how to eliminate theoretical terms. It is a way to conceive the logical structure of a scientific theory, a way to logically understand the functioning of the theory and its theoretical terms. It is a way of theorising, not of eliminating. Ramsey compares his view of theories with the way we tell fairy tales. The statement 'There is an electron such that . . .' can be compared with 'Once upon a time there was a prince . . .'. In both cases we fill in the dotted lines with whatever we want to state about the entity in question. The electrons move in given paths, the prince is sure to live in a castle and is on the verge of killing an animal that never came under the protection of the World Wildlife Fund.

> They are not, therefore, strictly propositions by themselves just as the different sentences in a story beginning 'Once upon a time' have not complete meanings and so are not propositions by themselves.[19]

DYNAMICS AND INCOMMENSURABILITY

It should be quite clear by now that Ramsey sentences do not result in an inflexibility of the type that explicit definitions of theoretical terms do. Ramsey sentences indicate clearly the function of the theoretical terms of the theory, at the same time permitting the dynamic properties of the theory to be retained. New laws, definitions or rules of translation can be added to already formulated Ramsey sentences. The theoretical concept 'Utility' can be made more precise by adding yet another 'definition' to our dictionary. We can assume, for example, that utility cannot only be measured by means of games but also by using secondary preferences.[20]

The dynamic advantages of Ramsey sentences can be further illustrated by considering the dictionary and its definitions in our version of Carnap's example. Our dictionary contains definitions of, or rules of translation for, the three theoretical terms 'Temp', 'Press' and 'Mass'. The term 'Vel' is not found in the dictionary. But assume that we find it necessary to introduce such a term into the dictionary. This could be done by rewriting D.

$$(D^*) \; (\ldots \text{Temp} \ldots O_{Temp} \ldots) \; \& \; (\ldots \text{Press} \ldots O_{Press} \ldots)$$
$$\& \; (\ldots \text{Mass} \ldots O_{Mass} \ldots) \; \& \; (\ldots \text{Vel} \ldots O_{Vel} \ldots)$$
$$\& \ldots.$$

Taking T and D^* together we will get a new Ramsey sentence (TD^*), which describes in full our changed view of reality. A corresponding change would be impossible if all definitions were explicitly defined from the start. Ramsey discusses this advantage of his sentences.

> We have to think what else we might be going to add to our stock, or hoping to add, and consider whether $\alpha(0,3)$ would be retained to suit any further additions better than $\bar{\alpha}(0,3)$. . . . [W]e hope from the observed instances to find a law and then to fill in the unobserved ones according to that law, not at random beforehand.[21]

Thus, Ramsey's method provides us with a method of understanding how new theories are developed and created. We need not add to the stock of our theory until new experimental laws and facts are found. But when such results are obtained, the theory can and should be developed in accordance with the new findings (e.g., by introducing new theoretical terms) – that is, as long as what is added is added as clauses falling within the scope of the initial existential quantifiers. Ramsey explains the reason behind this proposal.

> So far, however, as *reasoning* is concerned, that the values of these functions are not complete propositions makes no difference, provided we interpret all logical combination as taking place within the scope of a single prefix $(\exists, \alpha, \beta, \gamma)$; e.g.
>
> $$\overline{\beta(n,3) \cdot \bar{\beta}(n,3)} \text{ must be } (\exists \beta): \overline{\beta(n,3) \cdot \bar{\beta}(n,3)},$$
>
> $$\text{not } (\exists \beta) \, \beta(n,3) \cdot (\exists \beta) \, \bar{\beta}(n,3).$$
>
> For we can reason about the characters in a story just as well as if they were really identified, provided we don't take part of what we say as about one story, part about another.[22]

Note that Ramsey's basic reason is that the two statements above are not logically equivalent.

Using the Ramsey sentences to develop a theory of indirect or indefinite descriptions is another way of coming to understand how these sentences can tell us something about the dynamics of scientific theories and scientific growth. Herbert Bohnert in his defence of what he calls 'Ramsey's elimination method' compares the way we build up Ramsey sentences with the way we slowly come to know other persons, not by actually meeting them but by being given bits and pieces of information about them, an idea which can be used also in the present context.[23] In conversation, some people have a tendency to mention the name of a person or persons they know, assuming or pretending that you know who they are, but you do not have the slightest idea who they might be. Such conversations are rather irritating, but can be psychologically explained. What you as the listener have to do is to adopt some strategy to deal with the situation. One way to proceed is to take these references to an unknown person as being about someone not yet explicitly defined, but rather about someone for whom the various remarks hold. Bohnert points out that the formal correlate of this is that of an existential sentence and that as the conversation continues, new remarks made by the speaker have to be added as clauses. Thus if our speaker repeatedly mentions a Smith whom we do not know and cannot guess who it might be, we would be led to a sentence like 'There is an x such that . . . ', where our information about x is only indicated by dots. Here we have the Ramsey method applied to individuals. However, the example clearly shows that Ramsey sentences can throw light on the problem of scientific growth in an interesting way.

But doesn't this idea also tell us something about incommensurability? Getting to know more about Smith by adding new sentences as clauses could be compared with getting to know more about, say, electrons. But making changes by adding new sentences as clauses or changing the dictionary will lead us to a new and, strictly speaking, incommensurable theory. But, of course, we are talking of the same Smith; it is just that we learn more about him. Naturally this alters the meaning, but it is still Smith we are referring to. In the same way it would be foolish to maintain that Thomson, determining the mass of his corpuscles, actually was measuring the mass of something other than the electron. It would be like saying that if Smith changed his name to Jones he would no longer be the same person.

It is obvious from Ramsey's discussion at the end of 'Theories' that he envisages the possibility of comparing not only the content of theories but also their formal construction:

> Two theories may be compatible without being equivalent, i.e. a set of facts might be found which agreed with both, and another set too which agreed with one but not with the other. The adherents of two such theories could quite well dispute, although neither affirmed anything the other denied.[24]

Unfortunately, Ramsey does not give any illustrations. It would have been interesting if he had taken up the incommensurability debate which was in full swing at the beginning of this century.[25] One is thus tempted to agree with what D. H. Mellor says, that we have not reached much further today than Ramsey in the understanding of the problem of incommensurability. Whether or not theories are incommensurable, the Ramsey sentences are the best tool we have to arrive at an understanding of why this is so.

THE REALISM–INSTRUMENTALISM DEBATE

A subject that philosophers of science have quibbled over for decades is whether scientific theories can be assigned a truth-value. Is quantum mechanics true/false or is the theory only an instrument for systematising what we feel to be the external world? A philosophical question of a similar kind but on the ontological level is presented if we reflect on the status of theoretical terms. Do electrons exist? Is there a state of inflation independent of our theoretical description of it? Do we possess a superego and are there really genes? Discussing this problem will, I believe, give a more profound understanding of Ramsey's view of the functioning of scientific theories and their terms.

A realist is one who is a realist on both the theoretical and the ontological level, that is, someone who believes that scientific theories can be assigned a truth-value and that the things the theoretical terms refer to actually exist. Quantum mechanics is either true or false. The theoretical terms used in quantum mechanics denote actual objects. Electrons, mesons and quarks exist independently of us and our theories. They have the same status as birds, pens and balls.

One may dismiss the plausibility of either theoretical realism or ontological realism, or both.[26] The outlook of particular interest to us in this context is total anti-realism or instrumentalism, that is, both theoretical and ontological anti-realism. An instrumentalist claims that theories are neither true nor false and that theoretical terms are merely instruments with the aid of which we can systematize experimental results. These instruments permit us – with mathematics as a tool – to move about between different sets of empirical results.

Ramsey's attitude towards theoretical realism is not clearly expressed in 'Theories'. But in Chapter 4 we noted that in 'General Propositions and Causality', written the same year as 'Theories', he advocates a form of theoretical instrumentalism. I will thus just briefly recapitulate a few important findings of that chapter. General propositions are not truth-value bearing. Scientific laws and hence theories constitute the system (or instrument) by which we meet the future – 'they are maps of neighbouring space by which we steer'. Or, expressed differently, theories are 'not judgements but rules for judging'. Ramsey's view is that they cannot be negated, they cannot be proved true or false, but they can be disagreed with by someone who does not adopt the theory in question.[27] The pragmatic alternative developed by Ramsey in his 'General Propositions and Causality' was, as we have seen, influenced by the works of Peirce, but also by his new conception of mathematics. In Chapters 6 and 7 we will see that Ramsey at the end of his short life slowly gave up logicism for a finitistic view of mathematics. He more or less gives up the fundamental axioms of logicism one at a time.[28] Thus, Ramsey's own view of theories is in this respect the opposite of those who have made his theory known, that is, the logical positivists. But this important fact is seldom if ever pointed out. Ramsey's problem was not, for example, the realist's that theories are not statements but open-sentence formulas (because the dictionary does not necessarily contain correspondence rules for all theoreticals), a fact which means that the view that theories carry truth-value does not hold. They are not statements since they do not fulfill the grammatical conditions for statements.

That Ramsey was an ontological anti-realist appears more obvious. A theoretical term acquires its meaning by its function in the theory. In the essay entitled 'Causal Qualities', a commentary on 'Theories', Ramsey clarifies his position:

> No proposition of the secondary system can be understood apart from the whole theory to which it belongs. If a man says 'Zeus hurls thunderbolts', that is not nonsense because Zeus does not appear in my theory, and is not definable in terms of my theory. I have to consider it as part of a theory and attend to its consequences, e.g. that sacrifices will bring the thunderbolts to an end.[29]

The theoretical term 'Zeus' is meaningless if it is not associated with a set of observable consequences, such as 'thunderbolts'. For the same reason, the concept 'mass' will not acquire any import until we have decided what other terms are to be included in our theory, what axioms we are going to accept and what dictionary we intended to use (i.e., when we have decided what the observable consequences are).

Some of the axioms Carnap's simple theory will presuppose are probably taken from the kinetic theory of gases. The dictionary of this theory, as we know, contains no definition, no rule of translation, of the term 'Vel', that is, if we assume that 'Vel' is to be defined as 'the velocity of a particular molecule'. 'Vel' in this sense is therefore a meaningless term.

In the dictionary of the kinetic theory of gases, on the other hand, is included a definition based on the average speed of all molecules. When we specified the original dictionary in our example, we did not bother to define 'Vel'. Nevertheless, we noted that the dynamic properties of the Ramsey sentence permit us to do so on a later occasion. If instead of 'Vel', we imagine terms such as 'electron', 'quark' or 'utility', we see how they acquire their functional meaning in the light of the whole theory.

But a measure of caution in interpreting Ramsey's text may be in order. Ramsey discusses the theoretical terms that a scientific theory presupposes, such as 'electrons' or 'Zeus'. In his view we cannot say anything meaningful about them outside the framework of the theory but notice that we have not said that electrons or Zeus do not exist; we say only that the entities we name 'electrons' or 'Zeus' gain their meaning because of their place in the theory. We must distinguish between a theory's terms and its concepts. If the terms 'electron' or 'Zeus' have a function in a particular theory, this does not directly answer the question whether electrons or Zeus really exists. If Ramsey's method is to be effective, the concepts and terms must be identified. It is thus quite conceivable that, using Ramsey sentences, one could argue in favour of both an instrumentalist and a realist position.[30]

Ramsey's view of the functioning of theories and their theoretical terms can thus be summarized as follows. Theories are not judgements, but rules for judging – they do not carry truth-value, but are instead to be considered the cognitive maps by which we steer. These cognitive maps are drawn in perspective with the aid of known empirical facts and laws. However, to be able to draw useful maps, maps that connect and explain the laws and consequences, we have to make use of theoretical concepts. Such maps will not only guarantee that we know our way in our own backyard, but also that we can successfully undertake more dangerous journeys into the unknown. That is, they give us the power to predict the future.

EMPIRICAL CONTENT

One very important question is whether the same class of observational consequences can be derived from the Ramsey sentence of the theory as from the original theory. Do the Ramsey sentence and the original theory have the same empirical content? The answer may seem obvious. Ramsey's cleverly formulated sentence results in the empirical content being preserved. But it is not trivial to prove this statement formally and Ramsey presents no proof in his essay. It may be worthwhile then to throw further light on the question.

Before we can answer the question about empirical content, we must split the question into two parts and try to prove that (i) each observational consequence of TD^R is an observational consequence of the original theory TD, and vice versa, (ii) each observational consequence of the original theory TD is an observational consequence of TD^R. We shall show that the original theory expressed in terms of the axioms (the theoretical laws) and the dictionary (with its definitions) has the same empirical content as the Ramsey sentence of the theory.

The first of these two statements is comparatively simple to prove. The Ramsey sentence is an existential generalization of the original theory and is thus implied by TD. But if TD implies TD^R, TD also implies all the observational consequences of TD^R.

It should be borne in mind that we have assumed the reasonableness of leaving the domain of elementary logic for a more recondite second-order logic. We accept that it is possible to quantify over sets or properties (there is a property E such that . . .) and not only over individuals. This is, of course, a complication accepted by advocates of Ramsey sentences and of Ramsey himself.

We now pass on to statement (ii), which is more difficult to prove, and I shall follow the proof that H. G. Bohnert has given. Different versions of Bohnert's proof have been discussed by I. Scheffler and W. Stegmüller, among others.[31]

Let us assume that L is a scientific language containing among other things a number of theoretical terms. TD in Carnap's example can be seen as a theory expressed in this language. Some of L's sentences s will contain theoretical terms: others will not. The sentence TD is an example of a sentence in L of the former type. Let $E_T(s)$ stand for a complete existential generalization of a given sentence s of L, that is, with respect to the theoretical terms. An example of a complete existential generalization of a sentence in L is, of course, TD^R. If s does not contain any theoretical terms, then s and $E_T(s)$ will be equivalent. If there are no theoretical terms we can replace with variables, there is no good reason for introducing existential quantifiers. $A_T(s)$ denotes the corresponding result of universally generalizing a sentence s, that is, with respect to the theoretical terms. Instead of sorting out the theoretical terms and replacing them with variables and linking them to existential quantifiers, we link them with universal quantifiers.

We now have available instruments for facilitating our work of providing a proof. We recall that we are going to try to prove that each purely observational sentence, denoted s_0, that is, not containing any theoretical terms, implied by any sentence s in L is also implied by $E_T(s)$.

We assumed that s implies s_0 and one of the basic rules of logic tells us that we can conclude that

$$A_T(s \to s_0),$$

where '$\to$' denotes the material implication 'if . . . then'.

The logic we now need for the proof can be found in any textbook. An elementary theorem states that

$$\forall x(Fx \to Gx) \to (\exists xFx \to \exists xGx).$$

If it is true for all x that if x is a philosopher he is from Gothenburg, we know that if there is a philosopher, there is someone from Gothenburg. We now assume that the corresponding theorem is valid when we pass on to a second-order logic, that is, that the theorem holds if we talk about sets or properties instead of individuals. Admittedly, this assumption is not totally innocent. In the following section we discuss the ontological problem this assumption poses. But the assumption means that we know that

$$A_T(s \to s_0) \to (E_T(s) \to E_T(s_0)).$$

We thus have grounds for asserting that

$$E_T(s) \to E_T(s_0),$$

since $s \to s_0$ is a logical truth.

But since we have assumed that s_0 does not contain any theoretical terms, $E_T(s_0)$ and s_0 are equivalent and we have

$$E_T(s) \to s_0.$$

Again notice that if we identify s with TD it follows that

$$E_T(TD) \to s_0.$$

But since we have constructed $E_T(TD)$ in such a way that this sentence is equivalent to TD's Ramsey sentence, it follows that

$$TD^R \to s_0.$$

The empirical theorems of TD are thus also empirical theorems of TD^R.

ONTOLOGICAL COMMITMENTS

One type of critique levelled against Ramsey's method of eliminating the theoretical concepts of a theory is that Ramsey sentences give rise to unacceptable ontological assumptions. When we replace our non-committal theoretical terms with existentially quantified predicate variables ranging over non-individuals, we rapidly expand our ontological commitment way beyond what can be accepted, at least for those of us with a strong nominalistic bent. To see exactly how the ontological commitments come creeping up on us, let us consider our own version of an example first discussed by Scheffler.[32]

In Evelyn Place at Princeton, there is wooden house with a brass plate by the entrance stating that the Austrian author Hermann Broch lived there at one time. The information on the plate could be expressed in the following way:

a. Hermann Broch was an author and lived in Evelyn Place.

By substituting the individual constant 'Hermann Broch' for the individual variable 'x', the sentence may be rephrased as an existential assertion:

b. ($\exists x$) (x was an author and x lived in Evelyn Place).

From an ontological standpoint, this is innocuous. Sentence (b) states that there exists an individual x such that he was both an author and lived at the above address, an existential assertion that not even a nominalist would shrink from.

Sentence (b) may be compared with the sentence *TD* above, that is, with the formulation of a theory as a conjunction of a set of axioms and a dictionary. We can take this analogy farther by rewriting (b) as a Ramsey sentence. For this to be feasible, it is necessary for (b) to contain a theoretical term. The most natural thing is to take 'author' as the theoretical term. We therefore substitute the variable A for the predicate 'author' and add on the corresponding existential quantifier.

c. ($\exists x$)($\exists A$)(Ax & x lived in Evelyn Place).

But the transition from (b) to the Ramsey sentence (c) is not as innocuous as the switch from (a) to the existential assertion (b). Unlike (b), the Ramsey sentence states that besides individuals there exist properties or classes. There is a property or class A such that x has this property or belongs to this class. Thus the Ramsey sentences force us to make stronger ontological claims than we may wish to go along with. The existence of this type of entity is rather controversial. To a nominalist, to someone for whom only particulars exist, the Ramsey sentence of a theory is totally unacceptable. But even taking other ontological standpoints, the entities

Ramsey postulates may be questioned. Two particular strategies are of interest in this connection. These correspond to two of the economic policies in political debate – either we tighten our belts or we solve the crisis by expanding. If we want to have an ontological squeeze, if we have a philosophical desire to minimize our ontological commitments, we should be hesitant about Ramsey's method of 'eliminating' theoretical terms. On the other hand, if we do tolerate that our ontological commitment is increased, the ontology that the Ramsey sentences generate is probably to be considered acceptable.

Ramsey does not discuss the ontological problems of his method in his unpublished manuscript 'Theories'. But since he tackled the problem of universals in detail in his essay 'Universals', published four years earlier, it must be assumed that his theory in that essay is applicable to the problems created (the essay is discussed at length Chapter 8). Ramsey denies that there is any point in the distinction between universals and particulars. In his view, there is no essential difference between a predicate's and a subject's incompleteness. Ramsey's theory of universals seems to result in Ramsey sentences not involving any extra ontological apparatus. No expanded ontology, that is, over and above the kind we are bound to assume anyway, is needed for Ramsey's method to be applicable. Those who have criticized Ramsey and his work on the grounds of an apparently superficial introduction of an extended ontology have not made themselves familiar with his work on the problem of universals.

THE IMPORTANCE OF THE RAMSEY SENTENCE TO THE PHILOSOPHY OF SCIENCE

Although Ramsey's theory of theories and ideas regarding the status of theoretical terms has been largely misinterpreted, the Ramsey sentences have proved a useful instrument for analyzing various problems in the philosophy of science. But, since I believe that this discussion is almost without exception based on a misinterpretation of Ramsey's paper as a theory of eliminating theoretical terms, and thus does not develop Ramsey's own ideas, I will not spend time on repeating the arguments here. What one can say is that Ramsey's basic idea, no matter how it is interpreted or how one chooses to formalize it logically, has been highly important to the philosophy of science, and still is.[33]

Chapter 6

Logic and mathematics

For a generation of philosophers Ramsey is probably best known as 'the one who revised the theory of types suggested in *Principia Mathematica*'. At least this is the impression one gets looking up what is said about him in philosophical dictionaries or works on the history of philosophy (more often than not, he is not even mentioned). But it should be clear by now that Ramsey has made significant contributions to various other areas of research. There are several reasons for emphasizing his contributions to formal logic and mathematics. In the 1920s and 1930s, many philosophers were occupied with digesting the new theses of *Principia Mathematica* and *Tractatus*. Ramsey's profound and important criticism of these two works of philosophy has, of course, contributed to his reputation. Another reason Ramsey is primarily known for his works on logic and mathematics might be the somewhat misleading title of the first edition of his collected papers. Braithwaite obviously thought it would be a good idea to let the first essay of the volume, 'The Foundations of Mathematics', give its name to the book. But a book with this title hardly entices a larger audience. And this is true regardless of how many other brilliant (non-formal) papers the book contains. The most likely reason for Ramsey's reputation as a logician is, however, the simple fact that his contributions to formal logic and mathematics are of a remarkable power.

In this chapter we study Ramsey's attempt to save *Principia Mathematica* and logicism from the attacks from Hilbert's and

Brouwer's camps. Braithwaite has the following to say about 'The Foundations of Mathematics' in his introduction to the book of the same title:

[It] is an attempt to reconstruct the system of *Principia Mathematica* so that its blemishes may be avoided but its excellencies retained.[1]

THEORIES OF TYPES

THE PARADOXES

A number of antinomies or paradoxes have had a great influence on the developments of modern logic.[2] Assume, for example, that I say 'I am lying'. Is this candid assertion true or false? If my assertion is true, it is obviously true that I am not speaking the truth. On the other hand, if it is false, it follows that the assertion is true. Since we assume the law of excluded middle to be valid, that every proposition is either true or false, the assertion leads to a paradox.

A similar, well-known and elegant paradox has been formulated by Kurt Grelling and has become known as Grelling's paradox (Ramsey, however, refers to it as Weyl's paradox). One can divide words that designate properties into two disjoint classes: (i) those that have the property they designate, and (ii) those that designate properties that do not belong to the words themselves. The former, the *autological* words, can be exemplified by a word like 'polysyllabical'. The word 'polysyllabical' is polysyllabical. Another frequent example of a word belonging to the other class, the *heterological* words, is 'monosyllabical'. This word is not monosyllabical, but polysyllabical. Grelling now asked the question: Is the word 'heterological' autological or heterological? If it is autological, it does not have the property it designates and is thus heterological. Assuming, on the other hand, that it is heterological, it has the property it designates and is therefore autological. This simple contradiction is Grelling's paradox.

Another paradox, and one which had a crucial influence on the developments of modern logic, is Russell's paradox. Russell discovered the paradox in 1901 and a year later he sent a short letter to Frege in which he described it. Yet another year later the paradox was published for the first time in the first edition of *The Principles of Mathematics*.[3] This death blow of Russell's to the heart of Frege's life's work may be expressed in the following way.

For the most common types of sets it is true that they themselves are not one of their members. The set of all apples is not an apple and thus not a member of the class of apples. This is not to say that all sets are of this kind. The set of all non-apples (things which cannot be called apples) is not an apple and is therefore one of its own members. The set of all the things I am thinking of is another example of a set which is one of its own members.

Let us now consider the set of all sets that are not members of themselves. Is this set a member of itself? Anyone who has just pondered over the paradoxical in the above-mentioned antinomies gets a distinct feeling that by asking this question we might be caught in a contradiction similar to those above. This is also the case. If the set is one of its own members, it is a member of the set of all sets that are not members of themselves, and is thus not one of its own members. On the other hand, if the set is not one of its own members, then it is not a member of the set of all sets that are not members of themselves, and hence it must be a member of itself. We thus realize that the set of all sets that are not members of themselves is a member of itself if and only if it is not a member of itself.

What, then, made Russell's paradox so extremely momentous? The reason for its significance is that the paradox reveals a contradiction in the core of the theory of classes which in the view of Frege and Russell underlies all branches of mathematics. Russell's paradox thus indicates serious problems within formal logic itself, which is thought to be the core of sound mathematical reasoning. The paradox was not the first paradox of set theory. Well-known paradoxes at the turn of the century were, for example, Burali-Forti's and Cantor's paradoxes, but logicians thought these paradoxes were the mathematicians' problem; they argued that these paradoxes are formulated within some area or other of mathematics and in its system of notation. It was thus up to the mathematicians to put their house in order. But Russell's paradox could not be dispatched in the same unconcerned way. The paradox gave logic as good a shake-up as it gave mathematics. It was no longer a question of keeping things neat and tidy; now they had to see to it that the entire house did not fall apart. Since Russell and Frege aimed at creating a formalistic system of universally acceptable logical laws from which the whole of mathematics could be derived, the paradox shows that these laws may not be as universal as they were first thought to be. One or other of the bearing walls of logic has to be replaced or strengthened, if we are not to be buried under the rubble of falling theorems.

Ramsey, who devoted great attention to Whitehead's and Russell's attempt to bring mathematics back to pure logic, saw that the above paradoxes could systematically be divided into two groups – a train of thought also present in the works of Peano. The first group consists of paradoxes that are solely formulated in mathematical or logical terms (or, to put it somewhat differently, solely in the notation of *Principia Mathematica*). Among this group of paradoxes we count, for example, Russell's paradox. These are *the logical paradoxes*. The other group of paradoxes is not purely logical and cannot be formulated in logical terms alone. They all contain, as Ramsey points out, some reference to thought, language or symbolism and may thus be due not to faulty logic or mathematics, but to faulty ideas concerning thought and language. In this group of paradoxes we count, for example, 'the Liar', where the notion of truth plays a crucial part, but also Grelling's paradox should be assigned to this group. These are *the semantic paradoxes*.

Logic and mathematics

THE SIMPLE THEORY OF TYPES

In *Principles of Mathematics* Russell not only presents his own paradox but also suggests how the paradox might be avoided. The suggestion, which is only a sketch, differs in some respects from the theory that Whitehead and Russell came to incorporate in *Principia Mathematica* and to which we return in the following section.[4]

The simple theory of types, extracted by history from Russell's sketch, can be formulated in terms of individuals and sets. In order to avoid the logical paradoxes we must stop or prohibit certain types of sets, for example, the set of all sets which are not members of themselves. The problem is solved by postulating a hierarchy of types and disallowing everything which cannot be recovered from it. At the bottom of the hierarchy we have the individuals of the system: a, b, c, and so on. These are of Type 0. With these individuals as a basis one can construct sets of individuals, for example, $\{a\}$, $\{b\}$, $\{a,c\}$ and $\{a,b,c\}$. These sets are all of Type 1, they are sets of individuals. Type 1 sets are the most basic type of sets. On the third level of the hierarchy we have sets of Type 2. A set of Type 2 is a set of sets of individuals. Two examples of this type of sets are $\{\{a\}\}$ and $\{\{a,c\},\{a,b,c\}\}$. In this way we can continue further and further up in the hierarchy and construct sets of Type 3 (sets of sets of sets of individuals) and of Type 4, and so on.

Russell's idea is that only sets which can be found at some stage in this hierarchy can be said to exist. The set $\{a,\{a,c\}\}$ is neither of Type 1, nor of Type 2 and is therefore an unacceptable construction. The set cannot be found at any level of the hierarchy. In addition to this ontological condition Russell introduces a condition of significance on formulas. An assertion that x is a member of y is meaningful if and only if the type of x is one less than the type of y. To say that $\{a,c\}$ is a member of $\{a,b,c\}$ is thus neither true nor false but a meaningless proposition. The sets are of the same type.[5]

It is now obvious that these two assumptions jointly eliminate the logical paradoxes. The assumption made by Russell's paradox of the set of all sets that are not members of themselves conflicts with both the ontological assumption and the assumption of the significance of formulas.

The criticism that has been levelled against the so-called simplified theory of types has been severe but in many respects just. I will not recapitulate the objections directed against the theory since they are of little relevance to the following chapters. What is of interest, however, is that Russell for *Principia Mathematica* preferred to develop his rough sketch of 1903 into a stronger and more elaborated theory – a theory which is also capable of handling the semantic paradoxes.

THE BRANCHED THEORY OF TYPES

The theory of types Russell presents and develops in the essay 'Mathematical Logic Based on a Theory of Types',[6] and which without any significant modifications was included in *Principia Mathematica,* has become known as the *branched* or *ramified* theory of types. The theory gains its force from a principle first suggested by the French mathematician Jules Henri Poincaré (Poincaré got the idea when he was pondering over Richard's solution to his own paradox.) Poincaré's principle, which Whitehead and Russell decided to call the vicious-circle principle, says that

[w]hatever involves *all* of a collection must not be one of the collection.[7]

Whitehead and Russell give an example of the principle with the aid of the law of the excluded middle – 'all propositions are true or false'. We have already noted that it seems to be an unrestricted application of this law that leads to some of the paradoxes. If we argue that the law itself is true or false, because the law of excluded middle is a proposition, we sin against Poincaré's vicious-circle principle. As Whitehead and Russell point out in *Principia Mathematica,* 'all propositions' must be limited in order to become a legitimate totality and such a limitation must guarantee that statements about the totality fall outside of it.

It is not part of my aim to analyse in detail the branched or the logical theory of types and how Russell tried to recover its parts from the above principle. Such a task would take up too much time and lies outside the objectives of this book. A rather condensed presentation of the core of the general theory is, however, necessary in order to grasp Ramsey's sweeping recast of the philosophical foundations of *Principia Mathematica*.

The theory of types introduces two hierarchical systems. The first system assumes that individuals, classes and classes of classes can be arranged in a hierarchical system. The second system is a system of propositional function. For those who are not acquainted with the world of *Principia Mathematica*, something has to be said about propositional functions and Whitehead's and Russell's choice of notation. A proposition such as 'Socrates is wise' is denoted fa. The individual a has the property f. A *propositional function* is obtained by replacing the term or name 'Socrates' by the variable x, that is, if we, for example, assert that 'x is wise'. But propositional functions can also be relations such as 'x loves y'. The former type of function is denoted fx and the latter $f(x,y)$. The circumflex is used to indicate that we are talking about the propositional function and not one of its values. The proposition fa as well as the more ambiguous fx are both values of the propositional function $f\hat{x}$. This theory also makes a distinction between what is called *real* and *apparent* variables. A variable such as x in the above propositional function is a real variable; it refers to any one of a number of entities within a given domain. Asserting a propositional function is not, according to *Principia Mathematica*, the same as asserting that a propositional function is true. The assertion that 'x is wise' should not be confounded with the assertion that 'x is wise' is true for all values of the propositional function (which is $(x)(x$ is wise$)$). In the latter case we have an assertion about the members of a definite domain: 'x' is not referring ambiguously; instead 'x' is an apparent variable.

Whitehead and Russell now try to unify these two hierarchical systems by deducing them from the vicious-circle principle. But since '[t]he propositional hierarchy is never required in practice, and is only relevant for the solution of paradoxes',[8] we can concentrate on the hierarchy for propositional functions. This is also in accordance with the presentation of the theory of logical types in *Principia Mathematica* and with Ramsey's discussion of the theory.

As we have seen, a paradox can be solved by showing that its premises, the arguments by which it is derived, are incorrect. One way is thus to prevent a function being one of its own arguments. We must simply prohibit some of the theoretically possible constructions of propositional functions. The theory of types discussed in this section assumes, in the same way as the simplified theory discussed in the previous section, the existence of a set of individuals, the bottom level of the system. Of significant importance for the theory of logical types is the notion of a *matrix*. A matrix can be described as a function lacking any occurrences of universal or existential quantifiers. From a given proposition or function we obtain the matrix of it by removing all occurrences of 'all' and 'some' from it. Thus, from the matrix $f(x,y)$ we can derive the functions $(x)f(x,y)$ and $(x)(y)f(x,y)$.

Functions which in this way are derived from matrices and which do not presume any totality other than that of individuals are called *first-order functions*. A first-order function is a function whose argument is an individual and whose value is a proposition which contains no apparent variables (as, e.g., Socrates is wise) or one which contains apparent variables referring only to individuals (as, e.g., $(x)(x$ is wise$)$).

Similarly, we have second-order matrices whose arguments are first-order functions and individuals, but do not contain any apparent variables. Tied to these matrices are *second-order* functions, that is, functions involving a first-order function or proposition as apparent variable – or, as it is put in *Principia Mathematica*, functions derived from the second-order matrices by turning some of the arguments into apparent variables. In *Principia Mathematica* we find a number of examples of second-order functions and their matrices. The functions $(x)g(f!\hat{z},x)$ and $(f)g(f!/\hat{z},x)$ are both derived from the matrix $g(f!\hat{z},x)$ and are functions of $f!\hat{z}$ and x, respectively. (Whitehead and Russell use the exclamation mark to denote any first-order function.) Not too much ingenuity is needed to continue this process and derive functions of any order from their corresponding matrices.

In this hierarchy of functions there is one sort of function of particular interest. A *predicative function* is a function whose order is next above that of its argument, and, if it has several variables, if there is one of its variables such that, when the other variables have values assigned to them, we obtain a predicative function.

The theory of types of *Principia Mathematica* is thus based on a number of ontological and semantic presumptions. The theory assumes, for example, that some assertions are meaningless. If we have two matrices and the first belongs to a higher type than the second matrix, or to the same type, then to say that the first matrix is one of the arguments of the second is meaningless. Two functions of the same order cannot have each other as arguments.[9]

That *Principia Mathematica's* theory of types has been called the branched theory of types is quite understandable. It is no longer a question of a hierarchy of functions but of a hierarchy of hierarchies of functions (plus a hierarchy of propositions, to be correct). But the system works, it solves the paradoxes and lets us see how it steers clear of Grelling's paradox.

We rewrite 'x is heterological' in *Principia Mathematica's* system of notation and get

$$(\exists f)(xR(f\hat{z})\&\text{-}fx),$$

which is denoted Fx. If we assume that $F('F')$, that is, that 'heterological' has the property it designates, we note that from '$F'R(F\hat{x})$ and $(\exists f)('F'R(f\hat{x}))$ we derive that $F('F')$ if and only if $-F('F')$. The problem is thus that we can derive

$(\exists f)('F'R(f\hat{x}))$ from '$F'R(F\hat{x})$. The theory of types essentially blocks the paradox by arguing that the former formula cannot be deduced from the latter. The idea is that we can never get $(\exists f)('F'R(f\hat{x}))$ since the meaning of 'F' is not a function included in the range of 'f'. To put it somewhat differently: what we do in the derivation of the paradox is to replace a predicate variable by a predicate constant. But this is an illegitimate procedure since 'F' is of a higher order than 'f', because a bound 'f' occurs in the definition of 'heterological'.

However, the price of getting rid of the unwanted paradoxes is rather high. The branched theory of types has a number of troublesome consequences. Parts of classical mathematics cannot be formulated with *Principia Mathematica*'s theory of types as a basis. For example, we cannot employ the useful theorem of a least upper bound for mathematical analysis. The basic reason is that the least upper bound of a collection of real numbers is of a higher order than the order of the real numbers whose least upper bound it is. And this of course causes problems for Dedekind's basic set-theoretical method of constructing the system of real numbers from the system of rational numbers. Another useful part of classical mathematics that has to be partly abandoned is the principle of mathematical induction, which cannot be stated in full generality. A problem which Ramsey is particularly interested in is that this theory of types puts a stop to a relatively simple definition of identity,[10] that is, by saying that two things are identical if they have all their properties in common. But in order to make this definition into a workable definition we must assume that there is a totality of functions of a given type over which the variable function (property) can range. But there is no such totality. In order to avoid these not too desirable results Whitehead and Russell introduce a new axiom which asserts that for any function, regardless of order, type and arguments, there is a formally equivalent predicative function. This axiom, the *Axiom of Reducibility*, allows the lost domains of classical mathematics to be recaptured. One way to express the content of

this axiom is to say that what it asserts is that the universal
and existential quantifiers are not needed.[11]

Ramsey was clearly disappointed with Whitehead's and Russell's method of 'solving' the paradoxes. He writes:

> These contradictions it was proposed to remove by what is
> called the Theory of Types, which consists really of two dis-
> tinct parts directed respectively against the two groups of con-
> tradictions. These two parts were unified by being both de-
> duced in a rather sloppy way from the 'vicious-circle princi-
> ple', but it seems to me essential to consider them separately.[12]

Ramsey accepts the solution of the logical paradoxes. That it
is possible to divide the functions into a hierarchy depending
on their arguments, and in this way block, for example, Russell's own paradox by arguing that the assertion that a set
can be one of its own members is neither true nor false but
meaningless, he finds incontestable. On the other hand,
Ramsey believes that the subdivision of functions of the
same type into a hierarchy of orders is rather doubtful and
artificial. Furthermore, he is uncertain about the additional
assumption this hierarchy of hierarchies leads to, that is, the
Axiom of Reducibility:

> This axiom there is no reason to suppose true; and if it were
> true, this would be a happy accident and not a logical necessi-
> ty, for it is not a tautology. . . . Such an axiom has no place in
> mathematics, and anything which cannot be proved without
> using it cannot be regarded as proved at all.[13]

Ramsey urges us not to use the Axiom of Reducibility, because if we do our mathematical proofs become worthless.
The proofs are worthless because the axiom is not a tautology. The Axiom of Reducibility is a disgrace to *Principia*

Mathematica and hardly in accordance with the fundamental principles of logicism.

In 'The Foundations of Mathematics' (1925) Ramsey therefore suggests a completely new theory of types – a theory which can dispense with the Axiom of Reducibility. This theory is sometimes humorously referred to as the *Ramseyfied theory of types*. Ramsey's essay can be viewed as an attempt to show that what is really needed is a simplified theory of types and that in this way one can provide *Principia Mathematica* with a much more solid foundation. Ramsey developed his theory at the time when Whitehead and Russell were working on the revision of the first edition of *Principia Mathematica*. Ramsey makes all references to the second edition of *Principia Mathematica* (which was published in 1925 and 1927) and in this edition Whitehead and Russell express their obligation to Ramsey for reading the whole manuscript and for contributing valuable criticisms and suggestions.

During the early 1920s Ramsey had spent a lot of time trying to understand Wittgenstein's world of ideas. He now saw a possibility to use what he had learnt from *Tractatus* in order to improve *Principia Mathematica*. Above all, it was Wittgenstein's theory of propositions that he found useful. Ramsey also realized that, given his fundamental division of the paradoxes into two distinct groups, they could be given radically different solutions. The logical paradoxes could be solved by a simplified version of the theory of types, by a theory which did not conform to Poincaré's principle.[14] As we will see later on, Ramsey's theory allows impredicative functions. The semantic paradoxes, which are the result of the ambiguity of their 'epistemic' elements, an ambiguity of no interest for logic or the foundations of mathematics, can thus be handled on their own. There is no need to make any reference to the vicious-circle principle.

An *elementary proposition* in Ramsey's terminology is a truth function of a finite number of atomic propositions. If p and q are both atomic propositions, $p\&q$ is an elementary truth function. A proposition such as $(x)fx$ is thus not elementary in this respect. Ramsey emphasizes that in some cases a proposition will be considered elementary, in others not. It all depends on how we write it. The proposition *fa*, for example, is an elementary proposition but the equivalent proposition *fa*&($\exists x$)*fx* is not elementary.

Ramsey wants to make the Axiom of Reducibility redundant by avoiding the constructive model suggested by Whitehead and Russell. His aim is to treat functions of functions as far as possible in the same way as functions over individuals. If *a* is one of the arguments of the function *fx*, we presume that *a* is the name of an individual. In this way we restrict the number of possible substitutions through a condition of meaning. All signs *a*, *b*, *c* and so on, must be names of individuals. Extending this idea, Ramsey argues that the symbols which can be substituted as arguments in more complex functions should also be determined by their meanings. But since functions derive their meaning from the meanings of the propositions which are their values, and are thus not names of single objects, Ramsey has to come up with some amount of ingenuity in order to carry the project through. Ramsey realizes that the problem is to fix the values of the more general functions in such a way that we can meaningfully talk about all and some of this set of propositions. His idea is to determine these propositions through a description of their sense or import.

An atomic function in Ramsey's system is the result of replacing by variables any of the names of individuals in an atomic proposition. The atomic function *fx* is thus the result of replacing the name *a* of an individual by the variable *x* in the atomic proposition *fa*. The domain of values of an atomic function of individuals is hereby delimited by the aid of atomic propositions. The next step is to generalize this procedure. If f_1, f_2, . . . is a set of functions, we say that a function *P* is a truth function of these functions if any value of *P* is the truth function of the values of these functions. The idea is that by this method we treat functions in accordance with our methods of constructing truth functions. The process leads to one of the central definitions of this theory of types. We shall define what is meant by a *predicative function*.

Ramsey emphasizes that it is important to bear in mind that the term 'predicative function' will not be used in the same way as it has been used by Whitehead and Russell. A predicative function of *Principia Mathematica*, in this theory, is the same as the elementary function.

A predicative function of individuals is a truth function whose arguments are all either atomic functions of individuals or atomic propositions. It should be noted, as is also pointed out by Ramsey, that if the domain of arguments of the predicative functions is finite, then these functions would be identical to the predicative functions of *Principia Mathematica*. In this context, one should bear in mind that the Axiom of Reducibility becomes redundant if the domain is finite – it is the assumption of an infinite number of arguments that enforces this restriction. It is now rather straightforward to generalize this idea to functions of functions.

The niceties of this procedure are that, given the presumptions of Ramsey's system, we can never create non-predicative functions. And this in turn has a pleasant consequence:

> Thus all the functions of individuals which occur in *Principia* are in our sense predicative and included in our variable [*f*], so that all need for an axiom of reducibility disappears.[15]

The general idea of this theory will be much better understood if it is 'applied' to one of the paradoxes above, for example, Grelling's paradox. This gives us a chance to ponder how the solution given by the Ramseyfied theory differs from that given by the ramified theory. And why these semantic paradoxes, which arise due to an ambiguity in the word 'meaning' can be avoided in logic without making reference to Poincaré's vicious-circle principle.

We defined Fx, 'x is heterological', as $(\exists f)(xR(f\hat{z})\&-fx)$ and noted that given the presumption that '$F'R(F\hat{x})$ we could derive that 'heterological' is heterological if and only if it is autological. The ramified theory of types escapes the difficulty by prohibiting some types of substitutions. It is unacceptable to construct certain types of functions. The *Ram-*

seyfied theory of types, on the other hand, argues that the basic premise itself is the root of our problems. According to Ramsey, it is a mistake to assume that the sense in which 'F' means $F\hat{x}$ is the sense in which 'x' means $f\hat{x}$ (i.e. it is a mistake to assume that the sense in which 'Heterological' means heterological is the same as the sense in which 'red'means red). We must carefully differ between how a symbol gets its meaning from what it means.

The paradoxes of the above prototype seem to arise because of some functions not being clearly specified. *Principia Mathematica*'s authors solve the problem by clearly and unambiguously stating how more general functions can be constructed from a set of elementary functions. Ramsey turns the problem around. It is not a question of how the functions are constructed but a question of meaning. A definite advantage of Ramsey's method is that we do not prohibit functions which are not constructible according to the rules of *Principia Mathematica*. One could say that Whitehead and Russell tried to escape the semantic paradoxes through a change in the syntax. Ramsey, however, realized that a semantic problem demands a semantic solution.

Ramsey's theory leads to two hierarchies: one hierarchy of propositions and another of functions, the second hierarchy being deducible from the first one. Propositions of order 0, the elementary propositions, are those containing no apparent variable. Propositions of order 1 contain an individual apparent variable and propositions of order n contain an apparent variable whose values are functions of type $n - 1$. The hierarchy of functions is as follows: Functions of order 0 are the matrices, containing no apparent variable; functions of order 1 containing an individual apparent variable and functions of order n containing an apparent variable whose values are propositions of order n. Ramsey's theory is thus a simple theory of types. If the tree of logicism, which has run wild, is to be able to withstand the rough winds of formalism and intuitionism it has to be considerably pruned and more firmly rooted in the philosophical mould.

One may wonder why Ramsey goes to all this trouble to

get rid of the branched theory of types. The Axiom of Reducibility explicitly says that the branched theory of types is redundant. What is needed is a simple theory for predicative functions. But then one should bear in mind that Ramsey's aim was not primarily to get rid of *Principia Mathematica's* theory of types but one of its consequences, that is, the Axiom of Reducibility. True, he considered the branched theory of types to be a rather sloppy construction, but the real problem was the axiom. The Axiom of Reducibility is not a tautology and thus there should be no place for it in a book on the foundations of mathematics.

Finally, it should be emphasized that the Ramseyfied theory of types neither can nor should be seen as a minor change or improvement of the ramified theory. It is true that Ramsey's theory does not have any consequences for mathematics different from those of *Principia Mathematica;* the two theories are formally equivalent. But Ramsey's theory provides *Principia Mathematica* with a new and considerably more solid foundation than the one it originally relied on. With Ramsey's theory as a basis, in principle we get a new *Principia Mathematica.* It has been said that 'the foundations of mathematics' constitute the peak, but also the end, of a tradition. The reasons behind such a statement must be that modern theories of types on several fundamental issues differ from the sort of theories Ramsey was working on. After Ramsey's death, theories of types have developed in a direction which may have been difficult to foresee or guess in 1925. He would probably have got further himself if he had not so willingly accepted Russell's conceptual system. An analysis of the notion of propositional functions, for example, would have been in place.

I conclude this section by letting Ramsey himself show how he believes one should solve the Liar.

(a) 'I am lying'.

This we should analyse as '($\exists "p",p$): I am saying "p". "p" means $p. -p'$. Here to get a definite meaning for *means* it is necessary to limit in some way the order of 'p'. Suppose 'p' is to be of the nth or lesser order. Then, symbolizing by [f_n] a function of *type n*, 'p' may be [($\exists f_n$).f_{n+1} (f_n)].

Hence $\exists$'p' involves [$\exists f_{n+1}$] and 'I am lying' in the sense of 'I am asserting a false proposition of order n' is at least of order $n + 1$ and does not contradict itself.[16]

TWO AXIOMS

Having succeeded in relieving *Principia Mathematica* of the Axiom of Reducibility, Ramsey casts a covetous eye in the direction of two other axioms – the Axiom of Infinity and the Multiplicative Axiom (i.e., the Axiom of Choice). These axioms are required if we are to be able to prove theorems within central parts of mathematics and set theory. What is the status of these non-logical axioms of the theory? Are they tautologies?

The axiom of infinity asserts that there are an infinite number of individuals. An alternative formulation of the axiom would assert that there are infinitely many named objects. But *Principia Mathematica* does not demand only an infinite number of individuals but also that these individuals are distinguishable from each other. This is the result of the definition of identity employed in this book; that is, it is said that x and y are identical when every elementary function (predicative in their system of notation) satisfied by x is also satisfied by y; or, two things are said to be identical if they have all their elementary properties in common.[17] But, as Ramsey points out, this is an empirical hypothesis. His theory, however, does not demand that there are infinitely many distinguishable individuals, only that there are infinitely many.

If one of the above theories of types is taken for granted we are unable to define the natural numbers unless we make use of the Axiom of Infinity. Russell followed Frege in his definition of the natural numbers. The definition, which is an iterative process, starts off with the empty set. We can then define the successor of 0 (i.e., 1) as the set of all one-individual sets, the successor of 1 (i.e., 2) as the set of all two-individual sets and so on. The problem is that if this process is not to collapse, the theory of types demands that for each new number that is defined, a corresponding number of individuals must be assumed to exist (distinguishable or not). A universe consisting of only 10 individuals would then result in an arithmetic of the type taught in the lower department of the comprehensive school. In a universe of this restricted kind, all natural numbers greater than 11 will disappear.

Ramsey gives us the following arguments in favour of the Axiom of Infinity.

> [T]he Axiom of Infinity . . . , if it is a tautology, cannot be proved, but must be taken as a primitive proposition. And this is the course which we must adopt, unless we prefer the view that all analysis is self-contradictory and meaningless. We do not have to assume that any particular set of things, e.g. atoms, is infinite, but merely that there is some infinite type which we can take to be the type of individuals.[18]

In spite of the fact that Ramsey tries to convince us of the acceptability of the Axiom of Infinity, you get a distinct feeling that this is a strange axiom and it is odd that the founders of logicism themselves wouldn't budge an inch when it came to this ontological assumption. Ramsey's arguments aren't all that strong and it is difficult not to interpret the axiom as an empirical one. But most of us are more or less convinced that mathematics lives its own life independent of the number of actual individuals in the universe.

According to Braithwaite, and this is also clear from some passages in Ramsey's later writings and from parts of his unpublished material, Ramsey gave up logicism and the Axiom of Infinity in 1929 for a finitistic view of mathematics. We have also seen, especially in Chapter 4, how Ramsey sometimes alludes to his new position.

> So too there may be an infinite totality, but what seem to be propositions about it are again variable hypotheticals and 'infinite collection' is really nonsense.[19]

Actually, it is interesting to note that one can see with some precision how Ramsey gradually departs from logicism by giving up its axioms one at a time. The Multiplicative Axiom or the Axiom of Choice, as we prefer to call it, says that for every family of non-empty sets there exists a function which picks out exactly one element from each one of this family of sets. The status of this axiom has been the object of a lot of controversy, especially at the beginning of this century. One of the reasons mathematicians and philosophers have taken a somewhat unenthusiastic attitude towards this axiom is the nonconstructive nature of the axiom. That existence in mathematics was considered to be synonymous with construction was a dominating view until the late nineteenth century.[20] Another reason that people have flinched from this, in my view, rather intuitively reasonable axiom is that it leads to some puzzling results. One of the most well-known theorems, which at first sight may be thought of as a paradoxical result, is the Banach–Tarski paradox. This theorem says that, by using the Axiom of Choice, one can cut a ball into a finite number of pieces that can be rearranged in such a way that two balls of the same size as the original ball are obtained.[21]

Ramsey argues that he cannot see any good reasons whatsoever to doubt the Axiom of Choice. Given that we accept his reformulation of *Principia Mathematica*, the axiom is a tautology.

> If by 'class' we mean, as I do, any set of things homogeneous in type not necessarily definable by a function which is not merely a function in extension, the Multiplicative Axiom seems to me the most evident tautology.[22]

But things look rather different if we maintain the original theory of Whitehead and Russell. Ramsey shows by an example that

> the Multiplicative Axiom, interpreted as it is in *Principia*, is not a tautology but logically doubtful.[23]

MATHEMATICAL PROPOSITIONS

What is the difference between a mathematical or logical truth of the type '2 + 2 = 4' and a common true assertion such as 'the sun will rise tomorrow'? One of Russell's basic beliefs was that any proposition which can be stated by solely using logical terms must be a mathematical or logical proposition. The idea is that logical and mathematical propositions are completely general propositions; as Ramsey puts it, they are not about particular things and relations, but about some or all things and relations. Bringing back mathematics to logic would then finally give us a profound understanding of the nature of mathematical truth. Our analysis of the Ramseyfied theory of types suggests that Ramsey didn't fully share this belief. It is not enough that a proposition is completely general for it to be counted as logical or mathematical.

> Take for example 'Any two things differ in at least thirty ways'; this is a completely general proposition, it could be expressed as an implication involving only logical constants and variables, and it may well be true. But as a mathematical or logical truth no one could regard it; it is utterly different from such a proposition as 'Any two things together with any other two things make four things', which is a logical and not merely an empirical truth.[24]

The class of completely general propositions is too large for our purposes. It does not only contain logical and mathematical propositions, but also propositions whose truth or falsehood is a purely empirical question.

An alternative to logicism's method of distinguishing mathematical truths from other true propositions can be found in *Tractatus*. Wittgenstein writes:

6.1 Die Sätze der Logik sind Tautologien.

What characterizes the logical propositions is that they are tautologies. No matter how much the world changes they will keep their truth-values. They have, so to speak, received empirical immunity.

But that all logical propositions are tautologies does not mean that all tautologies are logical propositions. The proposition, either the sun will rise tomorrow or it will not, is a tautology, but it is hardly to be considered a logical truth. The class of tautologies is likewise too large to be used to demarcate the logical or mathematical truths.

Ramsey saw that the problem could be solved by knotting together the rather distinct ideas of Russell and Wittgenstein. What distinguishes a mathematical or logical truth is certainly that when it comes to its content it is completely general. But this is not enough. The proposition in question must also in its form be a tautology.

> Their content must be completely generalized and their form tautological.[25]

The Axiom of Reducibility, for example, is certainly general enough, but it is definitely not a tautology. The axiom should therefore be deleted from logicism's repertoire as soon as possible. The Multiplicative Axiom, on the other hand, is completely general as well as a tautology, even if one may argue that Ramsey's arguments in favour of it being a tautology are rather weak.

Ramsey's view of mathematics at this time differs in several respects from that of Wittgenstein, and at the time of Ramsey's death their positions were probably diametrically apart. Ramsey believes that mathematics consists of tautologies and not, as Wittgenstein says, of 'equations'. About Wittgenstein's idea Ramsey has the following to say:

> I have spent a lot of time developing such a theory, and found that it was faced with what seemed to me insuperable difficulties.[26]

Let us leave out the criticisms of Ramsey's solution to this philosophical problem and instead be content with keeping this formulation in mind when we are pondering the mathematical truth discussed in Chapter 7. Isn't Ramsey's theorem completely general in its content as well as tautological in its form?

Chapter 7

Ramsey's theorem

In his essay entitled 'Mathematical Logic' written in 1926, Ramsey gives his opinion of the evolution of mathematical logic after the publication of *Principia Mathematica*. The essay is largely a defence of the ideas of logicism against the attacks by Hilbert's formalism and Brouwer's intuitionism. Ramsey had already criticized Hilbert and Brouwer in 'The Foundation of Mathematics', and 'Mathematical Logic' is only a popular version of this criticism.

> The theories of the intuitionists admittedly involve giving up many of the most fruitful methods of modern analysis, for no reason, as it seems to me, except that the methods fail to conform to their prejudice.[1]

Hilbert's view of mathematics as a game with marks is in Ramsey's eyes an impossible theory for an analysis of mathematical concepts.

> Thus '2' occurs not merely in '2 + 2 = 4', but also in 'It is 2 miles to the station', which is not a meaningless formula, but a significant proposition, in which '2' cannot conceivably be a meaningless mark. Nor can there be any doubt that '2' is used in the same sense in the two cases, for we can use '2 + 2 = 4' to infer from 'It is two miles to the station and two miles on to the Gogs' that 'It is four miles to the Gogs via the station', so that these ordinary meanings of two and four are clearly involved in '2 + 2 = 4'.[2]

Or, to double-back on the discussion in Chapter 6, the formalistic creation of concepts implies that we totally ignore the content of the mathematical propositions and concentrate on their form. Logicism did exactly the opposite. Russell stressed their content but ignored their form. Ramsey wanted both form and content to be taken into account. But in spite of his critical attitude to Hilbert's programme, Ramsey was drawn to one of the basic problems of formalism.

Hilbert believed that a proof theory could be worked out, a mathematical theory whereby it would be possible to show by finite means: (a) that a given axiomatic system is consistent (that not everything can be proved using the axioms), (b) that the axioms are independent of each other and (c) that the system of axioms is complete (all the truths of an axiomatized system can be derived from the axioms). The last point in Hilbert's programme is that it should be possible to find a method that could be used to determine in a mechanical way whether an arbitrary mathematical proposition can be proved in a theory or not. The problem of finding such a mechanical method has become known as the *Entscheidungsproblem* and this is the problem that attracted Ramsey's attention.

The fact that the *Entscheidungsproblem* inspired a mathematician of Ramsey's calibre will be understood if one considers briefly what a solution to the problem would mean to mathematics. A solution would entail, among other things, our being able to decide quite mechanically whether a given mathematical proposition is provable or not. If a general method of this kind were to exist, we would be able to find out, for example, whether Fermat's famous conjecture is correct or not.

In his essay entitled 'On a Problem of Formal Logic' (1928), Ramsey succeeded in working out a solution to the *Entscheidungsproblem* for a special case of first-order predicate calculus. But six years after Ramsey's death the American logician Alonzo Church proved that the general problem is unsolvable.[3] No general mechanical method of the kind Hilbert hoped for exists. Church's proof is based on Kurt Gödel's well-known theorem of 1931. We know today that Ramsey spent some time trying to solve the unsolvable. But his time was by no means wasted. In his efforts to arrive at a solution to the *Entscheidungsproblem*, Ramsey proves a mathematical theorem that he believes he needs in order to solve the general problem. This theorem, which was not needed for the general decision problem, has turned out to be unusually important and has given rise to a flourishing branch of mathematics. I shall try to give here a brief presentation of *Ramsey's theorem*, a theorem which, if Ramsey had known of Gödel's and Church's results, he would most likely never have made the efforts to prove, and at the same time give some indications of the nature of the branch of mathematics now called *Ramsey theory*.

RAMSEY'S THEOREM

What has become known as Ramsey's theorem is an exceedingly difficult (also for the professional mathematician I dare say), extremely beautiful and imaginative theorem of combinatorial analysis. The best way to approach the finite version of Ramsey's theorem is, of course, through some examples. And probably the best known, non-trivial, example is the following one: *In any collection of six people either three know each other or three of them do not know each other.* That this assertion holds is easily seen if we assume that you and five other persons are invited to a party. You do not know who the other guests are, but you do know that you must know at least three of them or not know at least three of them. If you know three of them, then if two of these three know each other our assertion holds. And if they do not know each other it still holds since then we have three people who do not know each other.[4]

Another way of exemplifying Ramsey's theorem is by means of graph theory.[5] Consider, for example, the following three points:

(a)

These three points form an *empty* graph – there are no lines drawn between the three points. But more interesting graphs can be found if we draw some or all of the possible lines between the points.

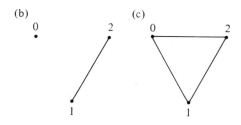

We say that (c) is a *complete* graph – each possible line is drawn between the three points.

In this context, empty and complete subgraphs of a graph are of special interest to us. If, for example, we have four points, we can draw a complete three-point subgraph in the following way:

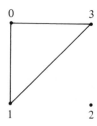

The special case of Ramsey's theory exemplified above tells us that if a graph has six or more points, then it either has a three-point empty subgraph, for example, {1,3,5},

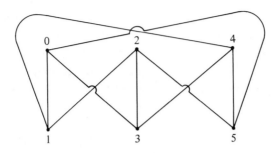

or a three-point complete subgraph, for example, {0,2,4}:

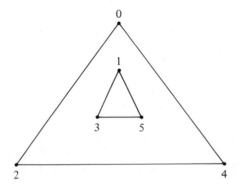

These two graphs only illustrate the assertion; they do not prove it. But that the assertion does not hold for graphs with only five points is proven by the following counter-example:

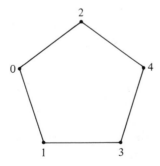

Arguments parallel with the one given above prove that a six-point graph is large enough. The special case of the finite version of Ramsey's theorem that we been studying so far can be generalized in a number of ways. First, one might simultaneously consider several and more complex relations besides 'knowing'. We may colour our graphs in more than two colours. Second, we might consider sets with more elements than pairs of people, knowing or not knowing each other, or pairs of points, connected or not connected by a line. But to see more exactly what Ramsey's theorem says demands some amount of formalism.

Let $[n]$ be a set of positive integers and let $[n]^k$ denote the set of subsets of $[n]$ of cardinality k (i.e., $\{X: X \subseteq \{1,2, \ldots, n\}, |X| = k\}$). By a partition of $[n]^k$ we mean a function $P:[n]^k \rightarrow r$, where r is a cardinal number. That is, in Ramsey's words, we divide the k-combinations of $[n]$, the subsets of $[n]$ that have exactly k members, into r mutually exclusive classes. Thus, the partitioning of $[n]^k$ corresponds to the colouring of the graphs.

If $P:[n]^k \rightarrow r$, a subset X of $[n]$ is said to be *homogeneous* for P if P is constant on $[X]^k$. A group of people who mutually know each other is a homogeneous group, and, similarly, a complete subgraph is a homogeneous set of points, a monochromatic graph.

We employ the useful arrow or Erdös's notation $n \rightarrow (l)^k_r$ for the assertion that: if the relation $n \rightarrow (l)^k_r$ holds, then there is a homogeneous subset of n for P of cardinality l.

Ramsey's theorem (finite version). For each finite k, r, and l, there is a finite n such that the relation $n \rightarrow (l)^k_r$ holds.

We can thus rewrite the assertion made by the two examples above in this notation. Both examples assert that for $k = 2$, $r = 2$ and $l = 3$, there is an n such that $n \rightarrow (3)^2_2$. In this case, $n = 6$ is the minimal n such that the relation holds, and this number is often referred to as the *Ramsey number*. That is to say, the Ramsey number is the minimal value of the *Ramsey function* $R_k(l,r) = \min\{n_0: \text{for } n \geq n_0, n \rightarrow (l)^k_r\}$. Ramsey's theorem thus simply states that $R(.\,,.)$ is a well-defined function.

The question of how small an n will work is still an open question and a lot of research effort is spent on finding exact values of the Ramsey function for small values of k and l. But the problem is extremely difficult and very few exact values are known. Actually only six exact values are known at the moment. For example, no exact values of $R_k(l,2)$ are known for $k \geq 3$! One major difficulty is that the Ramsey functions grow extremely rapidly. People have tried to find estimates which could serve as upper and lower bounds to the Ramsey functions. However, these estimates do not give too good a value.[6]

The infinite version of Ramsey's theorem, which is what *Ramsey's theorem* (or what he called *Theorem A*) actually is, says that for positive integers k and r, the combinatorial principle above holds when n and l are infinite sets; that is, $\omega \rightarrow (\omega)_r^k$.[7] In proving his theorem, Ramsey made explicit use of the axiom of choice (the axiom of selections). Today it is known that for countable sets this axiom is not needed to establish a proof. We also know that the axiom of choice implies Ramsey's theorem, but does not follow from it.[8]

TRUE BUT NOT PROVABLE

Gödel taught us that if a formal system is strong enough to contain the traditional arithmetic, then a formula exists which is true but not provable within the system. We thus know that not all true number theoretical propositions are provable with the Peano axiomatisation of arithmetics as a basis. Gödel proved, to use von Wright's words, 'that the *logical-mathematical area of truth is wider than that of the logical-mathematical proof*'.[9]

Although Gödel's proof is exceedingly inaccessible, the essential features can still be made understandable.[10] Inventing a smart system of numbering, Gödel showed how each sign, each formula and each proof of a formal system **S** can be assigned a uniquely determined number. These *Gödel numbers* are codified by the use of primes and in such a way that we know that two signs, formulas or proofs cannot be assigned the same number, but also the other way around – that is, given a Gödel number, we can determine which sign, formula or proof it represents. By decomposing the integers into prime factors, we can determine, for example, exactly which formula corresponds to a given Gödel number.

By means of Gödel numbers we can succeed in a complete arithmetisation of a formal system **S**. But Gödel showed that this method can also be employed at the meta-mathematical level. It is not only what we can say *within* the system that can be arithmetised but also what we can say *about* the system. Roughly speaking, one proceeds by uniquely projecting each statement *about* the system **S** (each meta-mathematical statement) onto a statement *within* **S**. The niceties of this method are that relations between statements of a meta-mathematical nature can be analysed as purely arithmetical relations. This means that a meta-mathematical statement of the type 'the formula with Gödel number y is not provable' corresponds to a purely arithmetical statement (such as $x/2$ $\leq x$, for positive integers).

'Provable' is a notion of great significance to Gödel's work. That a mathematical statement is provable means that, with the axioms of the formal system as a point of departure, we have a sequence of successively dependent formulas that lead us toward the proposition. The mathematical statement that a given formula is provable can thus be studied as an arithmetical relation between two Gödel numbers, that is, as a relation between the Gödel number for the proof and the Gödel number for the statement. This relation is commonly denoted 'Bew(x,y)' (after the German word *Beweisbar*).

What does it then mean that a formula is *unprovable*, say, the formula whose Gödel number is y? That a formula is not provable means that with the axioms as our basis we cannot find a train of formulas leading on to the formula whose Gödel number is y. Since each train of formulas, each proof, has a unique Gödel number, we can within **S** assume that '$(x) - \text{Bew}(x,y)$' stands for the mathematical statement 'the formula with Gödel number y is unprovable'. There is simply no Gödel number x such that the relation Bew(x,y) is satisfied.

Gödel succeeded in the remarkable achievement of finding a special case of the formula '(x) − Bew(x,y)', such that if the formula is provable its negation is also provable, and vice versa. If one makes the reasonable assumption that S should be free from contradiction, this has as a consequence that the formula is undecidable. Let us denote this special case '(x) − Bew(x,g)'.

The conclusion that 'if the formula is provable, it is unprovable; and if it is unprovable, it is provable' makes us think about the various paradoxes discussed in Chapter 6. Gödel also worked with 'the Liar' and 'Richard's paradox' in mind, but steered clear of the pitfalls.

The interesting point is that by assuming the consistency of arithmetic Gödel was able to prove that it is not provable that '(x) − Bew(x,g)'. But Gödel still had a titbit to offer. Again one could say roughly that if an unprovable formula says of itself that it is unprovable, then it is obviously true. Gödel showed not only that arithmetic contains an undecidable formula but also that this formula is true − a formula which is true but unprovable.

Thus a Gödel sentence means a sentence which is true but not provable within a given formal system. The sentence '(x) − Bew(x,g)' is but one example of such a sentence. But sentences which say that they are unprovable are, from the mathematician's point of view, rather strange sentences. Have they anything to do with a number theoreticians' everyday work? Isn't the main thing after all to prove the 'interesting' theorems, such as Fermat's last theorem? One may thus ask oneself if there really exist interesting and important mathematical theorems which are true but not provable. Since Gödel's theorem first became widely known, logicians and mathematicians have spent a lot of research effort on finding an example of a Gödel sentence. And quite recently L. Harrington and J. Paris proved that

Ramsey's theorem is a Gödel sentence![11]

It is not the above-mentioned finite version of Ramsey's theorem, but the following extension of it, which is true but not provable in Peano arithmetic.

Let us say that a set X of positive integers is *large* if X is non-empty, and such that if x is its least element, X has at least x elements; that is, X is *large* if $|X| \geq \min(X)$. The set $\{3, 9, 8, 95\}$, for example, is large, but the set $\{5, 29, 32\}$ is not. Following Paris and Harrington, we use the notation $n \overset{*}{\to} (l)^k_r$ to mean that for every partition $P:[n]^k \to r$ there is a large homogeneous set for P of cardinality at least l; that is, a large monochromatic set exists.

Given the infinite Ramsey theorem, it is not all that difficult to prove the following theorem:

For all positive integers k, r and l, there is a finite n such that $n \overset{*}{\to} (l)^k_r$.

Suppose that we are planning a party. We are not concerned about who is invited, as long as it is a huge party. We thus use the telephone directory and number the invited persons consecutively. Ramsey's theorem now tells us that there is a number n such that if we invite the first n persons in the telephone directory, we can find a group of people such that they either mutually know each other or such that the people of this group do not know each other and the number of persons in this group is larger than the least number we assigned to any one of them.[12]

Thus, had it not been for the assumption of a large homogeneous set, this theorem would have been identical to the usual finite version of Ramsey's theorem (which is provable in Peano arithmetic). But the main theorem of Paris and Harrington says that in Peano arithmetic

$$(k)(r)(l)(\exists n)(n \overset{*}{\to} (l)^k_r)$$

is unprovable; that is, their extension of the finite version of Ramsey's theorem is true but unprovable.

This is not the best context to discuss the details of this interesting theorem and its proof-theoretical basis. However, it might still be of some value to briefly note that what is at the bottom of this is the extremely rapidly growing Ramsey functions. If we think of Peano arithmetic as an apple tree, the roots of the tree are the axioms and the beautiful red apples are the theorems of the theory, respectively. We could then picture a proof of a theorem as using a longer or shorter ladder to climb up in the tree and pick one of the apples. Steadily we place the ladder at the root of the tree and use it to pick the apples we desire. But not all apples can be reached by this method (actually this is what Gödel's theorem tells us). Some of them can't be reached because it is simply too bushy where they are, others because the ladders we have aren't high enough and others still because they simply are not on this tree. Pictured in this way what we have is a ladder which we can use to pick the apple corresponding to the finite version of Ramsey's theorem (this theorem is provable in Peano arithmetic); however, no ladder is long enough so that the apple corresponding to the above combinatorial principle can be reached. Furthermore, such a ladder can never be built; this apple is simply too high up in the tree. Finally, the infinite version of Ramsey's theorem is an example of an apple which cannot be reached because it is on another tree (the infinite version of the theorem cannot be formulated within Peano arithmetic).

It is rather tempting to summarize and conclude this chapter in the following way:

Trying to solve the unsolvable, Ramsey proved the unprovable.

Chapter 8

Universals

We now turn to one of the central problems of metaphysics, namely, the classical problem of universals. Ramsey writes on the subject in his first essay of some length, 'Universals', which was published in *Mind* in 1925, and he returns to the problem in an essay written for a symposium with H. W. B. Joseph and Richard Braithwaite, entitled 'Universals and the "Method of Analysis"'.

Ramsey was interested in the problem of universals because his investigations of the foundations of mathematics more or less forced him to take this metaphysical problem seriously – which is more than one can say about most philosophers today, who try to escape it by not discussing it. However, one does not need to be dealing with the foundations of mathematics to see how central the problem of universals is. It can be approached in various ways.

If I lift my eyes for a moment from the yellow screen of the word-processor and look around my office, I will find a number of things which are yellow, too. On the bookshelves there are a number of yellow books; true, the shade of yellow varies, but nonetheless they are all yellow, and on the desk there are a couple of typical government-owned yellow pencils. These books, pencils and the yellow screen differ in a number of ways; yet they have a common characteristic – yellowness. The property these particulars all share is a universal. The particulars, it is argued, can only be in one place at a time; universals can be in many places at the same time.

But the problem of universals also comes creeping upon us from other directions. We use, for example, proper names to refer to particular things. 'Frank Plumpton Ramsey' is the name of a philosopher who was active in a city named 'Cambridge' at the turn of this century. But our language also consists of words like 'yellow', 'wise' and 'punctual'. But, unlike 'Frank Plumpton Ramsey' and 'Cambridge', these words are not names of any particular things. Thus, one argues, if now giving a name to some particular thing or property means that this particular thing or property exists, we have a problem when it comes to words such as 'wise' or 'punctual'. We can solve the problem by assuming that what must exist are universals and that these words are the names of these universals.

If we accept the reasonable in the distinction between universals and particulars, questions arise concerning the status of universals and their relation to the particular things. Realism, or, if one prefers, a Platonic theory of universals, maintains that universals exist independent of our mind and thoughts. Universals exist ante rem in a world of their own or in the consciousness of God, independent of ourselves. We cannot create new universals, for example, by creating new theories with new conceptual systems. What we can do is to 'discover' already existing universals. This way of looking at universals makes us 'explorers' in a transcendental world of ideas. As an alternative to the realistic theory of universals we have conceptualism, which argues, one may say, that we are not explorers but rather inventors. It is we who create or invent the universals. Given the various particular things, we conceptualize different universals. Finally, we have the nominalists, who completely deny the existence of universals. Universals are no more and no less than collections of particulars. Thus, the only thing that we can assume to exist is particular things.

The problem of universals is of crucial importance when it comes to discussing the foundations of mathematics. What, in fact, are the mathematical symbols referring to? When we draw a circle on a piece of paper we are aware of the fact that this circle is just a more or less good approximation of a perfect circle. But in what sense do perfect circles exist?

Working with *Principia Mathematica* and related problems forced Russell to try to come up with a solution to the problem of universals. Russell advocated a theory closely related to that developed by Plato, that is, a realistic theory of universals, which the Axiom of Reducibility definitely shows. This theory was, of course, questioned by the defenders of intuitionism and formalism, who can be said to take a conceptualistic and nominalistic view of the matter, respectively. But it was definitely Russell's work and then above all *Principia Mathematica* that was the source of inspiration for Ramsey and that enticed him to work on the problem.

'Universals' is a 20-page paper which in substance consists of a criticism of Russell's theory of universals and particulars, but which also deals with and criticises the theories advocated by Johnson and Wittgenstein. Unfortunately, Ramsey's own ideas have been put in the shade by far too detailed discussion of these theories. Ramsey himself tackles the problem of universals by questioning the fundamental distinction between universals and particulars. What are our reasons for making this distinction? They can be psychological, physical or purely logical. Ramsey argues that neither psychological nor physical arguments in favour of the distinction are tenable and therefore if there are any arguments in favour of it they must be logical. After a detailed analysis he finds, however, that we neither have any logical reasons to maintain this distinction nor consequently do we have any reasons at all to keep this distinction. It is rather so that

> the whole theory of particulars and universals is due to mistaking for a fundamental characteristic of reality what is merely a characteristic of language.[1]

Ramsey's arguments in favour of the thesis are most convincing. If we want to analyse a simple sentence such as 'Socrates is wise' we split it into two components – subject and predicate. 'Socrates' is the subject and 'wise' the predicate. Without reflecting on it, we thus assume that it is the subject part of the sentence that we are talking about. We are saying something about Socrates. We say that he is wise. But the sentence 'Socrates is wise' can also be formulated 'Wisdom is a characteristic of Socrates'. Reformulated in this way, wisdom is no longer the predicate but the subject of the sentence.

What Ramsey attempts to show is that if there is no defensible asymmetry regarding the function of a subject and a predicate in a given sentence, if there is no essential difference between the completeness of a predicate and of a subject, then we do not have any logical reasons for making a distinction between universals and particulars. Ramsey formulates his thesis as follows:

> Both the disputed theories make an important assumption which, to my mind, has only to be questioned to be doubted. They assume a fundamental antithesis between subject and predicate, that if a proposition consists of two terms copulated, these two terms must be functioning in different ways, one as a subject, the other as predicate. Thus in 'Socrates is wise', Socrates is the subject, wisdom is the predicate. But suppose we turn the proposition round and say 'Wisdom is a characteristic of Socrates', then wisdom, formerly the predicate, is now the subject. Now it seems to me as clear as anything can be in philosophy that the two sentences 'Socrates is wise', 'Wisdom is a characteristic of Socrates' assert the same fact and express the same proposition. They are not, of course, the same sentence, but they have the same meaning, just as two sentences in two different languages can have the same meaning. Which sentence we use is a matter either of literary style, or of the point of view from which we approach the fact. If the centre of our interest is Socrates we say 'Socrates is wise', if we are discussing wisdom we may say 'Wisdom is a characteristic of Socrates'; but whichever we say we mean the same thing. Now of one of these sentences 'Socrates' is the subject, of the other 'wisdom'; and so which of the two is subject, which predicate, depends upon what particular sentence we use to express our proposition, and has nothing to do

with the logical nature of Socrates or wisdom, but is a matter entirely for grammarians. In the same way, with a sufficiently elastic language any proposition can be so expressed that any of its terms is the subject. Hence there is no essential distinction between the subject of a proposition and its predicate, and no fundamental classification of objects can be based upon such a distinction.[2]

It is, of course, the theories of Russell and Johnson that Ramsey alludes to at the beginning of this quotation. Russell builds his theory in 'On the Relation of Universals and Particulars' on a number of explicitly given distinctions. One of these is that between verbs and nouns, that is, between subjects and predicates. The distinction leads to a theory in which particulars differ from universals in that they can only occur as subjects or terms of relations in a sentence. Universals, on the other hand, function as predicates or relations. Another difference is that particulars occur in time and they exist in space. Universals do not – they exist independent of space and time. Johnson argues in Part I of *Logic* that the subject–predicate distinction, noun–adjective in his terminology, not only corresponds to, but also explains the distinction and relation between universals and particulars. A universal is an adjective used to characterize a given particular and a particular is a substantive which is characterizable by a universal.[3]

It is important for our understanding of Ramsey's thesis to comprehend the significance *Principia Mathematica* has had for his conclusions. In *Principia Mathematica* universals always occur as propositional functions. A propositional function $f\hat{x}$ determines the domain of values of the function fx, but also the domain of functions of the function $g(f\hat{x})$. Let us take 'Socrates is wise' to give an example of what is meant by this. Replacing the term or name 'Socrates' by the variable 'x' gives us a set of propositions of the type 'a is wise'; that is, the domain of values to the function 'x is wise', that is, fx. But 'wise' occurs as a constituent of more propositions than can be generated by changing the argument of the propositional function 'x is wise'. As examples we can take 'Either Socrates or Plato is wise', 'If Socrates is wise, Plato is too', and so on. The wider class of propositions thus obtained can be denoted g('wise') or $g(f\hat{x})$. Individuals, too, determine domains of propositions. We can, for example, vary 'wise' and get propositions like 'Socrates is stupid'. That is, we get the domain of functions f(Socrates), where f is variable. This domain thus corresponds to the domain of functions of a particular function; it corresponds to $g(f\hat{x})$. As Ramsey points out, we can also get a counterpart to a narrower domain fx, by using a variable quality, but mathematicians find no need for such a construct.

According to Ramsey, our reasons for this asymmetry are as bad as those for the illusory asymmetry between the function of a subject and a predicate.

But what is this difference between individuals and functions due to? Again simply to the fact that certain things do not interest the mathematician. Anyone who was interested not only in classes of things, but also in their qualities, would want to distinguish from among the others those functions which were names; and if we called the objects of which they are names qualities, and denoted a variable quality by q, we should have not only the range $[fa]$ but also the narrower range qa, and the difference analogous to that between 'Socrates' and 'wisdom' would have disappeared. We should have complete symmetry between qualities and individuals; each could have names which could stand alone, each would determine two ranges of propositions, for a would determine the ranges qa and $[fa]$, where q and $[f]$ are variables, and q would determine the ranges qx and $[fq]$, where x and $[f]$ are variables.

So were it not for the mathematician's biassed interest he would invent a symbolism which was completely symmetrical as regards individuals and qualities; and it becomes clear that there is no sense in the words individual and quality; all we are talking about is two different types of objects, such that two objects, one of each type, could be sole constituents of an atomic fact. The two types being in every way symmetrically related, nothing can be meant by calling one type the type of individuals and the other that of qualities, and these two words are devoid of connotation.[4]

Personally, I find Ramsey's logical and linguistic analysis of the problem of universals utterly convincing. The linguistic asymmetry between subject and predicate, or the corresponding logical asymmetry, are but an illusion. In this case the bonds of our languages feel exceptionally heavy.

Using this insight, Ramsey went on to reject complex universals, to deny the existence of, for example, negative, relational and compound properties. The gist of Ramsey's argument is directed against the supposition that all propositions have to be of a subject–predicate form. Let us consider the proposition that the printer is to the left of the computer. One could then imagine three related propositions: first, that the relation 'being to the left of' holds between the printer and the computer; second, that the printer has the complex property of 'being to the left of the printer'; third, that the computer has the complex property which something has if the printer is to the left of it. But then, besides the fact that the printer is to the left of the computer two additional facts must exist. We must have the fact that the printer has the property of being to the left of the computer, but also the fact that the computer has the property of having the printer to its left. However, as Ramsey points out, they are not three propositions, but one proposition, for they all say the same thing, namely, that the printer is to the left of the computer. There are not three facts but only one, namely, the fact that the printer is to the left of the computer. Thus, as Ramsey puts it,

> the theory of complex universals is responsible for an incomprehensible trinity, as senseless as that of theology.[5]

Let us, to emphasize this point, consider a particular thing which is both green and blue. This particular thing has the property of being green and it has the property of being blue. Thus we have at least two properties, but is there a third property as well, the property of being green and blue.

Or to put the question somewhat differently, is this particular thing grue? Does the property grue exist? The answer is negative. If 'grue' were the name of a complex property, then the two propositions – the particular is green, and the particular is grue and it is blue – would have to be different propositions, but they are not, they both say the same thing, namely that the particular is both green and blue. Extending this argument, we thus note how the new riddle of induction is dissolved.[6]

D. H. Mellor (personal communication) has pointed out that one should also note that Ramsey's theory stops the regress argument against realism about universals. The realist explains the existence of a fact by referring to the existence of particulars and universals. Assume, for example, that a is F but that b is not F. We have two particulars, a and b; but why then is it not a fact that b is F? The obvious answer is that a has the property F whereas b does not. There is a relation R which holds between a and F, but not between b and F. This relation is a universal. Thus, the realist will argue for the existence of the fact aRF by referring to the existence of a, F and R. But the question thus arises: Why is it not a fact that bRF? – both a and b exist. Again the obvious answer is that there is a relation, R^*, which holds between a, F and R, but not between b, F and R, and so on.

This vicious regress of universals arises – it is vicious since at no stage does postulating another universal explain why it is a fact that a is F but not a fact that b is F – because we are trying to reconstruct facts from independently conceived universals and particulars. But Ramsey's theory tells us that universals and particulars are constructions out of facts, not the other way around. Thus we do not need a universal to recombine F and a; they were never separated in the first place.

Ramsey's theory is, however, far from universally accepted. There are critical voices. Michael Dummett, for example, in his book *Frege: Philosophy of Language*, has tried to point out the shortcomings of Ramsey's theory.[7] Dummett's criticism of Ramsey is based on Aristotle's dictum that a quality has a contrary but a substance does not. What this means is that for any predicate, there is another predicate with exactly the opposite truth-values. If we have a predicate, for example, 'wise', we can, it is thought, introduce a new predicate 'foolish' by stipulating that for every proper name these two predicates have opposite truth-values. The predicate 'foolish' is thus the contrary to the predicate 'wise'. But, says Dummett, we cannot in the same way for a given name, for example 'Socrates', introduce a new name 'Nonsocrates' by stipulating that for every predicate f, 'f(Nonsocrates)' and 'It is not the case that f(Socrates) is to have the same truth-values. Thus, the predicate 'wise' has a contrary but the name 'Socrates' does not.

I am not at all convinced by this argument. Ramsey's penetrating analysis of complex properties tells us that notwise is no more a real property than Nonsocrates is a real particular. In Chapter 2 we saw that in 'Facts and Propositions', written two years after 'Universals', he makes use of this argument discussing the redundancy theory. What he there argues is that 'not' cannot name some element in a fact, 'for if it were, "not-not-p" would have to be about the object not and so different in meaning from "p" '.[8] He thinks it hard to 'believe that from one fact, e.g. that a thing is red, it should be possible to infer an infinite number of different facts, such as that it is not not-red, and that it is both red and not not-red'.[9] We are instead simply saying the same thing in a number of different ways. One should keep in mind, it is argued, that it is only an accident of our symbolism that we have the word 'not'. Again Ramsey makes us realize that 'the whole theory of particulars and universals is due to mistaking for a fundamental characteristic of reality what is merely a characteristic of language'.[10] There are no complex properties in general and no negative properties in particular.

Another argument against Ramsey's thesis is that Ramsey has not completely proved that there is a complete symmetry regarding the functioning of a subject and a predicate. Can we say that 'Wisdom socratesizes'? There seems to be no problem with these expressions except that we generally do not use them in our language, except perhaps in poetry. However, in a sufficiently elastic language such sentences would be perfectly acceptable and would be easily understood. I believe that Ramsey would argue 'Wisdom socratesizes' and 'Wisdom is a characteristic of Socrates' assert the same fact and express the same proposition.

Being convinced that Ramsey's thesis is correct – we have no logical reasons for upholding the distinction between universals and particulars – we may still be doubtful about whether there really are no other fundamental reasons for making the distinction. As mentioned earlier, Ramsey dismisses in a few lines psychological and physical arguments in favour of the distinction. Of these two it is the latter alternative that has received the greatest attention. The way the problem of universals was introduced above indicates that it is easy to think of the distinction between particulars and universals as based on their relations to space and time. In his review of *The Foundations of Mathematics*, Russell discusses Ramsey's analysis of the problem of universals. Russell says that ever since the original publication of the paper he has been unable to make up his mind as to the truth and falsity of the theory. He agrees with Ramsey regarding the argument for symmetry, but he says that he does not feel convinced that Ramsey is right as to the source of the difference felt between universals and particulars and that the question remains open.[11]

If we should thus try to find another source of the difference we feel between universals and particulars, the most obvious alternative is to consider their relations to space and time.[12] Most of us do feel that particulars occur in time and exist in space. The yellow pencils on my desk occur in a well-defined part of reality. The property which they all share, 'yellowness', does not, however, have the same relation to space and time. A particular, a pencil or Socrates, forms a unique curve through space and time. From the day they come in to being until they are obliterated, particulars leave unique traces which can be followed through space and time.

But a universal, like 'yellowness' or 'wisdom', cannot be traced by its footsteps. Or more directly, some objects, like pencils, can only be at one place at a time; others, like yellow and wisdom, can be in many places at the same time, or in the same place at the same time. But quantum theory tells us that the entire universe is entirely made up of quantum particles which are completely identical and indistinguishable particles. Thus a state function for two electrons can determine the probability for finding an electron here and another there, but it is impossible to say which electron is which. Since the probability distribution is completely unchanged by changing particles we know that the state functions of two identical particles must either be an even or an odd function of the distance between them. The sign is a property of the type of particle. The so-called spin-statistics theorem now tells us that for integer spin particles we need a state function with positive sign and for half-integer spin particles a state function with negative sign. Thus, for electrons the sign must always be negative and for photons positive. Since the state function for two photons is always symmetric, it need not vanish when the distance between the photons is o, that is, when the photons are in the same state or, let us say, when they are occupying the same point at the same time. This is not true for electrons which do not satisfy Einstein–Bose statistics but Fermi–Dirac statistics. All this is standard, but it is of interest for our discussion of the problem of universals. If we can have particulars which are indiscernible and which can be in the same state at the same time then, the above argument loses most of its weight. Leaving classical physics behind for quantum theory makes it necessary to give up our hopes of basing the distinction between particulars and universals on their relation to space and time. Generally, I feel rather uncomfortable taking quantum physics as an argument for a philosophical standpoint, but in this case I feel it is without objections.

Chapter 9
Economics

Sometimes it can be pleasant and stimulating to turn to fresh fields of research – to try to apply one's knowledge to other areas. The philosopher who has grown weary of his own subject may look upon the experimental elements of psychology as tempting. Now and then such escapades turn out to be extremely successful. But more often than not the attempts evoke no more than an appreciative word from friendly colleagues in other disciplines.

Under the influence of the Cambridge economists J. M. Keynes and A. Pigou, Ramsey decided to test his mathematical and philosophical knowledge in the field of economics at the end of the 1920s. What Ramsey achieved were two essays of the highest class. Both 'A Contribution to the Theory of Taxation' (1927) and 'A Mathematical Theory of Saving' (1928) have given rise to new and flourishing schools of economic theory. The former essay is the point of departure for the theory of optimal taxation and the latter lays the foundations for the theory of optimal saving.

But it is perhaps primarily the essay on saving that has been noticed and discussed in the literature of economics. According to Keynes, who must be considered a competent judge, this essay is:

one of the most remarkable contributions to mathematical economics ever made, both in respect of the intrinsic importance and difficulty of its subject, the power and elegance of the technical methods employed, and the clear purity of illumination with which the writer's mind is felt by the reader to play about its subject.[1]

In this chapter I give a brief presentation of Ramsey's economic works. The discussion of the theory of optimal saving contains a number of formulae that may be considered difficult but one can quite simply bypass these and yet have a general view of the theory. One reason this section is more mathematical than the others is that Ramsey's way of formalising the theory of optimal saving is of interest. He was the first to apply the calculus of variations to an economic problem. Another reason is that by way of conclusion I want to show how Ramsey's theory of optimal saving can be linked with the risk theory formulated within the framework of traditional utility theory; that is, I want to show that two comparatively different economic theories can be brought together in an interesting way. But let us first study the theory of optimal taxation.

OPTIMAL TAXATION

Ramsey's first work in economics, 'A Contribution to the Theory of Taxation' published in the *Economic Journal* in 1927, lays the foundation for a theory of optimal taxation. The economic question dealt with in the essay is as follows:

[A] given revenue is to be raised by proportionate taxes on some or all uses of income, the taxes on different uses being possibly at different rates; how should these rates be adjusted in order that the decrement of utility may be a minimum?[2]

The person who suggested to Ramsey that he should try to come up with a solution to this problem was the Cambridge economist Arthur Pigou. From 1908 to 1943, Pigou was professor of political economy at Cambridge. When he was only thirty, he was appointed to the chair as successor to Alfred Marshall. Pigou was a devoted advocate of Marshall's classical economic theories in every respect and is said to have lived in the firm conviction that all economic theory of any value was contained in Marshall's works. Collaboration with Ramsey taught Pigou the lesson that even a Marshall could be wrong. Ramsey's results concerning optimal taxation are in conflict with some of Marshall's ideas. But as Pigou expressed it, 'Where a Marshall is caught the trap must be subtle indeed!'[3] In his book *A Study of Public Finance* (from which this quotation is taken), Pigou gives a very careful presentation of Ramsey's theoretical results and below I shall confine myself to Ramsey's and Pigou's texts.

To avoid complicating the issue, let us assume that the society we are studying only produces and consumes five types of commodities: bread, butter, coffee, roast beef and cars. Our problem can then be seen as how to raise the purchase tax on these five commodities in such a way that we minimize the utility decrease that the increased tax burden entails for the individual. A rise in tax payments always means that the private citizen takes a loss since his economic opportunities are cut back.

Ramsey shows that, given a number of economic assumptions (we shall return to these later on), the tax increase should be made according to the following principles:

The taxes should be such as to diminish the production of all commodities in the same proportion.[4]

If we want to minimize the loss, not to say the suffering, that levying heavier taxes entails for the private citizen, the change in taxation should be made in such a way that the relation between the production of the individual commodities is retained. If a rise in taxes means a drastic reduction in butter production, many slices of bread will be eaten without butter. A tax increase that causes fewer slices of bread to be available, but all with butter on them as before, is therefore to be preferred. We also want to avoid a surplus of butter being the result of the tax change: Butter without bread is just as bad as bread without butter. If prior to the tax increase there was a pat of butter for every slice of bread, we should make sure that this relation is maintained even after the tax increase.

Ramsey's results are valid for all types of goods, irrespective of their mutual relations. It does not matter, for example, if the demand for one commodity depends on the demand for another, as in the case of bread and butter, or if there is no such dependence, as in the case of bread and cars.

The question now arises whether a general increase in a proportional purchase tax really entails an equally large percentage cut in the production of all commodities. Certain articles are considerably more sensitive to price than others. A rise in the purchase tax of 1 or 2 per cent may mean, for example, that the consumption of essential commodities such as butter, bread and coffee remains the same or falls marginally. But the same tax increase may also mean that the consumption of luxury goods like cars and roast beef drops dramatically.

Roast beef is probably one of the articles that are sensitive to prices where an increase in price by 1 or 2 per cent will lead to a considerable drop in consumption. If we are to increase taxes in accordance with Ramsey's findings, we have to take account of factors of this kind. The more sensitive to prices a commodity is, the more cautious we must be in taxing it, and vice versa; the more insensitive to price increases the demand for a certain commodity is, the higher the proportion of the total tax levied on that particular commodity. Perhaps coffee is the perfect commodity to tax (at least here in Sweden). I have the impression that the price elasticity of coffee is more or less zero. The Swedes seem to be so dependent on their breakfast coffee, morning coffee, coffee after a meal, and so on, that people are prepared to pay almost any price per kilo.

What Ramsey's theory of optimal taxation shows is that if our aim is to minimize the utility loss brought about by increased taxation for the individual, then we should not use a non-differentiated purchase tax as an instrument for raising the nation's revenue. The result of an increase in purchase tax is that the production relation between different commodities will change because different commodities have a different elasticity of price, and thus there is no minimizing the utility loss for the individual. The reason why we do not have a much more differentiated scale of taxes, as this theory demands, is something that an amateur may only speculate upon. One reason is probably the amount of red tape such a system would in all probability involve. It is, for example, on the totally unrealistic assumption that the demand and supply schedules are all completely independent that a simple formula for the rate of tax on any commodity can be worked out. In general such a formula would need to involve factors describing the character of the interdependencies of existing demand and supply, thus resulting in a quite complex formula. Another reason is that although luxury goods are far more sensitive to price than essential commodities, it seems more logical to tax them, no matter how much pleasure they give the private citizen, rather than taxing essentials; that is, we want to do just the opposite of the recommendations of the theory. A tax increase may also enable us to attain a number of politically desirable goals. We can influence the pattern of consumption. By putting more tax on goods that high-income groups consume, we may attain an acceptable redistribution of income. What Ramsey's theory states is that to minimize the citizen's utility loss the tax increase must be made in such a way that the pattern of consumption is maintained. It does not require much reflection to realize that such a tax strategy will fall prey to our politicians' ambitions to redistribute income and change our preferences.

But in order to deduce the theorems that we used above, we need to make some assumptions. Ramsey assumes that it is possible to ignore the effects following from different individuals having different utility functions. Therefore, he assumes that the marginal utility is the same for each individual. This assumption naturally affects the universality of the result, but the assumption simultaneously gives rise to a not uninteresting scenario. Furthermore, it is assumed that we have a functioning pure market economy. Another assumption of Ramsey's is that the tax revenue allocated is spent by the state in the same way as it would have been if this revenue had never been collected. The reason for this is that it is not desirable that the tax revenue affect the mutual production relations between different commodities. However, one can have a system whereby the state spends its money on things that the individual cannot consume. Some of the tax revenue can therefore be used for various purposes, such as aid or defence without the validity of the theoretical results being affected.

Besides these assumptions, Ramsey's theory has a limitation that must be mentioned. If it is not assumed that a utility function has a certain curvature, that it is quadratic, the result obtained is only valid for infinitesimal tax increases, or approximately correct for 'small' tax increases. But if we assume that the utility function is quadratic – which would mean that the supply and demand curves are straight lines – the result holds regardless of the size of the tax increase.

Considered from the angle of utility theory, it might also be asserted that the assumption that the utility function is quadratic is not entirely wrong. A quadratic utility function mirrors the intuitive ideas we have about the shape of the utility curve. The value distances diminish as the rate of prosperity increases. The value distance or the utility distance between receiving 10,000 pounds and 20,000 pounds is considerably greater than the corresponding distance between receiving a million pounds and receiving a million plus 10,000 pounds. The trouble with a quadratic utility curve is that there is strong evidence that it correctly reflects only part of an individual's utility function. Our levels of aspiration have a decisive impact on the curvature of the utility curve. Perhaps it is true that we need or want to have 10,000 pounds. We may need a new car or we may be thinking of buying a sailing boat. If 10,000 pounds is our level of aspiration, this will mean that the value distances up to that point will be on the increase, but after that point the value distances will be diminishing. In that case the utility curve will look roughly like a diagonally extended 'S'. Ramsey's theory thus demands that we do not have any articulated levels of aspiration, which is hardly the case. It is in our nature to aspire and the absence of aspirations is almost a sign of being unwell. In spite of this objection, one can claim that it is perfectly all right to assume that the utility function is quadratic. In the majority of situations the real relations will be approximated with good results.

But Ramsey's result is valid even if we do not assume that the utility function is quadratic, but in that case it works only for infinitesimal taxes. For arbitrary utility functions, the theory is approximately correct for 'small' tax increases. What constitutes a small increase in tax is exceedingly relative. As Ramsey emphasizes, the unknown factor is the curvature of the supply and demand curves. It may turn out, for example, that 'a tax of 500% on whisky could . . . be regarded as small'.[5]

Finally, it must be pointed out that what at first sight might seem a serious limitation in the applicability of Ramsey's results, is really no limitation at all. Ramsey's rule for optimal taxation assumes that only a proportional purchase tax can be used. Usually, however, a progressive or linear income tax is considered more appropriate for redistribution purposes. This is true. However, Ramsey only discusses the aggregates, thus nothing prohibits us from using a progressive or linear income tax.[6]

OPTIMAL SAVING

THEORY

Keynes, who shared Ramsey's interest in questions concerning the foundations of probability theory and whose book *A Treatise of Probability* had lured Ramsey into that field, must have come to the same conclusion as Pigou about Ramsey's latent talent for economics. Keynes encouraged Ramsey to use his mathematical skill to try to find a solution to a tricky economic problem:

How much of its income should a nation save?

By making a number of simplifying assumptions Ramsey shows that there is a ready remedy:

> The rate of saving multiplied by the marginal utility of money should always be equal to the amount by which the total net rate of enjoyment of utility falls short of the maximum possible rate of enjoyment.[7]

Ramsey describes with great precision the assumptions he made in deriving this rule. One assumption he is forced to make is that society in some sense is stationary. The population does not change in number and these citizens always appreciate the good things of life to the same extent and always have the same aversion to labour. The society we study also goes on for ever.

These assumptions are unrealistic, of course, and Ramsey discusses certain attenuations for them. Much of the research based on Ramsey's work has also largely been directed at weakening the assumptions, thereby making generalizations of his results feasible.

Another assumption that Ramsey has to make is that money always brings greater enjoyment or utility but that there is a limit to this happiness. But does more money always mean more happiness or utility? If we have more money, we can buy more things, take time off work or do something else we enjoy. But it is also reasonable to assume that with the help of money we can achieve a finite level of satisfaction. To attain an infinite degree of utility, something quite different is needed. In utility theory and in economic contexts it is therefore customary to presume that money always gives an enhanced degree of utility, but that the marginal utility decreases. We come close to a maximum attainable level of utility without perhaps ever actually getting there. This maximum level of utility is what Ramsey calls 'Bliss'. It might be said that as evidence Ramsey assumes that we never achieve bliss but only come closer and closer to it and more slowly.

In planning the economy for future years we decide to spend x pounds and to save z pounds. The same afternoon as we draw up these guidelines, we go into town and suddenly realize that we want to consume goods for another few pounds. For the sake of simplicity, let us say that we want to buy goods for one more pound. When we get home, we take out our yearly budget and try to work out the setback this increase in consumption would cause. If we spend another pound, this means that it will take us longer to attain bliss – in economic terms – to reach the limit beyond which more money really does have marginal value. We will not, as we had planned, be able to save z pounds during the year; instead another $\frac{1}{z}$ year will be needed for us to increase our savings by this amount. (If we decide to save 12 pounds a year, and then change our minds and save only 11, then we have to save for one year plus $\frac{1}{12}$ of a year, that is, a year and a month before we have increased our savings by 12 pounds). If we choose to spend another pound, we shall achieve bliss $\frac{1}{z}$ of a year later than would have been possible had we forgone increased consumption and thus kept to the original budget.

But increased consumption not only means that it will take us longer to achieve bliss. We must not forget that a certain amount of labour is needed to scrape together the amount we have at our disposal and can decide to save or spend. This stint of labour must be related to the utility of enjoyment consumption brings. The excess of utility or happiness we get out of spending x pounds is equal to the utility of spending x pounds ($U(x)$) minus the disutility of labour ($V(a)$), that is, $U(x) - V(a)$. The disadvantage of spending 1 pound more is thus

$$\frac{B - (U(x) - V(a))}{z},$$

where 'B' stands for bliss.

If we equate this value with the marginal utility of money or consumption ($u(x) = dU(x)/dx$) and rewrite the formula somewhat differently, we get

$$z = \frac{B - (U(x) - V(a))}{u(x)}.$$

This is the rule for saving that Ramsey arrives at. The only difference is that saving z pounds is replaced in the general case by the corresponding limiting value. That is, we talk about the rate of saving:

> [The] rate of saving multiplied by marginal utility of consumption should always equal bliss minus actual rate of utility enjoyed.[8]

Although the arguments above for this rule have certain educational advantages, I think that Ramsey's own line of attack may be salutary despite its complexity. Ramsey assumes that the two variable factors of production in a society, that is, labour and capital, can be represented by the two continuous functions, $a(t)$ and $c(t)$. These functions tell us the rate of labour in society and its capital at time t, respectively. Furthermore, it is assumed that we have a continuous function stating what the consumption of society looks like over time. This function we denote $x(t)$.

Our personal income can be considered to be based on two factors – how much we earn and how much return we get on our savings – in the same way as a nation's income can be seen as a function of these two factors. We thus denote the income function $f(a,c)$ (or more precisely $f(a(t), c(t))$). The income society has at a given juncture may either be saved or consumed. But the consumption must not exceed the nation's income. We do not permit the country to have a consumption policy resulting in debt. We assume then that

$$f(a,c) = x + \frac{dc}{dt}; \tag{1}$$

that is, savings (the rate of growth of capital dc/dt) plus consumption equals income.

From society's point of view it is a matter of stipulating the labour input to be made by citizens and the saving by the society in such a way as to maximize the net utility over time.

We want the net utility, the difference between the utility of consumption and disutility of labour, to be as great as possible. So an attempt is made to find a labour function $a(t)$ and a capital function $c(t)$ (the consumption function $x(t)$ according to (1) is equal to $f(a,c) - dc/dt$) such that

$$\int_{t_0}^{\infty} (U(x) - V(a))dt \quad \text{is maximized.}$$

Formulated somewhat differently, we want the difference between bliss and net utility to be as small as possible over time. That is, we want to minimize:

$$\int_{t_0}^{\infty} (B - (U(x) - V(a)))dt.$$

With the aid of some mathematics and given the fact that the accumulated capital in the society at juncture t_0 is known and that the curvature of the utility function when t approaches infinity is also known – it can be shown that the rate of saving (dc/dt) should be equal to what the above-mentioned rule says:

$$\frac{dc}{dt} = \frac{B - (U(x) - V(a))}{u(x)};$$

the rate of saving multiplied by the marginal utility of consumption equals the amount by which the net utility falls short of bliss.

But to be able to find a labour function and a capital function which maximize the total utility over time, one or two conditions must be satisfied besides condition (1). The first of these conditions says that the contribution made by the marginal products of labour input to income, the efficiency of our labour or, if your like, our wages, is equal to the ratio of the marginal disutility of labour to the marginal utility of consumption:

$$\frac{\partial f}{\partial a} = \frac{v(a)}{u(x)}, \tag{2}$$

where $v(a)$ $(=dV(a)/da)$ denotes the marginal disutility of labour and $u(x)$ $(=dU(x)/dx)$ the marginal utility of consumption.

The third condition Ramsey needs to deduce his rule for optimal saving says that the proportional rate at which the marginal utility of consumption decreases over time is given by the level of interest. How much of the income growth is interest is represented by $\partial f/\partial c$, the contribution of marginal capital increase to income at a certain juncture, and this value is the rate of interest at that juncture:

$$\frac{\partial f}{\partial c} = -\frac{1}{u(x(t))}\frac{d}{dt}\{u(x(t))\}. \tag{3}$$

Condition (3) tells us that consumption is going to increase up to the point that the marginal utility of consumption vanishes, or until the rate of interest becomes zero. When this state has been reached, we have achieved bliss, the state in which neither more consumption nor positive interest rates can contribute to an enhanced level of utility.

GENERALIZATIONS AND CRITICISM

Ramsey's theory can, of course, be generalized in different directions. One of several possibilities mentioned by Ramsey himself is the introduction of a discount factor reflecting uncertainty of the future. Things seldom have the same value today as they will have in the remote future. A hundred pounds today will not have the same value as 100 pounds a few years hence, but just as economists discount money it would seem reasonable to discount utilities. To arrive at a more realistic economic theory, therefore, we need to introduce some discount factor.

Ramsey's theory has been criticized in various quarters. It may be questioned whether his results really are as robust as they seem. One problem is whether bliss is really attained at some finite level of consumption or whether one can merely suppose that we approach this level asymptotically. In the former case, Ramsey's method can be used to achieve the optimal saving program. But as S. Chakravarty has shown, we have no guarantee that an optimal solution always exists if bliss corresponds to a level of utility that cannot be attained.[9]

Another criticism of a more philosophical nature that can be levelled against the theory has to do with measurement theory. As we noticed in Chapter 1, it is difficult to determine the utility functions Ramsey needs for his argument. The problems are serious enough on the individual level, but they are even more complicated, if that is possible, when it comes to establishing collective utility functions generated from the utility functions of separate individuals. We must be able to establish functions of this type if Ramsey's method is to have any practical significance.

Ramsey's utility function $U(.)$ is supposed to tell us what the social utility of a particular level of consumption is. But this utility function must be generated out of the personal utility assessments made by the members of that society. The problem is that you and I perhaps have diametrically opposed opinions on the utility of a certain level of consumption. The ready spender appreciates every opportunity to make a purchase, but for the person to whom material things have little value the same opportunity is a nuisance. The problem is that we not only have to be able to say the citizens agree that more is better, we must also be able to represent the intensity of their preferences. To illustrate the problem further let us look at a simple case.

We assume that the collective we are studying consists of only two people, John and Mary. John enjoys going to the cinema very much but hates going to the theatre. At the theatre he always feels let down. Mary, on the other hand, prefers going to the theatre, but enjoys going to the cinema almost as much. It would thus seem as if the utility difference between going to the cinema and going to the theatre is greater for John than for Mary. Is it possible to use this piece of information to arrive at a societal utility function? Should the collective be encouraged to go to the cinema? I would maintain that a compromise between John's and Mary's preferences is impossible and that the attempts made only indicate that the basic assumptions of utility theory have not been understood. A compromise of this kind means that we can compare John's utility assessments with Mary's, that we know, for example, that the utility John assigns to a night out at the cinema is greater than the utility Mary assigns to it, and so on. But such comparison calls for a common point of reference, a 'zero point', a commodity, an outcome or a level of consumption that we know is evaluated exactly the same by John and Mary. We quickly realize the pointlessness of looking for a 'zero point' if we think about the way in which an individual's personal utility function is arrived at. Expressed differently and more concisely, one might say that two interval scales cannot be made into a ratio scale, however much we try. I shall not go into this criticism in detail here but refer the reader to the discussion in Chapter 1.

Nevertheless, there is a way out of the difficulty. One can, of course, conceive of a society that has a utility function which can be determined without reference to its citizens' personal utility functions. A utility function like this is reflected in the different political decisions made. However, the irrationality of politics will also be reflected in the appearance of the function. Political preferences and actual conduct do not always go hand in hand. But perhaps a society's preferences are sturdy enough to be represented by a relatively uniform class of utility functions. In that case, we can use Ramsey's theory of optimal saving in an interesting fashion. Every utility function results in an optimum strategy and since it is probably better to save too much than too little one should choose the strategy that leads to bliss fastest. But to sum up: it may be said that Ramsey's assumptions about the existence of two social utility functions $U(.)$ and $V(.)$ (disutility) are extremely problematic.

I have not analyzed in detail Ramsey's theory of saving. Someone who is more familiar with the workings of economic theory would be able to carry out that task much better. What one can observe as a layman is that Ramsey's theory ought to have a number of interesting applications outside the purely monetary field. One application is found in modern risk theory. When we build nuclear power plants, roads or airports we can work on the assumption that a certain number of people will be killed every year as a result of these activities. We know, for instance, that about 750 people die in road accidents every year in Sweden. Our decision makers usually also have a good idea of what it would cost to reduce this figure to, say, 700 deaths per year. But since no measures are taken to improve road safety, it must be assumed that the cost of saving another human life in this sector is considered too high.

If a number of sectors of society are analyzed – such as the traffic sector, the building sector and the industrial sector – it will be found that the cost of saving one more human life varies considerably from sector to sector. I myself probably lead a fairly safe life in comparison with a truck driver or a bus driver. One interesting question then is how to distribute the scarce economic resources we possess in the best possible way so that the greatest number of human lives will be saved. It is perhaps not at all reasonable to expend money on better road safety, but it is quite possible that improvements in the working environment for several groups would yield much better dividends. How does Ramsey's theory of how much a nation should save enter into it? Ramsey's theory applied to the field of risk theory could tell us something about how we ought to allocate the means we have at our disposal in the best possible way to save more lives. The theory would be able to show which programmes are optimal ones in this field.

RISK AND OPTIMAL SAVING

In this section we shall be dealing with a more technical problem. We shall try to find a connection between risk aversion and the rate of saving. In Chapter 1 we touched on the definition of the concept of risk aversion that is generally applied in economic contexts. It is usually said that risk-aversive behaviour occurs if one chooses the expected value of a fair game rather than the game itself. Assume that the game gives one pound with a 50 per cent chance and 0 pounds with a 50 per cent chance. This game has an expected value of 50 pence. If 50 pence in cash is preferred to participating in the game, the person who has made this choice is said to be risk-aversive. In principle this means that a person is risk-aversive if the marginal utility decreases.

K. Arrow and J. Pratt, who are usually associated with this definition of risk aversion, thus link the risk concept with a property of the utility function.[10] More precisely, Arrow and Pratt propose the following definition of risk:

$$(\text{Risk}) \quad R(x) = \frac{-\dfrac{d^2U}{dx^2}}{\dfrac{dU}{dx}}$$

This is a definition which has obvious advantages since it avoids some transformation problems. The reason why we are unable to use the simpler dU/dx is that the utility function is only determined up to a positive linear transformation.

If we have two utility functions U_1 and U_2 with the risk functions R_1 and R_2 defined as above, we say that U_1 is more risk-aversive than U_2 at x if $R_1(x) > R_2(x)$. This gives an opportunity to compare formally two utility functions with respect to risk.

In his essay Pratt shows that for two utility functions and two risk functions the following interesting connection holds:
$R_1(x) > R_2(x)$ if and only if

$$\frac{U_1(x_3) - U_1(x)}{U_1(x) - U_1(x_1)} < \frac{U_2(x_3) - U_2(x)}{U_2(x) - U_2(x_1)}$$

for all x_1, x_2, x and x_3 such that $x_1 < x_2 \leq x < x_3$.

I do not give the proof for this theorem but refer the reader to Pratt's work. Those who have just been engaged in trying to digest Ramsey's theory of optimal saving might well ask what Arrow's and Pratt's risk theory has to do with it. My idea is that we should be interested in comparing a nation's need to save with its risk behaviour. *Should a risk-aversive nation save more or less than a risk-prone one?* According to Ramsey's theory, we must assume that a nation has a collective utility function and such a function has, of course, a corresponding risk function which entitles us to ask the question.

For two nations with the utility functions U_1 and U_2 we can now show that

if $R_1(x) > R_2(x)$,

then

$$\frac{B - (U_1(x) - V(a))}{u_1(x)} < \frac{B - (U_2(x) - V(a))}{u_2(x)}.$$

Or, expressed somewhat differently, we can show that

$$\frac{dc_1}{dt} < \frac{dc_2}{dt}$$

if $R_1 > R_2$.

If one nation is more risk-aversive than another nation, the first nation needs to save less than the second, according to the theory. Intuitively, the theorem seems quite logical. A risk-aversive nation quite simply does not take any major risks and can thus accumulate money at a more moderate rate to attain bliss. A nation with a more risk-seeking financial policy, on the other hand, may encounter serious setbacks, and in that case it is advisable to have a higher rate of saving. This higher rate will thereby compensate for the more risk-prone behaviour as regards financial policy. To prove the above proposition more formally, we first make use of Pratt's theorem. We divide the denominators of both terms by $x_1 - x_2$ and let x_2 tend to x_1. We then get

$$\frac{(U_1(x_3) - V(a)) - (U_1(x) - V(a))}{u_1(x_1)}$$

$$\leq \frac{(U_2(x_3) - V(a)) - (U_2(x) - V(a))}{u_2(x_1)}$$

If we now let x_3 approach infinity, we find that $U_1(x_3) - V(a)$ and $U_2(x_3) - V(a)$ approach B. The theorem follows if finally we notice that the difference is obtained when x_1 approaches x.

What this result entails for political economy, I am unable to say. The theorem, however, interestingly links together two apparently quite different theories, that is, Ramsey's theory of optimal saving and the modern utility theoretical risk theory. It is an open question whether the reverse implication holds – if we can say anything about risk aversion using a comparison with respect to capital growth. The difficulty in proving this implication lies in the fact that the number of causal factors influencing saving must be restricted by a number of reasonable conditions. Another limitation is that the theorem is not valid if we break down the collective utility function into its constituent parts.[11]

Chapter 10
Biographical glimpses

The title of this chapter indicates that this is not intended to
be a complete biographical portrait of Frank Ramsey. Such a
task would be difficult to carry out for various reasons. There
is hardly anything written about him and what there is gives
a sketchy outline. Moreover, for obvious reasons, there are
few people now living who knew Ramsey and who would be
able to straighten out the many queries we have. I have
instead preferred to put together parts of the biographical
fragments to be found in the literature. I hope that these
glimpses will give some impression of the whole person.[1]
    In writing this chapter I have drawn greatly on D. H.
Mellor's excellent radio programme 'Better than the Stars',
which was broadcast by BBC Radio 3 on 27 February 1978 on
the occasion of the seventy-fifth anniversary of Ramsey's
birth.

BIOGRAPHICAL DATA

Frank Plumpton Ramsey was born on 22 February 1903 and
died at the age of 26 on 19 January 1930. Ramsey suffered
from a chronic and increasingly serious liver complaint, contracted jaundice after an operation and died at Guy's Hospi-
tal in London. He left a wife, Lettice Ramsey and two
daughters. Frank Ramsey came from a distinctly academic
background, his brother became Archbishop of Canterbury
and his two sisters also received a solid university education.

Ramsey's mother was active in politics and he inherited from her a very profound social awareness.

EDUCATION

Ramsey's father, who was a mathematician, perceived his son's aptitude for abstract problems at a very early stage and encouraged him to develop his talent. Besides being educated at home, he had a genuinely English education, attending first Winchester, one of England's leading public schools, and then taking a degree in mathematics at Trinity College, Cambridge, in the summer of 1923. He got first-class honours and became the most outstanding mathematics graduate at Cambridge. Ramsey never went on to write a Ph.D. thesis and I do not know whether the idea had even occurred to him.

In 1921 Ramsey became acquainted with J. M. Keynes through his friend Richard Braithwaite and thanks to Keynes's influence Ramsey became a Fellow of King's in 1924 at the age of only 21. Two years later he was made a lecturer in mathematics at Cambridge.

For many of us it takes some time for our talents to be revealed – in some cases they are never disclosed. But in Ramsey's case it was quite clear early on that he had an unusually keen and agile intellect. There is an illuminating story told about him by I. A. Richards in the broadcast mentioned above.

Well, my old friend C. K. Ogden had a very queer place called 'Top Hole', named after a war cartoon, above MacFisheries in Petty Cury, and one afternoon there – a tap on the door, and in came this tall ungainly, rather gangling boy. We knew who he was instantly – he looked so like his mother – and in no time he was at home. He was at Winchester, where he'd been for some time with no one doing much more than saying 'The library is yours, just do what you want'. He was recognised clearly at Winchester as quite one of the wonders; and there he was. And we chatted along for some time, and then he turned to Ogden and said: 'Do you know, I've been thinking I ought to learn German. How do you learn German?'. Ogden leaped up instantly, rushed to the shelf, got him a very thorough German grammar and a dictionary – Anglo-German dictionary – and hunted on the shelves and found a very abstruse work in German – Mach's *Analysis of Sensations* – and said 'You are obviously interested in this, and all you do is read the book. That's all, use the grammar, and use the dictionary, and come and tell us what you think.' Believe it or not, within ten days Frank was back, saying that Mach had misstated this, and that he ought to have developed that argument more fully, it wasn't satisfactory. He'd learned German – not to speak it, but to read it – in almost hardly over a week.[2]

Others confirm Ramsey's intellectual precocity. In the obituary he wrote on Ramsey's death, Keynes tells how even early on Ramsey exercised an influence on the economic theories being formulated at Cambridge during this period. One of Ramsey's earliest works, 'The Douglas Proposals', also forcibly shows that Ramsey had a bent for economic questions.

> From a very early age, about sixteen I think, this precocious mind was intensely interested in economic problems. Economists living in Cambridge have been accustomed from his undergraduate days to try their theories on the keen edge of his critical and logical faculties. If he had followed the easier path of mere inclination, I am not sure that he would not have exchanged the tormenting exercises of the foundations of thought and of psychology, where the mind tries to catch its own tail, for the delightful paths of our own most agreeable branch of the moral sciences, in which theory and fact, intuitive imagination and practical judgment, are blended in a manner comfortable to the human intellect.
>
> When he did descend from his accustomed stony heights, he still lived without effort in a rarer atmosphere than most economists care to breathe, and handled the technical apparatus of our science with the easy grace of one accustomed to something far more difficult.[3]

Someone else who respected Ramsey as a thinker was G. E. Moore.

The philosophy of F. P. Ramsey

He was an extraordinarily clear thinker: no-one could avoid more easily than he the sort of confusions of thought to which even the best philosophers are liable, and he was capable of apprehending clearly and observing consistently, the subtlest distinctions. He had, moreover, an exceptional power of drawing conclusions from a complicated set of facts: he could see what followed from them all taken together, or at least what might follow, in cases where others could draw no conclusions whatever. And, with all this, he produced the impression of also possessing the soundest common sense: his subtlety and ingenuity did not lead him, as it seems to have led some philosophers, to deny obvious facts. He had, moreover, so it seemed to me, an excellent sense of proportion: he could see which problems were the most fundamental, and it was these in which he was most interested and which he was most anxious to solve. For all these reasons, and perhaps for others as well, I almost always felt, with regard to any subject which we discussed, that he understood it much better than I did, and where (as was often the case) he failed to convince me, I generally thought the probability was that he was right and I wrong, and that my failure to agree with him was due to lack of mental power on my part.[4]

THE PERSON

The photographs in existence show him as being powerfully built and tall. He was a good 6 feet 3 inches and weighed about 17 stone. He had rather a round face, prominent cheekbones and a wide mouth. His eyes were hidden behind a pair of small, round spectacles of the kind in fashion today. Ramsey's hair, which judging by the photographs was always unkempt, thinned out with the years. As regards his style of dress, it is said that he preferred a more easy-going and relaxed style to being well-dressed in a formal sense.

As an individual, Ramsey is said to have been both shy and friendly. He had no need to assert himself. Besides Ramsey's friendly manner, his gurgling and infectious laugh seems to be what his friends remember most clearly. What I have said is brought out in the excellent picture Keynes paints in his obituary:

> The loss of Ramsey is, therefore, to his friends, for whom his personal qualities joined most harmoniously with his intellectual powers, one which it will take them long to forget. His bulky Johnsonian frame, his spontaneous gurgling laugh, the simplicity of his feelings and reactions, half-alarming sometimes and occasionally almost cruel in their directness and literalness, his honesty of mind and heart, his modesty, and the amazing, easy efficiency of the intellectual machine which ground away behind his wide temples and broad, smiling face, have been taken from us at the height of their excellence and before their harvest of work and life could be gathered in.[5]

We also get a glimpse of Ramsey's personality through his own happy attitude towards life as it can be discerned in a paper read to the Apostles, a Cambridge discussion society in 1925.

> Where I seem to differ from some of my friends is in attaching little importance to physical size. I don't feel the least humble before the vastness of the heavens. The stars may be large, but they cannot think or love; and these are qualities which impress me far more than size does. I take no credit for weighing nearly seventeen stone.
>
> My picture of the world is drawn in perspective, and not like a model to scale. The foreground is occupied by human beings and the stars are all as small as threepenny bits. I don't really believe in astronomy, except as a complicated description of part of the course of human and possibly animal sensation. I apply my perspective not merely to space but also to time. In time the world will cool and everything will die; but that is a long time off still, and its present value at compound discount is almost nothing. Nor is the present less valuable because the future will be blank. Humanity, which fills the foreground of my picture, I find interesting and on the whole admirable. I find, just now at least, the world a pleasant and exciting place. You may find it depressing; I am sorry for you, and you despise me. But I have reason and you have none; you would only have a reason for despising me if your feeling

corresponded to the fact in a way mine didn't. But neither can correspond to the fact. The fact is not good or bad; it is just that it thrills me but depresses you. On the other hand, I pity you with reason, because it is pleasanter to be thrilled than to be depressed, and not merely pleasanter but better for all one's activities.[6]

COLLEAGUES

At the beginning of this century Cambridge was, as we have noted so many times in this book, one of the foremost universities in the field of philosophical research. It was there that philosophers such as W. E. Johnson, Bertrand Russell, A. N. Whitehead, G. E. Moore and the economist J. M. Keynes worked. These philosophers crucially influenced our way of looking at philosophy, mathematics and economics. But I should also like to add to the group of Cambridge thinkers Ludwig Wittgenstein, although he belongs to a somewhat later phase. With the *Tractatus*, he made sure that professional philosophers were fully occupied, and, for better and worse, he also forced Cambridge into a special pattern of philosophical thought.

Ramsey was born in the same year as Russell's *The Principles of Mathematics* came out. Keynes writes that one has the feeling that from his nursery not far from Magdalene, Ramsey unconsciously absorbed all that was written and said at Trinity, alluding to the work of Russell and others. But remarkably enough, Ramsey, who grew up surrounded by heavy philosophical names, was almost self-taught. The only one who in some measure could be called his teacher is Moore. But even Moore was more of an equal in discussion than a teacher, as the above quotation suggests. This is not to say that Johnson, Russell and Keynes lacked influence on Ramsey's intellectual maturity. As we noted in the preceding chapters, Ramsey often used these thinkers as a launching pad for his own research. But the one who, in this respect, had the greatest importance for his philosophy is perhaps Wittgenstein. Not that Ramsey blindly accepted his philosophy. Ramsey was far too clear-sighted not to perceive the defects of *Tractatus* at an early stage. All the same, a work can be a source of inspiration, even if one does not accept the writer's theses. The defects of a theory may induce efforts to find something better. Personally, I believe that Wittgenstein was far more influenced by Ramsey than Ramsey was influenced by Wittgenstein. Since there is also a good deal of material about their relationship (as a result of the great interest in Wittgenstein) while corresponding material about Ramsey's other colleagues is largely lacking, I shall give a more detailed account of their relationship.

In 1922 Wittgenstein's *Logisch-Philosophiche Abhandlung* of 1921 was published in a bi-lingual version, this time under the title *Tractatus Logico-Philosophicus*, a title which Moore seems to have suggested. Wittgenstein's aphoristic style caused many, including Moore, to doubt whether it was possible to translate the book at all. Ramsey was extremely interested in Wittgenstein's text and Ogden suggested to him that he should try to translate it. At this time, Ramsey was only 18 years old, so perhaps the incident with Mach's text a few years earlier prompted Ogden to believe that Ramsey, if anyone, would be able to translate it. During the winter of 1921–2 Ramsey went now and again to the university typing office and dictated straight off a translation of the *Tractatus* to the office secretary. Having Ramsey translate the book proved to be a stroke of genius. *Tractatus* was published in 1922, C. K. Ogden being the editor.

But it was not until 1923 that Ramsey had the opportunity to meet Wittgenstein. Ogden wrote to Wittgenstein, who was at the time at Puchberg (a small Alpine village to which he had retreated), and explained that Ramsey would like to meet him. In a letter to Ramsey, Wittgenstein says:

> I've got a letter from Mr. Ogden the other day saying that you may possibly come to Vienna in one of these next months. Now as you have so excellently translated the Tractatus into English I've no doubt you will be able to translate a letter too and therefore I'm going to write the rest of this one in German.[7]

Ramsey went to visit Wittgenstein for a week or two and had the chance of discussing the difficulties he had with the *Tractatus*. In an often-quoted letter to his mother, he describes life in Puchberg in a most delightful fashion:

Wittgenstein is a teacher in the Village school. He is very poor, at least he lives very economically. He has one *tiny* room whitewashed, containing a bed, washstand, small table and one hard chair and that is all there is room for. His evening meal which I shared last night is rather unpleasant coarse bread, butter and cocoa. His school hours are 8 to 12 or 1 and he seems to be free all the afternoon.

He looks younger than he can possibly be; but he says he has bad eyes and a cold. But his general appearance is athletic. In explaining his philosophy he is excited and makes vigorous gestures but relieves the tension by a charming laugh. He has blue eyes.

He is prepared to give 4 to 5 hours a day to explaining his book. I have had two days and got through 7 (+ identical forward references) out of 80 pages. And when the book is done I shall try to pump him for ideas for its further development which I shall attempt. He says he himself will do nothing more, not because he is bored, but because his mind is no longer flexible. He says no one can do more than 5 or 10 years work at philosophy. (His book took 7). And he is sure Russell will do nothing more important. His idea of his book is not that anyone by reading it will understand his ideas, but that some day someone will think them out again for himself, and will derive great pleasure from finding in this book their exact expressions. I think he exaggerates his own verbal inspiration, it is much more careful than I supposed but I think it reflects the way the ideas came to him which might not be the same with another man.

He has already answered my chief difficulty which I have puzzled over for a year and given up in despair myself and decided he had not seen. (It is not in the 1st 7 pages but arose by the way.) He is great. I used to think Moore a great man but beside W!

He says I shall forget everything he explains in a few days; Moore in Norway said he understood W completely and when he got back to England was no wiser than when he started.

It's terrible when he says 'Is that clear' and I say 'no' and he says 'Damn it's *horrid* to go through that again'. Sometimes he says I can't see that now we must leave it. He often forgot the meaning of what he wrote within 5 min[ute]s, and then remembered it later. Some of his sentences are intentionally ambiguous having an ordinary meaning and a more difficult meaning which he also believes.

He is, I can see, a little annoyed that Russell is doing a new edit[ion] of Principia because he thought he had shown R that it was so wrong that a new edition would be futile. It must be done altogether afresh. He had a week with Russell 4 y[ea]rs ago. (September 20, 1923).[8]

Ramsey's and Wittgenstein's conversations resulted in both the English translation and the German original being altered, alterations that were made in the second edition of the *Tractatus* which came out 1923.

There are a few other letters from Ramsey to Wittgenstein from this period in existence. In one of the letters Ramsey reveals that he tried to figure out whether the continuum hypothesis was true or false.

Ramsey went back to Vienna in March 1924 to see Wittgenstein again. But he does not seem to have had much satisfaction from the conversations with him on the four occasions that they met. After that, they seem to have lost touch. At home in Cambridge, Ramsey tried to arrange financial backing for Wittgenstein to come to Cambridge and do research. He also seems to have worked hard to give Wittgenstein the necessary academic qualifications he needed to get a post at the university (the result of his efforts was that *Tractatus* was finally accepted as a Ph.D. thesis). When Wittgenstein moved to Cambridge in 1929, he and Ramsey resumed their acquaintance and are said to have met often and discussed philosophy.

Notes

PREFACE

1. P. 259, 127 or 111. References of this type are to *The Foundations of Mathematics and Other Logical Essays*, ed. R. B. Braithwaite, Routledge & Kegan Paul, London 1931; *Foundations: Essays in Philosophy, Logic, Mathematics and Economics*, ed. D. H. Mellor, Routledge & Kegan Paul, London 1978, *Philosophical Papers*, ed. D. H. Mellor, Cambridge University Press, Cambridge 1990, respectively.

INTRODUCTION

1. See D. H. Mellor, 'The Eponymous F. P. Ramsey', *Journal of Graph Theory*, 7 (1983), 9–13.
2. P. x, Basil Blackwell, Oxford 1953.
3. This example was given by R. B. Braithwaite in D. H. Mellor's radio program, 'Better than the Stars', BBC Radio 3, 27 February 1978.
4. Princeton University Press, Princeton 1944.
5. 'The Eponymous F. P. Ramsey', 12.

CHAPTER 1

1. Ramsey's paper has been discussed by, e.g., R. C. Jeffrey, *The Logic of Decision*, New York 1965, 2d ed., Chicago 1983; and K. Berka, "Ramsey's Logic of Partial Belief', *Theorie a Metoda*, 6 (1974), 67–84. See also *Decision, Probability, and Utility* ed. P. Gärdenfors and N.-E. Sahlin, Cambridge University Press 1987.

2. For a discussion of the historical developments of probability theory and for further references, see I. Hacking, *The Emergence of Probability,* Cambridge University Press 1975; and I. Todhunter, *A History of Mathematical Probability,* Chelsea Publishing Company, New York 1965.

3. Macmillan, London 1921. See also Ramsey's 'Mr Keynes on Probability', *Cambridge Magazine,* 11 (1922), 3–5.

4. P. 177, 79 or 73. References of this type are to *The Foundations of Mathematics and Other Logical Essays,* ed. R. B. Braithwaite, Routledge & Kegan Paul, London 1931; *Foundations: Essays in Philosophy, Logic, Mathematics and Economics,* ed. D. H. Mellor, Routledge & Kegan Paul, London 1978, *Philosophical Papers,* ed. D. H. Mellor, Cambridge University Press, Cambridge 1990, respectively.

   Ramsey follows Wittgenstein's distinction between atomic and non-atomic propositions. An atomic proposition can be true or false independent of the truth and falsity of any other atomic proposition. And a non-atomic proposition is a truth-functional compound of atomic ones. A non-atomic proposition is said to be *ethically neutral* if all its atomic truth arguments are ethically neutral. As we shall see in Chapter 4, Ramsey abandoned parts of Wittgenstein's theory in his paper 'General Propositions and Causality', which was written three years after the one discussed in this chapter.

5. The preference relation S can be defined in terms of P, i.e., aSb, if and only if $-(a$P$b)\&-(b$P$a)$, presuming a complete ordering to guarantee indifference in the sense of equality in value or preference.

6. P. 178, 80 or 74.

7. See D. Davidson, P. Suppes and S. Siegel, *Decision Making,* Stanford 1957; and J. A. Glaze, 'The Association of Nonsense Syllables', *Journal of Genetic Psychology,* 35 (1928), 255–67.

8. 'Preference among Preferences as a Method for Obtaining a Higher Ordered Metric Scale', *British Journal of Mathematical and Statistical Psychology,* 34 (1981), 62–75.

9. 'An Axiomatization of Utility Based on the Notion of Utility Differences', *Management Science,* 1 (1955), 259–70.

10. *The Foundations of Decision Logic,* Lund 1980, 77–82.

11. 'Preference among Preferences', *Journal of Philosophy,* 71 (1974), 377–91.

12. 'Freedom of the Will and the Concept of a Person', *Journal of Philosophy,* **68** (1971), 5–20.
13. See P. Suppes, 'The Role of Subjective Probability and Utility in Decision-making', in *Proceedings from 3rd Berkeley Symposium on Mathematics, Statistics and Probability,* ed. I. Neyman, University of California Press 1956, 61–73. Suppes's terminology is 'structure' and 'rationality' axioms.
14. See D. Kahneman, P. Slovic and A. Tversky, *Judgment under Uncertainty: Heuristics and Biases,* Cambridge University Press, New York 1982.
15. See N.-E. Sahlin, 'The Significance of Empirical Evidence for Developments in the Foundations of Decision Theory', in *Theory and Experiment,* ed. D. Batens and J. P. van Bendegem, Reidel, Dordrecht 1988, 103–21.
16. This is still another of the dice constructed in the light of Glaze's experimental results.
17. Since the distinction between the two kinds of axioms is somewhat slippery, one may well argue that there are conditions under which these axioms must be viewed as structural axioms. If, for example, we question ordering, axiom R3 could be taken to be a structural rather than a rationality axiom. For Ramsey, however, these axioms are *rationality axioms* – axioms which will, if we follow them, lead to sound behaviour.
18. This means that the utility function $u'(.)$ obtained from $u(.)$ by multiplication with a positive constant k and adding another constant l represents the same basic preferences.
19. Note that $a_{\frac{1}{2}}$ and $p_{\frac{1}{2}}$ generally are different propositions.
20. Pp. 179–80, 81–2 or 75–6.
21. A well-known problem with Ramsey's definition of probability is that it fails to handle state-dependent utilities (which is also true for the alternative suggestions by Savage and de Finetti). Ramsey assumes that the utility of a is the same as the utility of $a\&p$ and the same as utility of $a\&-p$ (see the above discussion of ethically neutral propositions and compare with (i)). That is, we must assume that the utility of 'becoming a clergyman' is the same as the utility of 'becoming a clergyman and the economic situation will improve'.
22. P. 180, 82 or 76.
23. Ibid.
24. Ramsey prefers to prove that the obtained measure of degree

of belief has the following properties: (1) $P(p) + P(-p) = 1$, (2) $P(p/q) + P(-p/q) = 1$, (3) $P(p\&q) = P(p)P(q/p)$ and $P(p\&q) + P(p\&-q) = P(p)$. Proving (1) and (2) is straightforward, and (4) follows when (3) is proved. That (3) is satisfied can be shown by the same method as was used above. What we have not proved is that $P(p/q) = P(p\&q)/P(p)$, i.e., Ramsey's (3). The proof is given in Ramsey's paper.

25. P. 183, 85 or 79.
26. *The Matter of Chance*, Cambridge University Press 1971, 31. The question of bettable propositions was raised in A. Shimony, 'Coherence and the Axioms of Confirmation', *Journal of Symbolic Logic*, **20** (1955), 1–28.
27. 'Foresight: Its Logical Laws, Its Subjective Sources', in *Studies in Subjective Probability*, ed. H. E. Kyburg and H. E. Smoker, Huntington, New York 1980, 62.
28. We assumed that (50 pence)$\mathbf{P}$(1 pound; $p_{\frac{1}{2}}$; nothing). This preference implies that u(50 pence) $> \frac{1}{2}u$(1 pound) $+ \frac{1}{2}u$(nothing). This in turn means that u(50 pence) $- u$(nothing) $> u$(1 pound) $- u$(50 pence); i.e., the marginal utility is decreasing. We have, of course, assumed that (1 pound)$\mathbf{P}$(50 pence)$\mathbf{P}$(nothing). For a presentation and discussion of this definition of risk aversion see, e.g., K. J. Arrow, *Essays in the Theory of Risk Bearing*, Amsterdam 1974. The definition is also discussed in more detail in Chapter 9.
29. I develop this criticism in 'Levels of Aspiration and Risk', *Philosophical Studies*, no. 24, Department of Philosophy, Lund University 1984.
30. See I. Hacking, *The Emergence of Probability*, Cambridge University Press, Cambridge 1975, 94.
31. P. 183, 85 or 79.
32. This type of problem is discussed, e.g., in *Decision, Probability, and Utility: Selected Readings*, ed. P. Gärdenfors and N.-E. Sahlin, Cambridge University Press, Cambridge 1987.
33. Pp. 182–3, 84–5 or 78–9.
34. P. 180, 82 or 76.
35. Theories based on this idea have been developed, e.g., by I. Levi, 'On Indeterminate Probabilities', *Journal of Philosophy*, **71** (1974), 391–418; and P. Gärdenfors and N.-E. Sahlin, 'Unreliable Probabilities, Risk Taking, and Decision Making', *Synthese*, **53** (1982), 361–86. Both articles are reprinted in *Decision, Probability, and Utility*.

36. Pp. 190–1, 92–3 or 86–7.
37. Frank Ramsey Collection, document number 007-06-02, Archives of Scientific Philosophy in the Twentieth Century, University of Pittsburgh.
38. Ramsey explicitly acknowledges a debt to Peirce, but the similarity between what he says and Peirce says is rather superficial. However, a full discussion of how Ramsey's view of propability relates to Peirce's view would fall outside the scope of this chapter.
39. P. 144, 46 or 40.
40. P. 206 (*The Foundations of Mathematics*) or 104 (*Philosophical Papers*). The note 'Chance' is not reprinted in *Foundations*.
41. P. 206 or 104.
42. P. 208 or 106.
43. See, for example, *Decision, Probability and Utility*.
44. For those interested in the history of Bayesianism and subjective probability theory, I conclude this chapter by mentioning that Ramsey in an unpublished note 'Weight or the value of knowledge' (Frank Ramsey Collection, document numbers 005-20-01 and 005-20-03, Archives of Scientific Philosophy in the Twentieth Century, University of Pittsburgh; this note is forthcoming, *British Journal for the Philosophy of Science*, **41** (1990)) gives a proof of the value of collecting evidence; i.e., there is a proof of this fact about 30 years earlier than the well-known and corresponding proofs of I. J. Good and L. J. Savage.
    Ramsey's proof is as follows:

Weight or the Value of Knowledge

Suppose a is an unknown proposition.

$\varphi(p)$ expectation of advantage in regard to a if I expect it with probability p.

Then $\varphi''(p) > 0$.

For: Suppose $x_1, x_2, \ldots$ are variables I can alter by my action.

Good to me if $a = f_1(x_1, x_2, \ldots)$

$$\bar{a} = f_2(x_1, x_2, \ldots)$$

If I expect a with prob[ability] p I act so as to maximise

$$pf_1 + (1 - p)f_2 \quad \text{for fixed given } p$$

i.e. I make

$$(1) \quad p(\partial f_1/\partial x_r) + (1 - p)(\partial f_2/\partial x_r) = 0,$$

$r = 1, 2, \ldots,$ and

$$(2)\ pd^2f_1 + (1 - p)d^2f_2 < 0$$
My expectation of advantage
$$\varphi(p) = pf_1 + (1 - p)f_2,$$
with x's def[ined] by (1).

In what follows I have cut out some details of the proof

$\varphi'(p) = f_1 - f_2$, whatever p.
$\varphi''(p) = d/dp\{f_1 - f_2\}$.

Now differentiating (1) w.r.t. $p[$, Ramsey finds that $\varphi''(p)] > 0$ by (2).

45. In a note, '*Reconsideration on Causality, Probability etc.*', dated September 1929 (Frank Ramsey Collection, document numbers 002-30-01 to 002-30-03), Ramsey expresses some doubts about his own theory:

> What is wrong with my probability is its externality. The 'form of thought' which makes it impossible to think illogically is a form which thought *haben soll*.

After a few remarks in German about some of Wittgenstein's familiar ideas on the topic, he continues:

> It is just like chess; in a game of chess you can't have 10 white queens on the board, [since] the emphasis is on *chess*. You can put them on the board if you like but that isn't chess.
> So also in thought you cannot have $p-p$; you can write that if you like but it would not be thought.
> But I think we can define chess. Can we define thought, and is there any such thing? What are its rules and who plays it? It isn't common; it is something to which we approximate by getting our language clear. 'All our everyday prop[osition]s are in order' is absolutely false, and shows the absurdity of interpreting logic as a part of natural science. All this is even clearer in my probability theory. Degree of belief is a useless scientific conception, and should not be introduced as one.

Note that Ramsey alludes to a remark he makes in the essay "Philosophy":

> A typical piece of scholasticism is Wittgenstein's view that all our everyday propositions are completely in order and that it is

impossible to think illogically. (This last is like saying that it is impossible to break the rules of bridge because if you break them you are not playing bridge but, as Mrs C. says, not-bridge.)

P. 269 (*The Foundations of Mathematics*) or 7 (*Philosophical Papers*).

CHAPTER 2

1. *Guitarr och dragharmonika*, 1891. Translated and interpreted by Muriel Larsson for this book.
2. *Nachgelassene Schriften*, Hamburg 1969, pp. 271–2. I found this reference in S. Blackburn, *Spreading the Word*, Oxford 1984.
3. Pt. I, pp. 52–3.
4. In his unpublished book manuscript, Ramsey mentions that he found the same idea in the works of Aristotle and Kant (Frank Ramsey Collection, document numbers 001-01-01 – 001-11-01, Archives of Scientific Philosophy in the Twentieth Century, University of Pittsburgh). This manuscript will be published as a book: F. P. Ramsey, *On Truth*, ed. N. Rescher and U. Majer, in press Reidel.
5. P. 142, 44 or 38.
6. Pp. 142–3, 44–5 or 38–9.
7. Clarendon Press, Oxford 1971, 11.
8. *Objects of Thought*, 12.
9. *Philosophy of Phenomenological Research*, 4 (1944), 341–76.
10. That is ($\exists p$) [Plato wrote p & (q) (if Plato wrote q, and $q \neq p$, then he wrote q after p) and p is true].
11. Tarski's first example, 'All consequences of true sentences are true', can be dealt with in the following way:

    For all p and for all q, if p, and if p then q, then q is true,

a sentence from which 'true' is easily eliminated.
12. One should not forget that Ramsey says 'Truth and falsity are ascribed primarily to propositions' (p. 142, 44 or 38) and that we now are talking about sentences.
13. *Objects of Thought*, 25.
14. 'Outline of a Theory of Truth', *Journal of Philosophy*, **72** (1975), 690–716.
15. *Philosophy of Logics*, Cambridge University Press, Cambridge

1978. See also 'Is Truth Flat or Bumpy?' in *Prospects for Pragmatism*, ed. D. H. Mellor, Cambridge University Press, Cambridge 1980.

16. See the discussion of general propositions in Chapter 4. According to Ramsey they are neither true nor false, as they carry no truth-value.
17. See 'Is Truth Flat or Bumpy?'
18. P. 187, 89 or 83.
19. P. 143, 45 or 39.
20. Harper & Row, New York 1961.
21. In *Inquiries into Truth and Interpretation*, Oxford 1984, 39.
22. See also J. L. Mackie, *Truth, Probability and Paradox*, Clarendon Press, Oxford 1973.
23. *Objects of Thought*, 37.
24. Ibid., 37.
25. P. 143, 45 or 39.
26. P. 275. The review of *Tractatus Logico-Philosophicus* was published in *Mind*, **32** (October 1923), 465–78 and is reprinted in *The Foundations of Mathematics*.
27. P. 138, 40 or 34.
28. R. M. Gale, 'Propositions, Judgments, Sentences, and Statements', in *Encyclopedia of Philosophy*, **6**, ed. Paul Edwards, Macmillan and Free Press, London 1967, 494–505.
29. P. 138, 40 or 34.
30. P. 140, 42 or 36.
31. In *Prospects for Pragmatism*, ed. D. H. Mellor, Cambridge University Press, Cambridge 1980. See also John Skorupski's, 'Ramsey on Belief', in the same volume.
32. See document number 001-11-01, i.e. *Ch III. Judgment* (or the same chapter in the published version of this script, *On Truth*, ed. N. Rescher and U. Majer, in press Reidel).
33. P. 143, 45 or 39.
34. P. 155, 57 or 51.
35. See the *Collected Papers of Charles Sanders Peirce*, ed. Charles Hartshorne and Paul Weiss, Cambridge, Mass. 1931–5, vol. 5, paras. 373, 400 and 27, respectively. I found these references in Hjalmar Wennerberg's *The Pragmatism of C. S. Peirce*, Library of Theoria, no. IX, Uppsala 1962, 121.
36. P. 144, 46 or 40.
37. This idea seems to me closely related to what is today referred to as a language of thought. See Jerry A. Fodor, *Representa-*

tions: Philosophical Essays on the Foundations of Cognitive Science,
MIT Press, Cambridge Mass. 1981.

38. Reading the manuscript one gets the feeling that these two
papers are simply condensed versions of what would have
been two or more chapters in the final book. I also believe that
'Facts and Propositions' contains most of what would have
become a complete theory of belief and truth. The book
manuscript is thus rather secondary in this context and
Ramsey was himself not that satisfied with it (as he indicates
in a letter to C. K. Ogden).

39. P. 145, 47 or 41.

40. P. 147, 49 or 43.

41. P. 146, 48 or 42.

42. P. 117, 22 or 13.

43. Pp. 147–8, 49–50 or 43–4.

44. Pp. 149–50, 51–2 or 45–6.

45. Ramsey's analysis of general propositions is also discussed in
Chapter 4.

46. P. 153, 55 or 49.

47. Ibid.

48. P. 238, 134 or 146.

49. Nonsense sentences or ungrounded sentences are dealt with
in a similar way. In this case we have sentences for which
there are no rational-action alternatives whatsoever.

50. See D. M. Armstrong, *Belief, Truth and Knowledge,* Cambridge
University Press, Cambridge 1973, 4; and David Hume, *A
Treatise of Human Nature,* bk. I, pt. III, sect. 7.

51. For a more detailed comparison, see D. J. O'Connor and Brian
Carr, *Introduction to the Theory of Knowledge,* Harvester Press,
Brighton 1982. Also D. M. Armstrong's *Belief, Truth and
Knowledge.*

52. See J. A. Fodor, *Representations* and Z. Pylyshyn, 'Computa-
tion and cognition: Issues in the foundations of cognitive science', *Behavioral and Brain Sciences,* 3 (1980), 111–32.

53. See Peter Gärdenfors, *Knowledge in Flux: Modeling the Dynamics of Epistemic States,* MIT Press, Cambridge, Mass. 1988.

CHAPTER 3

1. See, e.g., A. J. Ayer, *The Problem of Knowledge,* London 1956;
D. J. O'Connor & B. Carr, *Introduction to the Theory of Knowl-*

edge, Harvester Press 1982; and Plato's dialogue *Theaetetus,* e.g., Clarendon Press, Oxford 1973.

2. The gist of this example is found in B. Russell, *The Problems of Philosophy,* Oxford University Press (1912) 1986.

3. See Wilson's posthumously published book *Statement and Inference,* ed. A. S. L. Farquharson, Oxford 1926.

4. 'Is Justified True Belief Knowledge?' *Analysis* **23** (1963), 121–3. The essay is also included in the anthology *Knowledge and Belief,* ed. A. P. Griffiths, Oxford 1973. Russell's example can be found in chap. 13 of *The Problems of Philosophy.*

5. P. 258, 126 or 110.

6. P. 144, 46 or 40.

7. Oxford University Press (1912) 1986, 81.

8. One of Russell's examples is as follows: 'If a newspaper, by an intelligent anticipation, announces the result of a battle before any telegram giving the result has been received, it may by good fortune announce what afterwards turns out to be the right result, and it may produce belief in some of its less experienced readers. But in spite of the truth of their belief, they cannot be said to have knowledge' (p. 76).

9. P. 258, 126 or 110.

10. See R. E. Grandy, 'Ramsey, Reliability and Knowledge', in *Prospects for Pragmatism,* ed. D. H. Mellor, Cambridge 1980; D. Armstrong, *Belief, Truth and Knowledge,* Cambridge 1973; P. Unger, 'An Analysis of Factual Knowledge', *Journal of Philosophy,* **65** (1968), 157–69; and J. Watling, 'Inference from the Known to the Unknown', *Proceedings of the Aristotelian Society,* **55** (1954), 83–108.

11. 'A Causal Theory of Knowing', *Journal of Philosophy,* **64** (1967), 355–72.

12. P. 258, 126 or 110.

13. See the introduction (p. 24) to *Essays on Knowledge and Justification,* ed. G. S. Pappas and M. Swain, Cornell University Press, Ithaca 1978.

14. Harvard University Press 1983, chap. 3.

15. See M. Edman, 'Adding Independent Pieces of Evidence', in *Modality, Morality, and Other Problems of Sense and Nonsense,* Lund 1973; S. Halldén, 'Indiciemekanismer', *Tidskrift for Rettsvitenskap,* **86** (1973), 55–64; P. O. Ekelöf, *Rättegång IV,* femte upplagan, Stockholm 1982; and *Evidentiary Value,* ed. P. Gärdenfors, B. Hansson and N.-E. Sahlin, Lund 1983.

16. A discussion of examples showing how these two types of theories lead to different results can be found in N.-E. Sahlin, ' "How to Be 100% Certain 99.5% of the Time" ', *Journal of Philosophy*, **83** (1986), 91–111.

CHAPTER 4

1. Pp. 152–3, 54–5 or 48–9.
2. *Logic*, pt. II, Cambridge 1922, 59.
3. In the discussion for this chapter, I have relied greatly on J. O. Urmson, *Philosophical Analysis*, Oxford 1956.
4. P. 154, 56 or 50.
5. P. 238, 134 or 146.
6. Most likely Hermann Weyl's view of 'general propositions' has influenced Ramsey; see, e.g., U. Majer, 'Ramsey's Conception of Theories: An Intuitionistic Approach', *History of Philosophy Quarterly*, **6** (1989), 233–58.
7. P. 238, 134 or 146.
8. Ibid.
9. Ibid.
10. See *Logic*, pt. II, chap. 1.
11. See Braithwaite, 'The Idea of Necessary Connexion', *Mind* **36** (1927), 467–77, **37** (1928), 63–72.
12. Pp. 249–50, 145–6 or 157–8.
13. P. 131 (*Foundations*) or 143 (*Philosophical Papers*). The essay 'Universals of Law and of Fact' (1928) was not included in the volume of Ramsey's work edited by Braithwaite.
14. P. 131 or 143.
15. P. 242, 138 or 150. See also *Counterfactuals*, Blackwell, Oxford 1973.
16. P. 241, 137 or 149.
17. Ibid.
18. P. 244, 140 or 152.
19. Pp. 244–5, 140–1 or 152–3.
20. P. 253, 149 or 161.
21. See, for example, W. Quine, *Word and Object*, New York 1960.
22. See 'The Problem of Natural Laws' in *Prospects for Pragmatism*, ed. D. H. Mellor, Cambridge University Press, Cambridge 1980.
23. It is most likely that what Ramsey is discussing in the text

quoted next, and what has become known as the Ramsey test for conditionals, is not at all a test for conditional propositions. It is no more, no less, than the traditional theory for conditional probabilities (see his discussion of conditional probabilities in 'Truth and Probability').

24. Pp. 246–7, 142–3 or 154–5.

25. See 'A Theory of Conditionals' in *Causation and Conditionals*, ed. E. Sosa, Oxford University Press, Oxford 1975. The Ramsey test is discussed in a number of papers in the anthology *Ifs*, ed. W. L. Harper, R. Stalnaker and G. Pearce, Reidel, Dordrecht 1981.

26. See P. Gärdenfors, 'Belief Revisions and the Ramsey Test for Conditionals', *Philosophical Review*, 45 (1985), 81–93. A careful and critical analysis of this result is carried out by Isaac Levi in 'Iteration of Conditionals and the Ramsey Test', *Synthese*, 76 (1988), 49–81. Levi argues, for example, that if conditionals are neither true nor false they cannot be iterated and thus the conflict between (R) and (B) disappears. My position is that we have the same conflict even if we do not consider this type of proposition to carry truth-value; a concept of acceptability is all that is needed.

27. For an analysis of sentences like 'It is necessary that . . .' or 'It is possible that . . .' these dynamic factors are totally uninteresting.

28. The type of theories needed for a more formal formulation of these ideas can be found in, e.g., I. Levi, *The Enterprise of Knowledge*, MIT Press, Cambridge, Mass. 1980; and P. Gärdenfors and N.-E. Sahlin, 'Unreliable Probabilities, Risk Taking, and Decision Making', *Synthese*, 53 (1982), 361–86.

CHAPTER 5

1. See the first quotation in Chapter 10.

2. E. Nagel, *The Structure of Science*, Routledge & Kegan Paul, London 1974.

3. In my presentation of the traditional theory of the philosophy of science, in this section and in the following sections, I have drawn several examples from R. Carnap's book *Philosophical Foundations of Physics*, Basic Books, New York 1966. I have also relied on C. G. Hempel, *Philosophy of Natural Science*, Prentice-Hall, Englewood Cliffs, N.J. 1966, and Nagel's book. Another

important book is N. R. Campbell, *Physics: The Elements,* Cambridge University Press, Cambridge 1920, which I believe influenced Ramsey a great deal, although he did not fully accept its ideas.

4. See *Aspects of Scientific Explanation,* Free Press, New York 1965, 186.
5. Cambridge University Press, Cambridge (1953) 1968.
6. A good discussion of Ramsey's somewhat laborious example and of his paper can be found in U. Majer's paper 'Ramsey's Conception of Theories: An Intuitionistic Approach', *History of Philosophy Quarterly,* **6** (1989), 233–58.
7. P. 219, 108 or 119.
8. P. 220, 109 or 120.
9. Pp. 222–3, 111–12 or 122–3.
10. P. 230, 119 or 130.
11. See *Scientific Explanation,* Cambridge University Press, Cambridge 1968, 76.
12. See I. Hacking, *Representing and Intervening,* Cambridge University Press, Cambridge 1983.
13. *Philosophical Foundations of Physics,* 231.
14. See S. Toulmin and J. Goodfield, *The Architecture of Matter,* Penguin Books, Middlesex 1968, 283–5.
15. P. 230, 119 or 130. R. Tuomola, *Theoretical Concepts,* Springer, New York 1973, presents a number of examples of the above-mentioned type. Tuomola's book contains a detailed analysis of various possible interpretations of the Ramsey–Braithwaite thesis.
16. Ramsey begins the presentation and discussion of his own theory on p. 231, 120 or 131, and from that page on he does not use any words like 'elimination' or 'reduction', i.e., words that could suggest that he was trying to eliminate the theoretical terms. He simply had no such idea in mind.
17. P. 231, 120 or 131.
18. See *Philosophical Foundations of Physics,* pt. V, chap. 26. It should be kept in mind that Carnap's own interpretation of Ramsey's theory is on several points the opposite of the one advocated in this book.
19. P. 231, 120 or 131.
20. See Chapter 1.
21. P. 232, 121 or 132.
22. Ibid.

23. See 'In Defense of Ramsey's Elimination Method', *Journal of Philosophy*, **65** (1968), 275–9.

24. P. 233, 122 or 133.

25. See, e.g., H. Poincaré, *The Value of Science*, New York 1958.

26. In his book *Representing and Intervening*, Ian Hacking presents and discusses the ideas of representatives of different realist and anti-realist positions.

27. See the quotations directly connected to nn. 15 and 16 of Chapter 4.

28. U. Majer (Ibid.) shows that Ramsey is heavily influenced by the works of Heinrich Hertz and Hermann Weyl, a fact which is far from obvious if one reads Ramsey's published papers. However, reading what Ramsey says in his unpublished papers and notes, this line of intellectual influence becomes rather clear.

29. Pp. 260–1 (*The Foundation of Mathematics*) or 137–8 (*Philosophical Papers*). The essay is not included in *Foundations*.

30. See Braithwaite's book. D. Lewis, 'How to Define Theoretical Terms', *Journal of Philosophy*, **67** (1970), 427–46, uses Ramsey sentences to justify a realistic view of theoretical terms. For an instrumentalistic standpoint, see J. W. Cornman, 'Craig's Theorem, Ramsey's Theorem, and Scientific Instrumentalism', *Synthese*, **25** (1972), 82–128.

31. See H. G. Bohnert, 'In Defence of Ramsey's Elimination Method', *Journal of Philosophy*, **65** (1968), 275–81; I. Scheffler, *The Anatomy of Inquiry*, Knopf, New York 1963, and 'Reflections on the Ramsey Method', *Journal of Philosophy*, **65** (1968), 269–74; and W. Stegmüller, *Theorie und Erfahrung*, Springer, Berlin 1970.

32. *The Anatomy of Inquiry*, 205–7. But see also 'Reflections on the Ramsey Method', *Journal of Philosophy*, **65** (1968), 269–74; and Stegmüller, *Theorie und Erfahrung*, 431–7.

33. Ramsey's theory as a theory of elimination is discussed and developed in, e.g., J. Sneed, *The Logical Structure of Mathematical Physics*, Reidel, Dordrecht 1971; W. Stegmüller, *The Structure and Dynamics of Theories*, Springer, Berlin 1976; and J. W. N. Watkins, 'Metaphysics and the Advancement of Science', *British Journal for the Philosophy of Science*, **26** (1975), 91–121. For further references, see also Carnap, *Philosophical Foundations of Physics*; Scheffler, *The Anatomy of Inquiry*; and Tuomola, *Theoretical Concepts*.

CHAPTER 6

1. P. xi.
2. See, e.g., I. M. Copi, *The Theory of Logical Types*, Routledge & Kegan Paul, London 1971.
3. See *From Frege to Gödel*, ed. J. van Heijenoort, Harvard University Press, Cambridge, Mass. 1977, 124–8.
4. See S. Halldén, *The Logic of Nonsense*, Uppsala 1949 (especially pp. 124–5 and n. 6) for a discussion of alternative theories of types and for some important historical clarifications.
5. See *The Principles of Mathematics*, 523.
6. *American Journal of Mathematics*, **30** (1908), 222–62.
7. *Principia Mathematica*, 2d ed., Cambridge University Press 1973, 37. It should be pointed out that this principle can be interpreted in a number of different ways. See K. Gödel, 'Russell's Mathematical Logic', in *Philosophy of Mathematics*, ed. P. Benacerraf and H. Putnam, Cambridge 1985.
8. *Principia Mathematica*, 55. It is not obvious what ontological status propositional functions and propositions have according to Whitehead and Russell. See W. V. O. Quine, *Set Theory and Its Logic*, Harvard University Press, Cambridge Mass. 1970.
9. For a discussion of other semantic conditions see Halldén, *The Logic of Nonsense*.
10. Among Ramsey's unpublished manuscripts there is a longer paper called 'Identity' in which he discusses this problem in more detail; the paper (or, better, the notes) is rather formal and somewhat difficult to follow.
11. For a more detailed analysis of various theories of types see, e.g., J. Jörgensen, *A Treatise of Formal Logic*, Köpenhamn 1931, vol. III; K. Gödel, 'Russell's Mathematical Logic'; and Halldén, *Logic of Nonsense*.
12. P. 24, 175 or 187.
13. P. 28, 179 or 191.
14. See, e.g., pp. 41–2, 192–3 or 204–5.
15. P. 41, 192 or 204.
16. P. 48, 199 or 211.
17. See definition *13.01.
18. P. 61, 212 or 224.
19. P. 252, 148 or 160.
20. See T. J. Jech, "About the Axiom of Choice", in *Handbook of*

Mathematical Logic, ed. J. Barwise, North-Holland, New York 1978, pp. 345–70.
21. See ibid., 351.
22. Pp. 57–8, 208–9 or 220–1.
23. P. 59, 210 or 222.
24. P. 4, 155 or 167.
25. P. 5, 156 or 68.
26. P. 17, 168 or 180.

CHAPTER 7

1. P. 3, 154 or 166.
2. P. 2, 153 or 165.
3. See A. Church, *Introduction to Mathematical Logic*, Princeton University Press 1956.
4. See, e.g., R. L. Graham, B. L. Rothschild and J. H. Spencer, *Ramsey Theory*, Wiley, New York 1980. Note that it is enough that the relation of 'knowing' is symmetric; a transitive relation is not required.
5. See ibid.; and K. Kunen, 'Combinatorics', in *Handbook of Mathematical Logic*, ed. J. Barwise, New York 1978. I have borrowed most of Kunen's figures.
6. See R. L. Graham et al., 74–6.
7. I believe that Ramsey's own presentation of the theorem is educational:

> THEOREM A. Let Γ be an infinite class, and μ and r positive integers; and let all those sub-classes of Γ which have exactly r members, or, as we may say, let all r-combinations of the members of Γ be divided in any manner into μ mutually exclusive classes C_i $(i = 1, 2, \ldots, \mu)$, so that every r-combination is a member of one and only one C_i; then, assuming the Axiom of Selections, Γ must contain an infinite sub-class Δ such that all the r-combinations of the members of Δ belong to the same C_i.
> P. 82 or 233, not included in *Philosophical Papers*.

8. A discussion of the relation between Ramsey's theorem and various choice principles can be found in, for example, E. M. Kleinberg, 'The Independence of Ramsey's Theorem', *Journal of Symbolic Logic*, **34** (1969), 205–6; A. Blass, 'Ramsey's Theorem in the Hierarchy of Choice Principles', *Journal of Symbolic Logic*, **42** (1977), 387–90; and G. Lolli, 'On Ramsey's Theorem

and the Axiom of Choice', *Notre Dame Journal of Formal Logic*, **18** (1977), 599–601.

9. *Logik, filosofi och språk*, Stockholm 1971, 86.
10. For a detailed non-mathematical presentation of Gödel's theorem see, for example, B. Rosser, 'An Informal Exposition of Proofs of Gödel's Theorems and Church's Theorem', *Journal of Symbolic Logic*, **4** (1939), 53–60; and E. Nagel and J. R. Newman, *Gödel's Proof*, New York University Press 1958.
11. See J. Paris and L. Harrington, 'A Mathematical Incompleteness in Peano Arithmetic', in *Handbook of Mathematical Logic*, ed. J. Barwise, New York 1978; J. Paris 'Some Independence Results for Peano Arithmetic', *Journal of Symbolic Logic*, **43** (1978), 725–31; and J. Ketonen and R. Solovay, 'Rapidly Growing Ramsey Functions', *Annals of Mathematics*, **113** (1981), 267–314.
12. See D. Normann, 'Det uendelige – en matematisk nødvendighet', *Normat* (1984), 67.

CHAPTER 8

1. P. 117, 22 or 13.
2. P. 116, 21 or 12.
3. See 'On the Relations of Universals and Particulars', in *Logic and Knowledge*, ed. R. Marsh, London 1956, 104–24; and *Logic*, pt. I, Cambridge University Press 1921, 11.
4. P. 132, 37 or 28.
5. P. 118, 23 or 14.
6. See N. Goodman, *Fact, Fiction, and Forecast*, Hackett, Indianapolis 1979. Reinhardt Grossmann, *The Categorial Structure of the World*, Indiana University Press, Bloomington 1983, pt. II, chap. 2, also notes that Ramsey's theory can be applied to get rid of this problem. Grossmann shows how some other philosophical problems, stemming from the assumption that there are complex properties, disappear, once we have accepted the correctness of Ramsey's analysis. For example, it is pointed out that the view that there are individual essences becomes untenable (pp. 153–4).
7. Duckworth, 1973, 61–7.
8. P. 147, 49 or 43.
9. P. 146, 48 or 42.
10. P. 117, 22 or 13.

11. *Mind*, **40** (1931), 476–82.
12. One reason for mentioning this type of theory is that a theory with this intent was advocated by R. B. Braithwaite in an essay written for the above-mentioned symposium on universals. See *Aristotelian Society Supplementary Volume VI* (1926), 27–38.

CHAPTER 9

1. From Keynes's obituary on Ramsey published in *Economic Journal*, March 1930. See also *The Foundations of Mathematics*, x.
2. P. 242. Ramsey's essays on economics are printed only in *Foundations*, ed. D. H. Mellor.
3. P. 104 in *A Study of Public Finance*, London 1949.
4. P. 251.
5. P. 258.
6. For further reading and references, see W. J. Baumol and F. Bradford, 'Optimal Departures from Marginal Cost Pricing', *American Economic Review*, **60** (1970), 265–83; and A. Sandmo, 'Optimal Taxation', *Journal of Public Economics*, **6** (1976), 37–54.
7. P. 261.
8. P. 267.
9. See 'The Existence of an Optimum Savings Program'. *Econometrica*, **30** (1962), 178–87.
10. See *Essays in the Theory of Risk-Bearing*, London 1971; and 'Risk Aversion in the Small and in the Large', *Econometrica*, **32** (1964), 122–36.
11. More about Ramsey's theory will be found in, among others, R. G. D. Allen, *Mathematical Analysis for Economists*, London 1960; G. Hadley and M. C. Kemp, *Variational Methods in Economics*, London 1971; and *Essays on the Theory of Optimal Economic Growth*, ed. K. Shell, MIT Press 1967.

CHAPTER 10

1. I have gone through Ramsey's letters and notes and talked to his daughter Mrs Jane Burch and his sister Mrs Margaret Paul, and others who knew about his life. I have come to the conclusion that there is not enough material for a more detailed biography. Nor do I want Ramsey to suffer the same biographical misrepresentation as Wittgenstein.

J. M. Keynes's book *Essays in Biography,* Macmillan 1933, contains a good chapter on Ramsey.

2. But as is the case with all good biographical glimpses, this, too, is somewhat exaggerated. Ramsey's diary tells us that he had already begun to study German when the meeting discussed by Richards took place. The diary also tells us that it took Ramsey not a week but a month to read Mach, which is still an achievement.

3. See pp. 294–5 in Keynes, *Essays in Biography,* Macmillan 1933. The obituary was published in *Economic Journal,* March 1930, and a major part of it is reprinted in *The Foundations of Mathematics,* x–xi.

4. Quoted from Moore's introduction to *The Foundations of Mathematics,* p. vii.

5. See Keynes, 295–6.

6. Pp. 291–2 (*The Foundations of Mathematics*) or 249–50 *Philosophical Papers*).

7. L. Wittgenstein, *Letters to C. K. Ogden,* ed. G. H. von Wright, Basil Blackwell, Oxford 1973, 77. This book contains other letters from the Ramsey–Wittgenstein correspondence.

8. Ibid., 77–8.

Bibliography of F. P. Ramsey's works

Items marked *FM, F* or *PP* are reprinted or published for the first time in *The Foundations of Mathematics and Other Logical Essays (FM)*, ed. R. B. Braithwaite, Routledge & Kegan Paul, London 1931; in *Foundations: Essays in Philosophy, Logic, Mathematics and Economics (F)*, ed. D. H. Mellor, Routledge & Kegan Paul, London 1978; and in *Philosophical Papers (PP)*, ed. D. H. Mellor, Cambridge University Press, Cambridge 1990, respectively.

1922

'Mr Keynes on Probability'. *The Cambridge Magazine*, **11**, no. 1 (Decennial number, 1912–21; January 1922), pp. 3–5. Reprinted in *The British Journal for the Philosophy of Science*, **40** (1989).

'The Douglas Proposal'. *The Cambridge Magazine*, **11**, no. 1 (January 1922), pp. 74–6.

Review of W. E. Johnson's *Logic Part II*. *The New Statesman*, **19** (29 July 1922), pp. 469–70.

1923

Critical notice of L. Wittgenstein's *Tractatus Logico-Philosophicus*. *Mind*, **32**, no. 128 (October 1923), pp. 465–78. (*FM*)

1924

Review of C. K. Ogden and I. A. Richards's *The Meaning of Meaning*. *Mind*, **33**, no. 129 (January 1924), pp. 108–9.

1925

'The New Principia' (review of A. N. Whitehead and B. Russell's *Principia Mathematica*, vol. I, 2d ed.). *Nature*, **116**, no. 2908 (25 July 1925), pp. 127–8.

Review of the same book in *Mind*, **34**, no. 136 (October 1925), pp. 506–7.

'Universals', *Mind*, **34**, (October 1925), pp. 401–17. (*FM, F* and *PP*)

'The Foundations of Mathematics'. *Proceedings of the London Mathematical Society*, ser. 2, **25**, part 5 (read 12 November 1925), pp. 338–84. (*FM, F* and *PP*)

1926

'Mathematics: Mathematical Logic'. *The Encyclopædia Britannica*, supplementary volumes constituting 13th ed., **2** (1926), pp. 830–2.

'Universals and the "Method of Analysis" '. *Aristotelian Society Supplementary Volume*, **6** (July 1926), pp. 17–26. [Symposium with H. W. B. Joseph and R. B. Braithwaite]. (A few pages of this paper are reprinted in *FM* and *PP*, see 'Note on the Preceding Paper'.)

'Mathematical Logic'. *The Mathematical Gazette*, **13**, no. 184 (October 1926), pp. 185–94. [Paper read before the British Association, section A, Oxford, August 1926.] (*FM, F* and *PP*)

1927

'A Contribution to the Theory of Taxation'. *The Economic Journal*, **37**, no. 145 (March 1927), pp. 47–61. (*F*)

'Facts and Propositions'. *Aristotelian Society Supplementary Volume*, **7** (July 1927), pp. 153–70. [Symposium with G. E. Moore.] (*FM, F* and *PP*)

1928

'A Mathematical Theory of Saving'. *The Economic Journal*, **38**, no. 192 (December 1928), pp. 543–9. (*F*)

'On a Problem of Formal Logic'. *Proceedings of the London Mathematical Society*, ser. 2, **30** (read 13 December 1928), pp. 338–84. (*FM* and in *F* as 'Ramsey's Theorem')

1929

'Mathematics, Foundations of'. *The Encyclopædia Britannica*, 14th ed., **15** (1929), pp. 82–4.

'Russell, Bertrand Arthur William' (in part). *The Encyclopædia Britannica*, 14th ed., **19** (1929), p. 678.

POSTHUMOUSLY PUBLISHED PAPERS

1931

'Epilogue' (1925), in *FM* and *PP*. [Paper read to the Apostles, a Cambridge discussion society in 1925.]

'Truth and Probability' (1926), in *FM*, *F* and *PP*. [Parts of this paper were read to the Moral Sciences Club at Cambridge.]

'Reasonable Degree of Belief' (1928), in *FM* and *PP*.

'Statistics' (1928), in *FM* and *PP*.

'Chance' (1928), in *FM* and *PP*.

'Theories' (1929), in *FM, F* and *PP*.

'General Propositions and Causality' (1929), in *FM, F* and *PP*.

'Probability and Partial Belief' (1929), in *FM* and *PP*.

'Knowledge' (1929), in *FM, F* and *PP*.

'Causal Qualities' (1929), in *FM* and *PP*.

'Philosophy' (1929), in *FM* and *PP*.

1978

'Universals of Law and of Fact' (1928), in *F* and *PP*.

1987

'The "Long" and "Short" of It or a Failure of Logic'. *American Philosophical Quarterly*, **24**, no. 4 (October 1987), pp. 357–9. Ed. N. Rescher.

1989

'Principles of Finitist Mathematics'. *History of Philosophy Quarterly*, **6** (1989), pp. 255–8, appendix to U. Majer, 'Ramsey's Conception of Theories: An Intuitionistic Approach', pp. 233–58.

1990

On Truth, ed. N. Rescher and U. Majer, Reidel in press.

'Weight or the Value of Knowledge'. *The British Journal for the Philosophy of Science*, **41** (1990), pp. 1–3. Ed. N.-E. Sahlin.

Index of names

Index of names

Index of names

Index of names

Wennerberg, H., 237n
Whitehead, A. N., 8, 133, 159–80, 226, 250
Wilson, J. C., 85, 239n
Winet, M., 23–4, 231n
Wittgenstein, L., ix, 2, 6, 7, 14, 48–50, 66–7, 76–7, 102–4, 106, 111, 170, 178–9, 194, 226–9, 231n, 235n, 247n, 248n, 249

Young, T., 139